THE ART OF THE AMERICAN FOLK PREACHER

The Art of
the
American Folk Preacher

BRUCE A. ROSENBERG

New York   OXFORD UNIVERSITY PRESS   1970

Copyright © 1970 by Oxford University Press, Inc.
Library of Congress Catalogue Card Number: 77-111649
Printed in the United States of America

To
the Rev. Rubin Lacy
and
the Rev. Elihue H. Brown
and
the Congregation of
the Union Baptist Church
of Bakersfield, California,
whose God is not dead

Acknowledgments

In the scholarship with which I am more at home, that of the literature of the Middle Ages, every effort of research owes a great debt to the work of other scholars; in this book my debt is to the people themselves. In the former case, the proper expression of gratitude is in footnotes; in this book it must be in these few words.

My research for this project was made possible by a fellowship awarded by the American Council of Learned Societies, which allowed me free time in which to go into the churches, and provided funds with which to buy the recording equipment necessary for this study.

All the ministers I approached were generous of their time and showed me the greatest courtesy. I do not have the space to thank all of them, but I could not pass by without mentioning the names of the Reverends Rubin Lacy, Elihue H. Brown, D. J. McDowell, Rufus Hays, Dorance Manning, Fred Greening, T. R. Hanner, and Joseph Grooms. And I must thank those members of the Union Baptist Church of Bakersfield, California, who cheerfully and helpfully responded to my requests: Sister Brown, Sister Mary Olison and the deacons of Union Baptist; and Sister Lula Fortune of Evergreen, Virginia.

At the University of California at Santa Barbara the generous aid of Professor Clayton Wilson enabled me to describe this phenomenon musically. Professor David Young of the Classics Department was very helpful as a scholar of Homeric verse and as a friend.

Operations Manager Larry Daniels of radio station KUZZ, Bakersfield, aided me in my researches at his station, as did his counterpart Robert Stroh at WELK, Charlottesville.

Dr. Harry Abram and Dr. Mary Lou Abram of Charlottesville have been helpful in locating informants, as was Alan Jabbour of Durham.

Professor Robert M. Davis and Barbara Davis were invaluable to me in my trip through Oklahoma: they unearthed informants in the field, sustained me in their home, and made the routine quite pleasant. Scholars themselves, they were sensitive to another researcher's needs.

Edgar Bowers welcomed me in my journey's midst as one hopes mellowed friends will, nor more nor less.

Professors Donald K. Fry, Robert L. Kellogg, and Richard Bauman have made important contributions to the final form of this book. To them I owe a special debt of gratitude which, if spelled out, would embarrass them all.

Professor Francis Lee Utley encouraged this project from its beginning, read the final draft at its conclusion, and has assisted its progress in a hundred ways. As with all great teachers his obligation did not end with his student's graduation.

Thanks also to Roy Noorda who has the ideal qualities of the research assistant; did he not enjoy finding errors he might not have found as many.

This study also owes a great debt to the knowledge and cooperation of several people in the U.C.L.A. Folklore Group: Professor Robert Georges, Mr. David Evans, and Mr. Peter Welding.

Without Professor D. K. Wilgus this research could never have been done. At every stage I relied upon his advice and his counsel: in conception, in planning, in collecting, in classification, and in analysis, he gave me the benefit of his shrewdness, wisdom, and experience. Much of the credit for any value this study may have belongs to him. I have saved the mention of him for last because I owe him most.

State College, Pennsylvania   B.A.R.
March 1970

Contents

It is said that once, in London, England, there were a group of artists and entertainers—in the city—and by some scheme some enterprising person was able to get most of them together in one place, so as to demonstrate their gifts. And when all of them had gone through their routines, they came down to an orator and a minister. And both of them were requested to recite the Twenty-third Psalm. The orator employed all of his innate gifts of speech, called upon all of his skill, and gifts of oratory. And when he had finished his recitation of this psalm, the house went up in thunderous applause. And then the minister arose rather solemnly, and proceeded to recite the same passage. When he had finished it is said that nobody applauded, but there was hardly a dry eye left in the house. The M.C. upon commenting on the two who had recited this passage, said the orator recited this passage like a man who knew it and was gifted to recite it; but the minister recited like a man who knew the shepherd of which it speaks.

C. L. FRANKLIN
(*From a sermon on the Twenty-third Psalm.*)

PART ONE

I

Introduction

Albert B. Lord's epoch-making study of oral composition, *The Singer of Tales,* was the summing-up of decades of collection, analysis, and formulation by him and his mentor at Harvard, Milman Parry. The original intention of these men had been to learn something about the composition of the Homeric epics, and their quests led them on a scholarly odyssey to Yugoslavia where they recorded and interviewed the Serbo-Croatian *guslars,* supposedly the last remaining singers of oral epics in the West, who accompanied themselves on the single-stringed *gusle.* Even then, three decades ago, Lord thought that the oral epic tradition was in decay; the "disease" of literacy, to use Lord's later phrase, was "infecting" the oral singers, particularly since the literacy programs of the Communist regime.[1] Consequently, when this tradition finally died out, we also lost the possibility of field-testing Lord's hypotheses, and the legacy of the *guslars* in the West has been a mountain of conjecture as high as their homeland hills.

English scholars have applied the Parry-Lord theories of oral composition to Old English poetry, especially to *Beowulf,* sometimes with controversial results.[2] The early work done by Professor Francis P. Magoun, also of Harvard, and his disciples has substantially altered our understanding of Old English poetry and its composition; the speculation in this field, based upon a close analysis and often a trenchant reading of the available texts, is the most interesting and possibly the most important to be applied to Old English criticism in this century. Many of the

3

traditional theories of the Old English scholars have subsequently been modified and refined,[3] and such improvements were to be expected. As a result we have a clearer understanding of oral composition (especially in the case of performers who, though illiterate or nearly so, can recite epics of several thousand lines in length with great consistency over a number of years), we have a firmer apprehension of transitional texts (in which the oral and literate modes are blended), and of the nature of "formulaic" language. The close examination of available texts has so far yielded a rich harvest; yet those who have been dubious of some of Lord's original conclusions have had only speculation to rely upon, while Lord relies upon the data gathered over the past thirty-five years; and Magoun's conclusions rest upon the findings of Lord.

When the Serbo-Croatian epic tradition died, anyone interested in oral composition had to turn to the internal evidence of the texts themselves (or else learn the language of the Kirghiz nomads of central Asia and travel there). Hence the impetus for this study: not only to learn something more about the composition of epic verse specifically, if that were still possible, but to find an extant oral tradition which might further endow our conceptions about the nature of composition and transmission of such "illiteratures."

Milman Parry was working on the hypothesis that the epic singer composed his oral poems by the judicious manipulation of metrically consistent phrases, some memorized and some spontaneously composed, which enabled him to spin out stories at great length; yet his memory was such that the singer could also recite basically the same story months or even years later. These metrically consistent phrases Parry named "oral formulas," and defined them as "a group of words regularly employed under the same metrical conditions to express a given essential idea."[4] The reader who is confronted with this definition for the first time may perhaps realize its vagueness; the professional folklorist or student of Anglo-Saxon literature, who has been struggling with this definition ever since Parry wrote it, will attest to its slippery nature. For now we can offer no better description; but we shall attempt to in a later chapter.

The field research for this project began in Bakersfield, California, and ended there as well. In the intervening years I traveled to Oklahoma, Kentucky, North Carolina, and Virginia, in addition to other areas in south and central California. It was there that I found a tradition of oral composition that is vigorous, widespread, and available to study. Originally from the South, many preachers (most of whom are Negro) compose their sermons spontaneously by using techniques identical to those employed by Lord's *guslars*. The past fifty years have seen an accelerated migration on the part of these men to the East, the Far West, and many of the major cities of the Midwest; almost always these men carried their culture with them. The ministers seldom object to having their sermons recorded (the ones with whom I worked, at any rate), and if an analysis is done with care, Lord's work can be continued here in the United States. The biggest difference between the Yugoslavian oral epic and the American oral sermon is that the *guslars* sang narrative epics, while the American preachers chant another kind of narrative. And the lines of the sermons are less rigid metrically. But for the other aspects of composition, the two genres have much in common.

Almost of secondary interest to this research—but perhaps of primary interest to some folklorists—is the collection and study for its own sake of the spontaneous chanted sermon. So far as I know, no such an examination has ever been undertaken. Newman I. White, Alan Lomax, J. Mason Brewer, and a few others have published "oral" sermons, or fragments of sermons, but almost never with analytical comment.[5] To me White's sermon looks suspiciously literary; but literary or not, it is one of the few such recorded sermons even pretending to an authentic oral tradition. James Weldon Johnson was heavily influenced by preachers he had heard in his childhood when he wrote seven sermons for a book he called *God's Trombones*. But they are literary poems, not oral folk sermons, and moving though they may be they are not appropriate to this study.

However, in one way the starting point for this introduction to the sermon is Johnson's observation that the oral chanted sermons are the materials of folk art.[6] The sermons almost never rhyme, they seldom alliterate, the imagery is meager, yet they are poetic. The lines are metrical, the language is ordered, and the effect is often pleasing. If Harry Caplan is correct in calling preaching a "sacred art,"[7] then the oral sermon is certainly artistic. Its oral style echoes *Beowulf* or the *Nibelungenlied*; but it is usually not a conventional or sophisticated poetry. It often mediates between oratory and oral narrative and frequently mediates ineptly, but it is folk art for all of that. Johnson remembered hearing sermons which he thought were "passed along" from preacher to preacher and from region to region with only minor variations.[8] During this study it has not been possible to trace a sermon so thoroughly, but there is no doubt whatsoever that an active oral tradition of the chanted sermons is still alive. That tradition is now nationwide, and we have waited too long to study it.

The idea first occurred to me when, as a graduate student in Ohio, I would occasionally pick up evangelists' sermons on local radio stations. My first impulse, I must admit, was to turn the dial immediately; but the ear is quicker than the hand, and after a short time—during which I heard parts of several sermons—I thought that I was hearing the same phrases repeated, much as are formulas in *Beowulf*. At the Santa Barbara campus of the University of California, Professor David Young of the Classics Department one day happened to remark that he thought that J. Charles Jessup's sermons—performances he also admired—were heavily formulaic. Jessup, based in Gulfport, Louisiana, is carried to the Southern California area over radio station XERB, Los Angeles. Young is interested in formulaic approaches to literature through his studies of Homer. But what was crucial to this study was his independent corroboration of my hypothesis; after that, my work began in earnest.

Professor D. K. Wilgus of the University of California at Los Angeles supported this project from its conception, and it was he who provided my first contact. Several of his graduate students had been recording in the California interior, especially in Bakersfield and Ridgecrest, and they had first met the Rev. Rubin Lacy there. Their purpose was the collection of folk ballads; Lacy was a Blues singer in the late twenties and early thirties, and he and friends of his had proven helpful to the UCLA people. One of them, David Evans, had recorded parts of sermons, and from his description of them I felt certain that a visit to Lacy would be profitable. It was. Lacy was friendly and cooperative from the beginning and introduced me to several of his colleagues.

In my first recordings I kept the microphone with me in the congregation, in the first row. But the audience noise proved so distorting (because of the congregation's active participation in the service) that I eventually moved the microphone forward to the area of the pulpit. Usually the preacher preferred to have the microphone on the pulpit itself.[9]

With the microphone placed forward much greater fidelity was obtained; however, with a preacher who moved back and forth continually there was little to do except continually adjust the recording level. That generally worked out well so far as clarity was concerned, though sometimes at the expense of the effect of the sermon. Even with the microphone on the pulpit at least part of the audience is clearly audible. I mention this fact specifically because audience response is vital in an antiphonal service. Later we shall discuss the effect the congregation has on the preacher's performance: sometimes they are "filled with the Spirit" and at other times they are listless, bored, and unresponsive. The state of the audience is an important matter, and the headnotes to the sermons printed below reflect it. One cannot understand any sermon of this type adequately without knowing the responses of the congregation during that sermon.

My presence did not appear to alter significantly the performance of the service, and most important for my immediate purposes, the performance of the sermon. The very young children gave me sly and quizzical glances, but for the most part I was ignored by the adults. They shouted, clapped, and sang, paying no particular attention to me, but this was not always the case with the preachers. The first few visits to each church made a difference in the sermon, however slight. Lacy, for instance, saved his favorite numbers for me, which turned out to my advantage. Other preachers may have felt that because they were being recorded they should perform better; one man actually told me so, though jokingly. It is difficult for me to evaluate what difference these factors made in the "texts" I recorded and later analyzed, but I do not believe it was linguistically significant. Primarily this appears to be so because radio sermons which were monitored manifested the same linguistic characteristics as those which I personally attended. Then, after a short time the men did not pay special attention to me. Finally, having heard several successful sermons at the outset I had a concrete basis for comparison with later performances.

The only difficulty I did encounter was in the interviews, and that was the result of the nature of the subject: it is sacred matter and not always easily translatable into laymen's terms. I was told very early in my relationship with Lacy and the Rev. E. H. Brown that there was no use talking about the preacher's language because it all came from God. That was the end of it. When I recorded a traditional folk tale during one sermon the preacher was reluctant to discuss its source except in terms of the Holy Ghost. I later recorded a preacher in Virginia, the Rev. T. R. Hanner, using a striking metaphor during a sermon: "Out of His mouth/

Come a two-edge sword/ Cuttin' sin/ Both right and left." Lacy had used the identical metaphor months before in California; and while Revelation does have the two-edge sword it does not have the entire figure. Hanner was insistent that "the Lord" gave it to him, even in response to my suggestion that the specific diction might be humanly derived.

The basic plan of the study was to cover four geographic areas in the United States, and to fill in some of the spaces by monitoring radio broadcasts. Of the areas chosen, one should reflect a society in transition or dislocation (southern California); a stable portion of the South (Virginia and Georgia); a border area, preferably in the hills (Kentucky and Tennessee); and the middle Southwest, an area between the stable East and the demographically fluctuating Far West (Oklahoma City and Tulsa). Radio broadcasts from Mississippi and Texas are plentiful, and were frequently monitored. Within each area the procedure has been to get a sampling of about twenty men in the area, but also to concentrate on two or three and to know their styles thoroughly.[10] In Southern California the sermons of over twenty preachers were recorded, with the concentration on Lacy and Brown; ultimately, the difficulty is in deciding when the sample is sufficient. Since one can never be certain, recording was continued as a matter of routine, but so far as this study is concerned I have heeded the maxim of the famous Russian ethnologist, Vladimir Propp: when you stop finding new material, the collecting may be terminated. For the specific aspect of the sermon that was studied, I have not recently discovered new qualitative data.

II

The Church

Many Americans have never heard the kind of preaching this book is concerned with. I say this although no nationwide poll has been taken; but only one of all my colleagues and acquaintances had ever heard such a sermon—he grew up in a small North Carolina town—and even frequent churchgoers had never thought much about sermon styles. Most northern Presbyterians, to sharpen the contrast, think that nearly all preaching is from a prepared text, while just as many southern Baptists must assume that all sermons are delivered directly by their pastor without any manuscript at all. So at the outset a few fundamental distinctions must be made.

A man is either a manuscript preacher or a "spiritual" preacher—according to those who count themselves among the latter. This seems to me the most obvious beginning, and a distinction to which we must adhere if anything at all is to be said about sermon styles. Of course some men use note cards with the barest hints concerning the outlines of their sermons, which makes for an interesting "transitional" performance, but for the most part such men can be classed among the "spiritual" preachers so long as we are careful in our analysis of sermon structure to take their "text" into account: such a text may differ markedly from one that results from a purely spontaneous performance. Some men read part of their sermon and recite the rest spontaneously, but such a performance presents no problem in classification since the sermon itself is usually thus divided into two parts. Blending of styles occurs when the prepared

9

written text is partially abandoned by the preacher, who breaks away from the prose of his source into his natural rhythm, but the classification of such a phenomenon is pedantic. The result, however, is extremely useful in that it is a demonstration of the spontaneous creation of metrical lines. At the point at which the preacher begins to depart from his text for the sake of metrical consistency, the sermon—to use the language of the preachers—becomes "spiritual" (or "oral" or "spontaneous"), though often the sound recording of the performance and not merely the transcription is necessary to determine that point.

Spiritual sermons also are of two types—chanted and nonchanted—although the distinction here is not nearly so marked. The chanted spiritual sermon is the one with which this book is chiefly concerned: if the sermon is not chanted and the length and metrical consistency of each uttered line is not regularized, the formulas of which Parry and Lord spoke will not occur. The music of the performance creates the formula in that the preacher attempts to fit his language into a metrically consistent pattern. In the chanted sermon, the verses are preponderantly formulaic (in the Parry-Lord sense), there are extended passages with parallel syntax, and the constructions are direct with almost no periodicity.

Of the spiritual preachers in America, themselves a minority, only a few chant their sermons. These men are found largely in the South where they were born and where they learned to preach, though some now live in every major city in America. Although most of these men are Negro, there are whites in the eastern Kentucky hills and in parts of Ohio and Pennsylvania who still preach this way. Where the sermon first was chanted is very difficult to determine, owing to the scarcity of documents on this specific aspect of American religion, but certainly blacks have developed it most fully. In Kentucky, white "old-time country preachers," as their neighbors call them, were surprised to learn that the chanted sermon was not exclusively theirs.

The orally presented prose (nonchanted) sermon, on the other hand, has more of the characteristics of conventional oratory and even of conversational speech. In such performances logical development from sentence to sentence occurs more frequently than in chanted sermons, with fewer parallel developments and almost no memorized formulas. The language will have a rhythm of its own but it is regular, so formulas do not develop. The syntax is quite free in this kind of sermon, as flexible as conversation which, aside from the conventions of oratory and preaching, it resembles when transcribed. Most spiritual preachers are of this sort, especially those whose congregations are middle class. One such man, the evangelist Maxie Boren of Austin, Texas, found the chanting strange (yet interesting) though neither he nor any of his colleagues preached that way; among other things, he had not the musical ability.

We shall have to confront, finally, the matter of nomenclature, since it is simply too cumbersome to refer continually to a sermon as spontaneously composed, orally presented, and metrically ordered. Actually no one name is ideal. "Oral" does not distinguish the chanted sermon from the spoken; neither does "spontaneous," although occasionally in the forthcoming pages both are used when the context makes their meaning clear. To label a preformance "metrical" ignores its oral spontaneity. Francis Lee Utley has suggested "Pentacostal," probably because of the word's association with that phenomenon of verbal ecstasy, speaking in tongues; but many spiritual preachers do not belong to the Pentacostal Church. We do think of a denomination when we hear the word, and such a name might well be confusing. I opt for "chanted," for despite its obvious shortcomings it does describe the one feature of these sermons which is most important in this study.

To best describe the performance of the chanted sermon still more is needed than the flat statement that it is spontaneous and metrical. Therefore, I should like to relate the impression of Professor Alan Jabbour, now of the Library of Congress who, though armed with only scant knowledge of this project, was seeking informants for me in Durham, North Carolina; after attending the services of the Rev. W. T. Ratliff he sent me the following letter:

> Rev. Ratliff begins his sermon in normal, though stately and carefully measured, prose. As he gets into his subject, he gradually raises the intensity of his delivery (though with well-timed ups and downs). About one third of the way into his sermon the prose has verged into a very rhythmical delivery, punctuated into periods (more or less regular) by a sharp utterance which I suppose might be called a vehement grunt. I haven't timed these periods, but I would guess that they fall about every three seconds, sometimes less. Within the rhythmical framework, the rises and falls eventually build to a climax when he lapses into a sort of chant, still with the same punctuation, but with a recognizable tonic (tonal center).

Some of the congregation (who respond *ad libitum* throughout) here lapse into humming along with him. After this climax he breaks off dramatically into normal prose, then builds back again, and finally tapers off into a subdued normal delivery at the end.

Jabbour's letter was so accurate in its description of the kind of sermon I had been recording (it might well have been the description of over 90 per cent of them) that I recognized it at once, and asked him to arrange an interview for me. What was true of the South had been true of California, for the people I met in the San Joaquin were southerners practicing (in their terms) old-time, not new fangled, religion. This study began in the Negro churches of California and was extended back to the preachers' former land, where the faith came from. And the church service itself in California was much as I and Professor Jabbour found it in the South.

It would seem unlikely that all of the churches are hot all of the time, but it always feels that way. The buildings, often fibre or plywood siding nailed on wooden uprights which barely support the low ceiling, are in effect Dutch ovens. Everyone is sweating all the time. All during the services cardboard hand fans with mortuary advertisements on them are swished back and forth, giving the singing and the sermon an undertone of humming. If the congregation is prosperous the church will have a large swamp fan built into the wall, as noisy as an old Ford, which blows warm air around; but when it is 108 degrees even warm air pushed in one's face feels good. I think that everyone expects the service to be hot, for regardless of the weather, regardless of the swamp fan, nearly everyone flicks the mortuary fans in front of their faces.

The services are as informal as though the congregation felt that God was an old friend (a friend to whose house a jacket and tie are worn, however). No real effort is made to stop children from signaling and giggling at one another, or to stop the infants from crying. The women usually sit together on their side of the aisle toward the front with their young. The men, who are relaxed and jovial as they joke outside, come in at the last minute and sit near the back. At many services one or two of them sleep through the sermon. The preacher sweats more than anyone because he is as active as an actor strutting on a stage. He gesticulates, twists his face in theatrical masks, and waves his arms. Regularly he lifts his handkerchief to his mouth to clear his throat and to wipe the perspiration from his lips. If the sermon is especially effective the audience may dance in the aisles, fall on the floor, or speak in tongues, but most of the time their response is limited to relatively more sedate cries of "yes, Jesus" or "that's right," to clapping, and to controlled toe-tapping.

We can fairly characterize these contemporary services as conservative in that they attempt to conserve what the preacher and congregation consider to be the best of the past. On a national scale we now realize that the "past"—the relation of the Negro to American Protestantism—is a shameful one, but it will be useful to review a segment of it here. Our sketch must be brief and will touch upon the highlights of what we know about preachers in Colonial and pre-Civil war frontier days; our purpose will be to explore the possible origins of the chanted sermon.

New England must first be considered: although the settlers in this region paid scant attention to the religious needs of either slaves or freedmen, some Negro churches were eventually formed. The vast majority of slaves were never given Christian training by the Puritans,[1] and it is estimated that only a small porportion of the Negroes in the colonies were even nominal Christians.[2] Nevertheless, some Negroes were exposed to this faith of the white man—usually to foster docility and obedience—and we should not discount the possibility that, in part, the contemporary chanted sermon derives ultimately from such exposure.

In Philadelphia during the last quarter of the eighteenth century the remarkable Richard Allen bought his freedom from a sympathetic master in the same year of his conversion, and later established the Free African Society and the American Methodist Episcopal Church. Membership in this Church initially was small,[3] though in the second decade of the nineteenth century branches of the AME Church had been formed in in Baltimore, Wilmington, and several Pennsylvania and New Jersey towns. In 1820 there were 4,000 black Methodists in Philadelphia, half that number in Baltimore. Despite this impressive growth, however, Allen's influence in the South was checked by the hostility of southern planters who, after the Denmark Vesey insurrection of 1822, repressed the appearances of Allen's followers below the Mason-Dixon Line.[4]

We are thus tempted to discount Richard Allen's influence on the spontaneous chanted sermon, despite his undoubted importance in the early Negro church. There is no evidence, moreover, that his preaching or his services were characterized by the outpouring of the sort of emotion we have described. Nothing in contemporary descriptions of his style suggests the kind of performance witnessed, for example, by Professor Jabbour. Rather, he has been described by those who knew him as "a plain-spoken, matter-of-fact, young Negro. . . . His words were simple and instructive and sincere."[5]

The influence of New England religion may have been felt in the South in two ways, though, as we have seen, it is difficult to measure the intensity of that feeling. The first is in the structure of the Puritan sermon—what some modern ministers glibly call the "text-and-context" form. The preacher begins with a quotation from Scripture (the "text"), proceeds to explain it ("context"), raises a doctrine from the passage and then, in the section that most interests the preacher, applies that doctrine to every-day affairs. The structure of the sermon was simple and ordered by a straightforward setting forth of argument after argument, an arrangement which Perry Miller has likened to a lawyer's brief.[6] This pattern was followed with little variation for over a century following the settlement of New England, and we find that this pattern informs many chanted sermons.

The second important element to spring from New England is that of freely expressed passion in Divine worship; one thinks immediately of the "Baptist Whine" and of such men as James Davenport and George Whitfield (of whom David Garrick once said that he could bring an audience to tears merely by intoning the word "Mesopotamia").[7] The Anglicans attacked their more passionate colleagues for their vehement pathos, their histrionics, the "tuned voice" (of Whitfield), and there is ample evidence of this early theological quarrel.[8] Nowhere do we find the statement that the sermons of these men of the "New Lights" were chanted, as are those of the men who interest us here; however, the emotionalism, the free expression, and the "musical tone" of the preachers suggest that this aspect of the chanted oral sermon may begin in this context.

It was only during that wave of religious fervor in 1800 and 1801 called The Second Great Awakening, that large numbers of Negroes were proselytized and converted.[9] The Baptists and Methodists especially, out of favor in New England because of their "barking" and "jerking" and other "primitive traits,"[10] were prominent in this new wave of enthusiasm on the frontier. The Camp Meeting enlarged the physical scope (at least) of Divine service; for example, at Cane Ridge in 1801 over 20,000 worshippers gathered to pray, while during the sermons men and women danced and shouted aloud.[11]

The Methodists and Baptists succeeded with the whites as well as blacks in the South (while the Anglicans and Presbyterians failed in comparison) because of several sociological reasons. The Baptist preachers, for the most part lacking the education of their Anglican peers, appealed to those whom E. Franklin Frazier has termed as "the poor and the ignorant and the outcast."[12] The Baptists and Methodists emphasized feeling as a sign of conversion, and this doctrine was readily accepted by the socially repressed. The Protestant middle-class communions were already concerned with national and political issues; the "unrestrained emotionalism" of preaching the gospel continued among adherents of the Second Great Awakening and is, as we have seen, continuing today. The clergy of this movement, often circuit riders and farmer-preachers, were given easy access to the slaves since they usually taught a religion of consolation rather than of revolt against their white masters; several Episcopal planters are known to have requested Methodist preachers to come and console (i.e., quiet) their slaves.[13]

The Rev. Dr. Joseph Washington, Jr. has shown us[14] how the slaves thus received a substandard Christianity. The white preachers taught Christian morals—especially patience and endurance—to be sure, but not the tenets of faith or ethical concerns such as the immorality of slavery. But the hypnotizing effect of the Baptists was impelling, and very quickly many slaves took up preaching on their own. It is possible, therefore, that the chanted sermon as we know it today was also influenced by these first black "exhorters." On the issue of Negro worship the southern planters were of two minds. We have seen how they encouraged Methodists to preach to their slaves; yet it was often thought necessary to repress Negro preaching for fear of sedition and rebellion. Between 1830 and 1835 the fear of insurrection was so great that services without white supervision were prohibited: five or more slaves could not assemble in the absence of a white.[15] The historical evidence, therefore, suggests quite strongly that although many Negroes may have first witnessed Christianity from other Negroes, by far the majority in the South learned about it from whites.

The reasons for locating those areas which were most heavily proselytized during the Second Great Awakening as the birthplace of the chanted sermon are compelling. New Lights preaching in New England appears not to have reached many Negroes there, but was tremendously effective among the slaves after 1801. We find many descriptions of Negroes responding to the emotional fervor of the Baptist and Methodist preachers in the South, but seldom in the North; and the sermon with which this book is concerned appears to be primarily a southern phenomenon. Finally, if the border states were the locale where white preachers passed the chanted sermon along to their Negro brethren, one would expect to find whites reciting in this style. My field trips to eastern Kentucky showed this to be the case. Chanted sermons are well established in the area among whites who say that neither they nor their grandparents ever preached differently.

If there is any validity to the theory that we have just presented—that the chanted sermon as we today know it either began or was widely popularized during the Second Great Awakening—then its history is roughly parallel to that of the spiritual. Beginning, as Don Yoder has traced it,[16] in eighteenth-century New England, the spiritual migrated south where it was widely adopted (and adapted) by Negroes. By using popular tunes as the vehicle for evangelical hymns, the spiritual also developed the chorus which has come to characterize the camp-meeting spiritual. The practice of "lining out" hymns was common, probably because many of the congregation could not read but just as plausibly—as whites in Kentucky claim today—because hymnals were scarce: the leader sang out a line and the congregation responded by resinging the same line, often in their own melody. If a worshipper wished to sing harmony, or sing either his own words or melody, or if he wanted to shout, he was free to do so. This kind of antiphonal performance was already in the Negro work-song tradition and was readily adapted into black services.[17]

One is inclined to approach the origin of the chanted sermon by the circuitous route of the spiritual for several reasons. The sermons are repetitious in the same ways the spirituals are. And an extraordinary number of sermon lines come directly from spirituals; for instance, the following ten lines, taken verbatim from a sermon by the Rev. D. J. McDowell of Bakersfield (a former gospel singer) have several lines from spirituals:

> God is our refuge
> And strength
> A well-proved helpmate in trouble
> <u>I'm in trouble this evenin'</u>
> 5 <u>Yes I am</u>
>   <u>I said I'm in trouble this evenin'</u>

I need someone to go all night long
If you never hear me no more
Keep your hand in God's hand
10 He'll make a way for you

No doubt this borrowing will occur as long as sermons of this kind are preached.

There are other similarities: as we shall later see, the sermons are most often chanted in the pentatonic, a popular scale of Baptist hymnals. The rhythms are the same in spirituals and sermons, and the informal, concrete tone appropriate to a personal relation with one's God is present in both. Satan and God and all the saints are treated as real and living people, not as abstractions. So it is in the spiritual sermon, where one often hears the preacher say, "Jesus said to me last night."[18]

Functionally, the chanted sermon is an ideal conflation of the prose sermon and the spiritual. Both of the component genres are approved expressions of worship, and the conflated form has proved equally acceptable. We can never know for certain why the chanted sermon initially came to be wedded to music, but perhaps our common sense can provide a reasonable answer. Sermons can be dull, especially long sermons and particularly when they are solemnly intoned. We must remember that the first Negro preachers in America, like their white counterparts on the frontier, had little formal education and even less training in formal rhetoric or public speaking. We may speculate that chanting or singing was first used both to liven a potentially dull sermon and to establish a rhythm so as to make the performance as emotionally stimulating as the obviously successful spirituals. Singing is difficult to sustain in an extended form such as the sermons; so chanting is clearly a more practical expedient, though some talented preachers occasionally break into song for short periods. Whites in Kentucky today hum after each line of their spiritual sermons so as to establish rhythm. The congregation is moved to religious ecstasy by this form which embodies the emotional power of music and the (ostensibly) rational power of the spoken word. Musical instruments are not needed since the preacher's voice is the full orchestra.

If the chanted sermon is in fact a conflation of forms, one would expect to find transitional "texts" showing an intermediary form of the conflation more clearly; and such performances have been recorded. For the following "song" I am indebted to Charles Perdue, who recorded it in Rappahannock County, Virginia, in 1968. The singer's name is Newton Jackson who is, happily for this illustration, a deacon in his church. He is quite active in church affairs, and though it is not known whether he preaches extensively or not, Perdue thinks that he does. The first three verses as well as the last were sung; the twenty-six lines between were chanted in the style of the spiritual preacher:

How I got over,
How I got over,
My soul looked back and wondered,
How I got over.

How I got over,
How I got over,
You know, my soul looked back and wondered,
How I got over.

You know just as soon as I can see my Jesus
That, that made me free.
I'm glad that he suffered
And he died for you and me.

I want to thank Him 'cause He brought me,
I want to thank Him 'cause He taught me,
I want to thank Him because He kept me,
I want to thank Him 'cause He never left me,
I want to thank Him for the Holy Bible,
I want to thank Him for good old revival,
I want to thank Him for heavenly visions,
I want to thank Him for old time religion,
Don't you know, I'm gonna sing, "Hallelujah,"
Yeah, I'm gonna shout, "Glory,"
O, I'm gonna thank Him for what He's done for me,
Don't you know I'm gonna wear a diadem,
In the New Jerusalem.
Gonna walk the streets of gold,
Goin' to the homeland of the soul,
Gonna view the Hosts in white,

You know they travel both day and night,
Comin' up from every nation,
On the way to the great combination,
Comin' from the north, south, east, and west,
Yes, on the way to the land of rest,
You know I'm goin' to join the heavenly choir,
Well, gonna sing on and never get tired,
Hallelujah, you know I'm gonna sing, sing "Hallelujah,"
Yeah, I'm gonna shout, "Glory,"
O, I'm gonna thank Him for what He's done for me.

Well, it's how I got over,
How I got over,
Lord, my soul looked back and wondered,
How I got over.

This performance is part spiritual and part sermon, though the influence of the latter is not quite as strong as the fact that it was chanted in sermon style makes it appear. Although heavily repetitive in the style of the sermon, it appears to be largely memorized rather than entirely improvised. Most of the lines rhyme, suggesting strongly that Newton at least knew most, if not all, of the couplets by heart. Probably he knows additional rhymes which might be added to or substituted in this passage when it occurs in other performances, as his memory and other factors permit. To the extent that he was relatively free to add and to delete these rhymes, none of which are necessary to this sequence, the performance is spontaneous. The rhymes themselves are almost assuredly memorized as units, making the section in effect a short sermon. A conventional sermon would not be as highly memorized, more improvisation would occur, and (in authentic sermons) rhyme would be rarely used.

We should not think, however, that music necessarily came to the sermon historically through such transitional forms, though, as we have suggested, the idea seems plausible. Rather, what Newton's performance does illustrate is that among men whose religion has always been communicated by the chanted sermon, the singing of spirituals is intimately related to preaching and is religiously acceptable within the context of so serious a form as the sermon. Even if Newton's performance does not recapitulate the historical blending of prose sermon and spiritual, it is

illustrative of the attitude of the preachers interviewed toward the symbiotic roles of singing and preaching in their religion. As we shall later
see, one preacher volunteered his belief that Blues were suitable for
church as they often were as "truthful" as hymns. And it is no coinci-
dence that every man interviewed for this project was either a former
professional singer, choirmaster, or singer of some talent though perhaps
only with amateur status. As the first sermon to be chanted was the
product of a man with musical as well as oratorical genius, so the same
talents are obvious in the tradition today.

The principal informants in Bakersfield for this study were the Rev.
Elihue H. Brown, pastor of the Union Baptist Church, and the Rev.
Rubin Lacy, who had just given up his own church in Ridgecrest, California, and was then in Brown's congregation. Since then Lacy has been
pastoring in Corcoran. Brown was born near Helena, Arkansas, in 1916;
Lacy's first home was in Pelahatchie, Mississippi, where he was born in
1901. When I met Lacy in California he was preaching about once a
week, either at the Union Baptist or at one of the other churches in the
area. Lacy is otherwise unemployed and supplements his welfare money
with the "offerings" he gets for preaching. Sometimes he is paid a flat
five or six dollars for each service; at other times he gets half of the congregation's offering, the other half going to the host pastor.

Most of the men in Bakersfield (like preachers with small congregations around the country) cannot support themselves on their church
earnings, and hold other jobs. A few can: a handful in Bakersfield, and
some of the more popular men with larger followings in big cities. In the
main the preacher depends upon his skill as an orator to draw members
to his congregation. The Rev. Edmund Blair of the Omega Baptist
Church in Chicago is reported to have built up his congregation in a
few years from eight to 3,800. The Rev. D. J. McDowell (who does live
on his preaching and pastoral duties alone) believes that one must be
careful about what the congregation is told: "People don't like to be told
that they are bad." The part-time or free-lance preacher does not have to
worry as much about offending his audience, but neither will he disre-
gard their feelings. Even if he doesn't depend upon the congregation for
his living, his pride is involved in his popularity (i.e., he is ineffective
as God's minister if no one wants to hear him), and some money, after
all, is involved.

Every one of the preachers recorded during the course of this study was born in the South, though many of them now either live or spend much of their time elsewhere. Lacy attributes this movement to the eastern seaboard, Chicago and Detroit, and southern California simply to "civil rights." The situation is, of course, far more complex than that, but for the immediate purposes the important fact is that the effect has been to spread a portion of southern culture across the nation. Those who migrated to the North, East, and West wanted to worship in the old way, and brought their religion with them. The migration created a demand and encouraged other ministers to follow their flocks. The pastors went with their congregations or else formed new ones in the new land; the healers and evangelists found new areas for conversion and reform, and strengthened their foothold on both coasts and in the Midwest.

Functionally, the clergy in this study divided themselves into four groups: the pastors, the preachers, the healers, and the evangelists. Their authority is Ephesians 4:11: "And He gave some apostles; and some prophets; and some evangelists; and some pastors and teachers." The pastors run the local churches and tend to all the organizational and administrative matters concerned with keeping the congregation together. Preachers, on the other hand, may not be the head of their church and may have nothing to do with local administration; they have been given the gift of preaching and may do so anywhere. Some preachers are members of an organized church, as Lacy is a member of the Rev. Elihue Brown's Union Baptist Church of Bakersfield. But Lacy often gives guest sermons at Brown's church and at others in the area. The preachers believe that Paul was the first of their number. Healers can be, though often they are not, limited to a specific church: A. A. Allen, for intance, is not only interdenominational but interracial and international. Relatively little of Allen's time is spent at his home base in Miracle Valley, Arizona. The evangelists almost never have a church of their own; their role is to bring converts to the churches of the pastors. However, most churches have "evangelistic services" on Sunday evenings, and more often than not they are led by the local pastor.

In practice it is nearly impossible to distinguish functions except at specific times and with individual men. Lacy calls Brown a pastor, yet Brown preaches often and skillfully at his own church, the Union Baptist, and at others as well. He spends many summers doing evangelistic work in his home state of Arkansas which is unrelated to the immediate welfare of his congregation. I would personally classify A. A. Allen as a healer. His monthly magazine, *Miracle Magazine*, is devoted largely to his healing miracles, but Lacy has called him an evangelist. And no doubt the same ambiguity of roles is present in the evangelist Kathryn Kuhlman and the healer Oral Roberts.

Possibly because their roles are not clearly defined and their functions overlap, tensions are often strong among the various types of clergy, much as it was in the Middle Ages. Chaucer records the reputed licentiousness of Pardoners and Friars and some parish priests, and the ease of getting absolution from some of them for certain favors. And we know that after the thirteenth century tension existed between parish priests and the Franciscans and other preaching orders. Lacy at first denied, for the record, any conflict between pastors and evangelists. He was keeping his own house in order. But at another interview he said that his wife used to send money to A. A. Allen, money which might have gone to his own church. Lacy had forgotten his earlier statement, no doubt, but such conflicts are not hard to detect. Allen himself frequently attacks the established church clergy not only for their "false theology" but for their "greed." And I have heard, though not with such great frequency, similar attacks made by J. Charles Jessup (Gulfport, Miss.), and Neil Glasse and Brother Bob MacElroy, both of the Claremont-Ontario area in California.

Lacy defines pastors as "feeders"; they "feeds Christians," specifically their flock, with spiritual food. As Lacy explained to me, a "pastor" is a place where one feeds (actually meaning a "pasture"). When a "pastor" is dry, Lacy told me, there is no food for the flock.[19]

According to the clergymen I interviewed, the calling to the church comes from God. There is no other way. In nearly all instances, as was also the case with Lacy, Brown, and McDowell, the calling comes against the will of the preacher. On one occasion Lacy said that he did not want to preach when he first felt the spirit of God come to him, and he resisted for many years. He was a marginally successful Blues singer and had various odd jobs until 1932 when he was in a railroad accident. He says a voice came to him then and said, "The next time it will be death." Thereupon Lacy gave away his guitar and went into the Missionary Baptist Church to do the Lord's work. Yet he recalled that when he was very young he was considered "peculiar" and given to religious thought; his grandfather, by whom he was raised, was an "African Methodist" preacher.

A man may be called to do the Lord's work, but if he is to preach he must have "spiritual power." This feeling that one is divinely summoned is important in understanding sermon techniques. Only "spiritual power" allows a man to preach well; that can only come from God and "it don't take nothing but faith." (Yet at another interview Lacy said that a man could either be born to be a preacher, or else he could be called, but Lacy could not clearly distinguish between modes.) Lacy may well have been born to be a preacher; others, like J. Charles Jessup, appear to have been called. The story is told (not only by Jessup) that one day, while he lay upon "the bed of affliction," Jessup insisted on being locked in his room for forty days and forty nights, and that when he emerged he was a new man and one of God's ministers. Lacy tells another story about a friend who was deathly ill and who called out, "God, if you spare me I'll do what you want, and become a preacher." God did; and the man kept his promise.

The spiritual preacher finds ample scriptural support for his style of sermonizing. The preacher need not be learned, in fact should not be educated, except in the ways of the Bible:

> And, behold, I send the promise of my Father upon you: but tarry ye in the city of Jerusalem, until ye be endued with power from on high. (Luke 24:49)

The important point here is that the apostles are not instructed to school themselves or to attend a seminary, but are merely to "tarry" until the Spirit comes to them. The spiritual preacher's understanding of the Bible, the Truth, will come only and directly from God:

> Then opened he their understanding, that they might understand the scriptures. (Luke 24:45)

For the holy preacher there is only one fit subject, the kingdom of God:

> The law and the prophets were until John: since that time the kingdom of God is preached, and every man presseth into it. (Luke 16:16)

God is with the preacher at every moment, inspiring and informing his words:

Go ye therefore, and teach all nations, baptizing them in the name
of the Father, and of the Son, and of the Holy Ghost:
Teaching them to observe all things whatsoever I have commanded
you: and, lo, I am with you alway, even unto the end of the world.
A-men. (Matthew 28:19-20)

And the Holy Spirit shall forever be his comfort:

Then had the churches rest throughout all Judea and Galilee and
Samaria, and were edified; and walking in the fear of the Lord, and
in the comfort of the Holy Ghost, were multiplied. (Acts 9:31)

The matter of being born to be a preacher and being called is no different from what the laity think of as the preacher's education. I have
already mentioned that Lacy was raised by his preacher grandfather and
as a child was thought to be destined to be a clergyman. He said that at
the age of seven he used to "practice preach" and would give sermons
to the birds and the trees (like St. Francis?) in Pelahatchie, Mississippi.
At that time, he said, he used to "mock" people he heard in the area,
especially "Lee Hardy" and "Old Man Atkin." In other words, he grew
up in a clerical tradition where preaching, like gospel singing, was a vital
part of his life. He got religion at home, like most Negro Baptist children
he went to church more than once a week, and he also went to revivals
and other camp meetings. When the Spirit of God finally moved him to
take the cloth in 1932, he could draw upon a very rich and very vigorous
tradition.

That tradition[20] is with us today, seemingly as vigorous as ever. Lacy,
like many of his colleagues, still listens to radio sermons and watches
revivals on TV. He has heard a few sermons which have been recorded
(on the Battle and Chess labels). He goes to church three or four times
a week and hears not only his own pastor but guest preachers from
neighboring towns—Pixley, Delano, Taft, and Arvin. What he gets is
a cross section of styles from many places in the South and from many
transplanted southerners. That cross section of styles is within a definable
tradition. All of the men whom Lacy hears "live" do not prepare written
sermons: they chant (and sometimes sing), using stock phrases, stories,
and ideas. Lacy not only learns and assimilates the language of his colleagues, but contributes his own innovations to the tradition.

In another culture, Albert B. Lord has identified three stages in the development of the singing career of the Yugoslav *guslars*. At first the *guslar* is a nonparticipating listener, learning the stories, songs, and language of the performing singers. The second stage begins when the apprentice first begins to sing. The final stage, according to Lord, is when the singer has become accomplished enough to move freely in his tradition.[21] Roughly the same paradigm can be used for the preachers. At first, as a young child, he sits in church and learns the stories of the Bible, the popular sermon topics, the melody and rhythm of gospel songs (and more importantly the melody and rhythm of his pastor's chanted sermons), and, however unconsciously, many of the phrases which will later become formulas. The incipient preacher will also hear sermons and gospel singing at home on the radio; recently he can hear them on records and even more recently he can see other preachers on television. All these aspects of style and lessons of theology he absorbs as a child, whether he has it in his mind ever to become a preacher or not.

A second stage often comes when the apprentice involves himself with church work so that he attends services more frequently. The Rev. Mr. Brown sang in a choir for several years before stepping forward to the pulpit, and during that time the music of songs and sermons became firmly ingrained in him. Many preachers are former deacons of the church who began their new role gradually by reciting short prayers before the sermon proper;[22] when the prayer has been mastered a short sermon may be attempted, perhaps in front of the children's Bible class. Gradually the assistant pastor can work into his church's schedule until he is ready to take a church on his own. The sermon of such an apprentice, William Robinson of the First Baptist of Santa Barbara, is included in this book. Lacy skipped this second stage, learning his music as a Blues singer; but his childhood was saturated with the music and rhythms of the church, and he attended services regularly while singing for his living.

The final stage begins when the preacher takes his own church; at this point he must feel that his repertoire is sufficient to sustain the congregation week after week, and that his skill is sufficient to master the intricacies of the individual sermon. He then becomes an active part of his tradition: he has mastered certain aspects of language and certain rhythms which he knows are sure to elicit a predictable response. The ratio of the interplay of free-floating materials (shaped by the preacher's imagination) to necessary elements makes a comparison with improvised jazz helpful. Rarely does the jazz musician completely improvise with no relation to the work he is currently playing; almost always he knows his score perfectly, has played it many times, and has thought about it even more frequently. When, during a performance, he breaks free of the limits of the standard notes, he has a good idea of what he is going to do, in at least general terms. But the important point of comparison is that the improvisation is possible only when the basic score has been mastered, however simple or difficult. Thus, in the same way, the preacher does not move away from what he knows well, even if his standard is his own text, until he has mastered his technique.

One could predict with certitude how a taped sermon by Detroit's C. L. Franklin or one by the Rev. Mr. Gatewood would be received; such sermons are in, are part of, the idiom.[23] And one could with equal certainty predict how flat a sermon by a white, northern Presbyterian would sound to a southern Baptist congregation. C. L. Franklin, filled with the Spirit of God, would impart that Spirit to any Negro congregation (whose own pastor was a spiritual preacher) even though they had never heard him before.[24]

III

Sermon Content and Structure

Every oral preacher insists that his sermon material comes from God. There is no question in his mind about that, and it is a touchy matter to try and discuss more secular sources. Lacy can sit at home for a week and think on and off about his sermon for the following Sunday, but he knows that God has driven him to deliver that particular sermon on that particular day, even to choosing the passages from Scripture that he will use or quote; and most important, at the moment of performance God, and God alone, will inspire him to say the words that he will actually use. The most articulate expression of that belief—the relation of inspiration to the spiritual sermon—comes not from Bakersfield, however, but from the Rev. Rufus Hays of Louisa, Virginia. Though not from Lacy's present or former home, Hays's opinion would be heartily endorsed by all spiritual preachers:

> As you concentrate and meditate open-hearted and mind, God can relate to you the interpretation properly, and He can bring out the message that He has in the particular points to the people that He has to speak of. As you know the Scriptures tells a story; they relates commands; they relates demands; you might be reading a particular experience of Israel. In that particular statement or conversation there is a point of verse; and the Spirit of the Lord dawns on you out of that particular point or passage of Scripture. The Lord utters deeper inspiration, maybe not relating to the same subject or thought that was spoken to Israel at that time, but that's the way God's word is . . .

What the preacher says comes from the Holy Ghost, but the preacher must be familiar with Scripture, for instance, in order to know how to interpret the Holy Ghost's message. Only after I came to know them better did Lacy and Brown discuss their sources. The most fertile field for religious ideas is the sermons of other preachers, especially ones the preacher has heard in his childhood. Then, scores of books are available which anthologize sermons either in their entirety or in outlines, and occasionally list suggestions for sermon themes.[1] And radio, phonograph records, and television church services are a third valuable source.

Exposure to the sermons of fellow preachers is extensive, even without the intensifying of that exposure through radio and television. For instance, Lacy and Brown usually go to Arkansas every year to participate in the revivals there; and of course they listen to the sermons of their colleagues who have made the same pilgrimage from other parts of the country. A man like Lacy is able to pick up ideas for sermon topics from preachers all over the South without doing extensive traveling himself. The annual Baptist conventions also bring the faithful together for several days of prayer and preaching. One of Lacy's favorite sermons, for instance, is an elaboration and application of the Old Testament parable "The Eagle Stirreth Up Her Nest." Lacy says that he heard "Lee Hardy" use it often. Perhaps; but this is an extremely popular sermon topic among southern Baptists, having been recorded on disc by C. L. Franklin, J. M. Gates, and Calvin P. Dixon. Lacy has heard records made by Franklin, although he doesn't remember which ones, and he might have heard the others.

Especially popular is "Dry Bones in the Valley" (from Ezekiel 37): Lacy and Brown can recite their own versions of it, and the story has also been recorded by Gates, Joe McCoy (as "Hallelujah Joe"), Elder Charles Beck, and the Rev. Leora Ross. A further indication of the popularity of this story may be seen in its version as a spiritual ("Ezekiel Saw the Wheel") and the popular *tour de force* of several years ago ("Dem Bones, Dem Bones, Dem Dry Bones"). Both traditions have been united by Lacy in a sermon recorded in 1967. Not only the repeated use of a specific passage from Scripture but the similarity of development of many of the sermons suggest at least an indirect influence within a tradition.

Other popular sermon topics are worthy of mention here: The Four Horsemen; the Twenty-third Psalm; Moses at the Red Sea; Dead (or Live) Cat on the Line; the Horse Paweth in the Valley; Jesus Will

Make It All Right; Jesus Will Lead You; The Prodigal Son; and The New Jerusalem.[2] Certain preachers favor certain stories and will use them more often, but most preachers with several years' experience will be able to preach on all these topics.

Now most preachers are not willing to admit that their ideas come from other men. Lacy, for instance, preached a sermon in June 1967 on a "Deck of Cards," which he at first claimed was his own invention; people in Bakersfield had never heard such an idea, he said. The sermon's basic theme was that the standard deck of cards has religious significance: the ace is the One God, the two suggests both books of the Bible, the three stands for the trinity, the four-spot corresponds to the four gospel writers, and so forth. When pressed by another member of the congregation, and remembering that he was in church, Lacy admitted that he got the idea from a talking Country and Western record made by T. Texas Tyler some time after World War II. The same story has since been recorded by Tex Williams, Tex Ritter, Ernest Tubb, Pee Wee King, Wink Martindale, even by Phil Harris. It has been satirized by Ferlin Husky (as "Simon Crum") in a version called "The Hillbilly Sucker and the Deck of Cards." Lacy recognized a good thing when he heard it and used Tyler's idea[3] in his sermon (the "Deck of Cards" sermon is printed in this book). The Rev. J. J. Freeman of Pixley, California, uses a particularly inventive theme for one of his favorite sermons, "The Postage Stamp," which compares man, and especially the church's pastor, to a postage stamp: man has his place in life, just as the stamp has its place on the envelope. The five-cent stamp (before the rise in postal rates) does the best job it can within its capability, just as man is bidden to do the best he can with the talents God has given him.[4] I have not been able to track down the source for Freeman's sermon, if one does exist, but I would guess that if it is original it will soon enter the tradition (if it has not done so already) when some other preacher adopts it.

A second major source is written sermon material, of which there is a thriving literature. Jabez D. Burns has written several books of sermons and sermon outlines which are very popular among the clergy I interviewed. Lacy has often preached on "God's Plowboy," comparing the minister to the farm laborer who fertilizes the (spiritual) soil, but who toils in the field in hopes of an ultimate reward. The theme comes from *Master Sermon Outlines* (Atlanta, n.d.); Lacy merely used the bare outline and several of the major points as a rough guide, as is usually the method when written sources are used. ("God's Plowboy" and its source

have been printed below.) Many southern Negro preachers are so ac-
customed to reciting orally and composing spontaneously that when they
read from a text the result is usually poor; in the performance of "God's
Plowboy" recorded in 1967, Lacy read three or four passages from Scripture contained in his source book, but extemporized the rest, while ad-
hering—as was mentioned earlier—generally to the book's outline.

One should also include among this kind of sermon those which are
read directly from the Bible. The Rev. Mr. Goins, from the Bakersfield
area, once preached on Genesis, reading directly from Scripture (though
one may be certain that he did not have to), gradually breaking into a
chant and away from a literal reading.

If we try to find out from the men themselves how they compose their
sermons, we again run into differing interpretations. "Manuscript"
preachers compose by the inspiration and perspiration method: about
90 per cent hard work to exploit 10 per cent good idea. But "spiritual"
preachers of the type under consideration are far harder to pin down.
The Rev. Mr. Brown has often said that his inspiration comes only from
God; Lacy corroborates this, insisting that no preparation is necessary
because the sermon is inspired: he simply has to step up to the pulpit
and he is "fed" directly from God. These explanations are typical; I have
since found the same idea invariably expressed throughout the South.

Yet at times Lacy could announce a week in advance what he was
going to talk about on the following Sunday morning and one time let
slip that he had been "thinkin'" and "workin' up" a particular sermon
for several days. On Sunday morning it is common for the men I interviewed to use many of the words, phrases, and even ideas that they are
going to use while preaching. One Sunday morning, Brown welcomed
me with the remark that he was thankful that "God's hand" had guided
me to Bakersfield, and he excused himself several minutes later, leaving
me in "the goods hands" of the deacon. His sermon an hour later was on
"Being in the Hands of God."

The spiritual preacher "works up" his sermon for several days or, if
time is short, for several hours before delivery by reviewing in his mind
the basic outline, much as Parry and Lord found that their Yugoslav informants "memorized" their epics by remembering the basic outlines and
filling in the story with formulas. The spiritual preacher has a stock
of themes for use in sermons as well as a stock of sermons which he can
use at will. Like the jazz musician of our earlier example, the preacher
does not experiment with his sermons until he has learned them well.

New sermons are added to the repertoire gradually, and then filled in with stock phrases and even stock passages of ten lines or more. This generalization will almost always hold despite Lacy's claim that the best way to preach is without warning of any kind: "if you got notice you mess up," but when you preach at the last minute you have got to depend upon God. Preliminary study time is used by such men as the Rev. Rufus Hays (of Louisa, Virginia) who gives a fifteen-minute "sermonette" over WELK, Charlottesville, and who studies the Bible in preparation for the day's message just before broadcast time.

Lacy has already been quoted as insisting that the preacher is fed by God, and he uses this faith to justify his mild contempt for those who use a manuscript. Yet in his sermon on "God's Plowboy" Lacy used *Master Sermon Outlines* and read the appropriate passages from Scripture. Brown does the same thing when he wants to be sure to repeat the quotation accurately. McDowell often uses a note card, reducing a twenty-minute sermon to a 5″ x 5″ card. Goins and others who have recited from the Bible begin with the book in front of them, and though the first several words may be quoted verbatim they soon break into their own idiomatic chant. For instance, Brown once began a sermon with: "In the beginning was the word. And the word was with God. And the word sure was God." In this case the idiomatic "sure was God" was added to regularize the meter of the line.

For the spiritual preacher, then, God works through an extensive tradition of sermon topics, derived from other preachers heard live, on radio, records, or television. Some of the topics are explications and comparisons of normally secular subjects, such as the deck of cards or the postage stamp. Others are explications of passages in the Bible. The preacher relies upon stock phrases and passages to fill out the skelton of the sermon, and develops the message through repetition. T. Texas Tyler's "Deck of Cards" record takes less than four minutes in performance. Lacy stretches it out to about eight minutes, but even that is still only one-third of the piece he calls his "Deck of Cards" sermon. He has recently said that he can use the "cards" portion of the sermon with almost any message preceding it, though preferably with commentary on "heart." He has used the "cards" portion so often that he can recite it nearly by heart, with only minor lexical variations. The rest of the sermon may not be so nearly organized or composed, but can be put together by techniques similar to those described by Parry, as we shall later see.

There is a famous literary precedence for Lacy's technique. Chaucer's

Pardoner could also preach on any topic spontaneously: "for I kan al by rote that I telle."[5] The Pardoner's technique is not oral formulaic, yet the suggestion is strong that he composes by the manipulation of traditional themes. But the Pardoner's story is a confession of cynicism; he preaches against certain vices in the tale, specifically, gluttony and swearing in order to increase the sinner's offering. His preaching is flexible; he can preach against any sin spontaneously because he has "by rote" learned what to say on every occasion. This historical comparison is important for several reasons. Primarily, it places Lacy and his colleagues in a human and Christian context which is relevant to their lives today. This context, which gives us many analogues to Lacy's situation, raises his problems and his skills out of the immediate milieu of his Bakersfield existence and enables us to see how he shares them with memorable characters of the past. And finally, these comparisons remind us that though the immediate focus is the American spiritual preacher, our ultimate concern is with a less chronologically and spatially limited human phenomenon.

We have seen how the Puritan sermon is based on a "text-context-application" pattern; if we are to judge from Middle English sermons collected in the Early English Text Society series (London, 1940), such was the basic pattern for the later Middle Ages. Once again we may see Lacy, with all his individual genius, still as part of a tradition which has been the common heritage of all of us for several centuries. For this pattern is exactly what many southern preachers, especially those under study, strive for in their own sermon organization.

The "text-and-context" organization, the exegetical sermon, has survived through the Renaissance and into our century where, as the Rev. Mr. Robert Howland of the Goleta, California, Presbyterian Church, has pointed out, it has been largely ignored by white middle-class churches. The pastors of those churches prefer topical sermons dealing with more secular matters such as civil rights, disarmament, our Asian wars, the "New Morality," and such quasi-secular topics (for Protestants) as birth control. This secularized sermon is another aspect of our heritage from the eighteenth century. The topical sermon occasionally uses scriptural evidence to support the main argument, but it is not at all thematically like the gospel preaching of many southern fundamentalist clergy. The northern middle-class churches are changing their sermon content; the southern churches, especially the Baptist and Methodist, are in this respect keeping alive Christian tradition of considerable antiquity.

One can see the structural patterns of which we have been speaking in several of the sermons collected in this volume. They are even more obvious in the sermons of the great, nationally known preachers such as the Rev. Mr. C. L. Franklin. Many of his sermons have been recorded by *Battle* and *Chess* Records in Detroit. Franklin is a master of organization, just as he is of drama. His sermon, "Moses at the Red Sea," in particular, and its applicability to those in his congregation who face or who have faced seemingly insurmountable difficulties—and their resolution by drawing upon the strength within themselves—has been created carefully by a man of great sensitivity and reason. J. Charles Jessup, though not Negro and not Baptist, strives for the text-context-application-resolution formula and usually achieves it. Lacy and Brown are far less tidy in their sermon organization, especially Lacy: witness his statement that he could begin his "Deck of Cards" sermon on almost any topic, though he tried to think of something that had to do with "heart." His opening quotation was: "The fool has said in his heart, 'there is no God.'" Both Lacy and Brown digress quite a bit, as did several other preachers in the area, occasionally getting completely off the subject. A sermon of thirty to forty minutes is, after all, difficult to keep on a single subject within a given framework. There is no continuing narrative thread to force the speaker to stay on the track. And it is in the nature of sermons to use examples, proverbs, parables, etc.; understandably, then, preachers who compose spontaneously by welding together such illustrative materials with set passages and phrases can be very easily led astray. In some of Brown's sermons one can hear him struggling to get back to the point after an ambiguous scriptural passage has led him to pursue some irrelevant theme.

When one first hears sermons of the type under consideration, little coherence is found in them. Even in transcribing them I could find little in the way of any principle of organization. Narratives are easier to organize; certain characters have to be introduced at certain points in the story and certain events have to take place. We learn something about Beowulf before he fights his first combat; he sets sail, is encountered by the coast-warden, is introduced to Hrothgar, and is twitted by Unferth before he engages Grendel in combat. The singer of such a tale will have little trouble remembering what is to happen because of the nature of the story: the singer is not likely to forget and place the Unferth episode after Beowulf has beaten the troll—it would not make sense.

But sermons need not have any such necessary consistency. Standardized narrative scenes whose language is memorized—Lord's "themes"—may be ornamental or essential. The former may be used in any given narrative depending upon the whim of the singer; essential themes may have to be used owing to the nature of the narrative. The sermon singer can be far more flexible: the sermon itself is usually based on a single line of Scripture, and not on an elaborate narrative. That single line may be expanded in many ways, and though the preacher may use passages that are similar in principle to Lord's themes, they are seldom necessary in the way that narrative themes are necessary.

A good illustration of this point is Lacy's sermon on "Dry Bones in the Valley" (printed below). The story from Ezekiel concerns the role of the prophet and preacher, and the fact that he was in the desert reminds Lacy of himself in the San Joaquin "desert." But Lacy is also an old man now and one of his favorite stories is about St. John as an old man. So he talked about John first in the sermon on "Dry Bones." Then he talked about "Old Man" Moses, gave a sermonized version of "Dem Bones," and finally got around to Ezekiel. Now little enough logic holds in this sermon, yet all these stories are related if we use the associational leaps in Lacy's mind as a guide. St. John's old age is not related to Ezekiel logically, but we have seen how the connection would be made by the preacher. The story of Moses follows; the connection? Moses as an old man led his people to salvation across the desert. The final passage Lacy knows he will have to reach has to do with bones, and that reminded him of the popular song about "Dem Bones." Finally he comes to Ezekiel. As narrative it is near chaos, though there are narrative passages in the separate stories of the sermon; as logic it is something of a disaster; and yet, in a subtle way, all the tales hold together.

But if they cohere in this sermon at least, they, or their order, are not essential to the sermon. No discussion of Ezekiel in the valley of dry bones needs a story of Moses in the desert. All that is necessary to such a sermon is the story of Ezekiel in the valley. The other stories—sometimes they are also themes—are ornamental (like the digressions in *Beowulf*?). Very few themes are essential in this art, so that the preacher has a greater thematic flexibility than the *guslar*. There is this difference: many of the *guslar's* themes are structured necessarily while nearly all of the preacher's are arbitrary and occur associationally.

IV
Chanting

What strangers to chanted sermons find most striking is that during most of the performance, and especially during the chanted portions, the congregation is actively involved in the service. They hum, sing aloud, yell, and join in the sermon as they choose, and almost always their timing is impeccable. The quality of the congregation appears to have a great effect upon the sermon, influencing the preacher's timing, his involvement in his delivery, and sometimes even the length of the performance. Such have been my observations despite Lacy's claim that it did not matter whether his audience numbered three or three hundred. He has said that he could preach alone in his own house with no audience, or could preach to me alone; but he never tried, or came near trying. Some preachers who do a lot of radio work where there is no congregation present have become less dependent on audience response, but with men who do both live and electronic preaching there is a difference in styles. In Lacy's case, after one sermon to a particularly deadening congregation he complained to Brown that he had to "carry it" by himself. For instance, his pacing and timing were nearly perfect in the 1967 "Deck of Cards" sermon, and the audience's response was so vigorous that many of Lacy's words were obscured by spontaneous shouts and singing. But in a later sermon on "Revelation" his timing broke down, he stumbled over his words like a drunk over foot-stools, and emotionally never got out of bed. His occasional efforts to rouse up the "spirit" of the congregation—by shouting, by singing some of the lines, and by calling "Amen!"—fell flat, and he himself was punctured and drifting.

Lacy's chanting failed because his congregation was not with him—had no empathy with him—that time. But Lacy was correct in theory: as he explains it, chanting seems to "attract people's attention," though that is a great understatement. Clearly, chanting builds up the emotions of the congregation as can no other means, and it is at such moments of emotional intensity that the Spirit of God is most noticeable. The sermons begin in prose and (should) end in song, passing through and pausing over various stages of chanting.[1] To illustrate this difference of style within the same sermon, I quote the following lines from the beginning and ending of two performances. The first selection is from a sermon delivered by Lacy on July 9, 1967:

[1] For the Lord's portion is His people
   Jacob is the lot of his inheritance
   He found them—watch this—in a desert land
   In the waste howling land
5 He led him about and He instructed him
   And kept him as an apple of His eye

I have set up Lacy's "sentences" in this transcription as though they were metrically consistent in order to compare them with the following chanted lines from the same sermon:

[1] Eagle has got an eye
   Look at the sun
   The beams of the sun
   All day long
5 Don't have to bat his eyes
   Don't turn his body around
   Jes' set there in one place
   Turn his neck around

The most obvious difference between these two passages is that the chanted lines are shorter, and usually have five or six syllables. But when one hears Lacy the difference is far more noticeable than the printed comparison indicates. The first passage is recited calmly, as though from a book: the cadence is casual, almost relaxed. But when the second passage was chanted or sung, the short lines, such as line 4, were drawn out;

metrically, "all" and "long" are given a time value of two or three syllables. Musically, the words are rendered *glissando* so that the time interval is made consistent with lines 3 and 5. And those lines with more than six syllables, such as line 6, are compressed by garbling and by shortening the notes to bring them nearer the standard.

Perhaps because of his experience as a professional singer, Lacy's chanting is more metrical (and more rhythmical) than some. Here is the beginning of a recent sermon on "Revelation":

1 I want you to understand this, it don't be mornin' all over the world
    at the same time
It don't be mornin' in the world—all over the world—at the same time
Sometime it's evenin' here when it's mornin' there
But I believe He's coming in the mornin'
5 I don't know what time He be here
But I believe He's comin' in the mornin'
And I know he's on his way
I know He's on His way because I seen too many signs
The average person don't care nothin' about God

The following lines are from the same sermon after Lacy had begun to chant:

1 And God told John—break a twig Amen!
And hold up a twig
As prove to you that I'm on the' island
And John broke a twig—God from Zion
5 And held the twig up on the island
And the four winds began to shake a twig
In old man John's hand
The Spirit kep' on callin' to John
God from Zion
10 And told old man John
Umm-hmm

In the second passage Lacy is alternating between a nine or ten-syllable line (such as lines 1, 3, 4, 5, 6, and 8) and the shorter half-line (or its metrical approximation) as in lines 2, 9, 10, and 11. Line 4 has been transcribed as a nine-syllable line, but might just as easily have been valued at two lines of five and four syllables.

Making a line-by-line transcription of the passages from the first part of any oral sermon is slightly harder than marking the limits of the chanted line. At first the "reading" is performed as though from a conventional manuscript with appropriate pauses at the end of each "sentence." Usually the sermons begin with a reading of Scripture and the preacher follows the Bible's punctuation. But these sermons are antiphonal in nature, and soon the audience's response—so active and cogently felt—actually delineates each line, each formula. Metrics govern. To punctuate the "beat" the congregation shouts "Amen!" "Oh yes," "Oh Lord," "that's all right," etc. Most of the time there is no doubt about the end of the phrase: the congregation clearly makes it known. Or else the preacher himself punctuates his lines with a gasp for breath that is usually so consistent it can be timed metrically.

These chanted passages are, as Lacy says, the times when God's Spirit has taken over completely. At such times he is being "fed" by God directly, is almost overcome by a "spiritual feeling," and tries to convey the Spirit to the congregation. At such moments, the preachers say, the words come so fast that they have to pause to straighten them out in their minds. Hence, say Lacy and Brown, the frequent use of such phrases as "Am I right this evenin'," "God from Zion," and "I want you to know." But more of that later.

The better to describe this chant in musical terms for those readers who have never heard a sermon sung—and who will never hear the field tapes—Professor Clayton Wilson of the Music Department at the University of California of Santa Barbara volunteered to notate the chants of Lacy and Brown musically. The phrases were selected for their musical quality and because they were also representative. The first two are from a sermon of Brown's:

Although these lines are used to illustrate their music, the first one is a stock phrase which Brown probably uses a dozen times a sermon. If read, one would give it six syllables, but the way Brown chants it the line has a value of seven and, depending upon how "know" is noted, possibly eight. Now the second line has eleven syllables when spoken, but when chanted—as noted by the triplets—the words are elided and compressed so that it has the value of about a seven count. Brown is happiest with a tetrameter line, but when a phrase is too short, as in the first example above, he lengthens it, and when the line is too long, he squeezes it musically to fit, or nearly fit, his meter.

Lacy's professional training has given him an advantage so far as concerns metrics. The following lines were taken from his sermon, "The Eagle Stirreth Up Her Nest:"

Lacy usually prefers a pentameter line or variations of it, especially two half-lines of six and four, or single half-lines of five syllables.

Professor Wilson also remarked that both men chanted in a pentatonic scale, as did most of the men recorded in this study, even when their chanting was barely distinguishable from the spoken part of the sermon. The scale is a common one in the Baptist hymnal—one would expect the preachers to be at home with it—and we found that the congregation also hummed or sang along in the same scale. On one occasion, before Brown chanted, "Oh I want you to know," one member of the congregation sang the same notes, anticipating his pastor by a second or two. This came to our attention because the singer's voice was interfering with Wilson's notation of Brown's music, and the same line had to be replayed quite often before it could be notated properly. But the same phenomenon happens often, so often that it strongly suggests that not only do the listeners know what ideas and phrases are to come next, but that they can also anticipate the preacher's music. In an antiphonal art such as this, music provides yet another means of mutual communication. But music may also provide a bridge between lines as an aid in composition: repeated phrases are often chanted to the same musical notes and may aid the preacher in the selection of the notes of the next line. And participation by the congregation in the performance brings additional rapport with the preacher on a level other than the linguistic one. The musical element of the sermon, then, not only aids the preacher with his metrics and arouses the emotions of the congregation, but helps them to anticipate the message. I use the word "message" with a certain care, for in few other arts is the message so clearly the medium as in this kind of preaching.

In a sense each preacher has his own "message," and that will vary from man to man even though the text for the day is the same. The music is *that* important. Lacy's short line and intense emotion (once he gets going) give his message a dramatic compulsion; Brown's longer line and even pacing give his sermons a lyrical quality appropriate to his lamenting tone; and the Rev. Mr. McDowell is capable of both drama and lyric and can use both within a single sermon. Each preacher has his own style, his own melody, timing, and tonal quality that help determine the quality of his message. A few, like McDowell, can vary that tone within a sermon, but too great variations seem to be distracting to the preacher's concentration.

It must be recalled in any discussion of the meter or rhythm of oral sermons that they all begin in prose and work toward metrical verse. The flow is not always smooth, the metrics may be poor (and may vary during the sermon), and the preacher may alternate between "prose" and metrical sections. It is sometimes difficult to know exactly when the preacher is chanting (rather than talking) or when he is singing (rather than chanting). It is, of course, a matter of degree. This is one of the reasons why visual scanning of transcribed sermons is often not significant as a descriptive technique. The most superficial look at any of the sermons shows that more lines are hyper- and hypometric than are "standard." This happens for reasons other than the preacher's unconcern about whether he is talking, chanting, or singing at any given moment.[2]

Most preachers do not seem to have a particularly strong desire to maintain the same meter throughout the sermons, and one often hears syncopated lines which, although not peculiar to Negroes, is characteristic of their music. This has been observed countless times in Negro ballads and it has apparently carried over to their religious literature. A syncopated beat, especially when used in a hyper- or hypometric line, will appear even more irregular when printed, though its time value may be the same as a regular line in performance. And, further confounding any attempts to scan this literature as one would text poetry is the Negro's well-known proclivity for improvisation. Gerould has commented on this trait in ballad studies[3] and it, too, is characteristic of the oral preaching style.

When Lacy said that he thought chanting "caught the attention" of the congregation, I asked him about the appropriateness of the Blues in church services.[4] His answer was simple. The Blues he defined as "a worryin' mind." Hence only the Christian could really sing the Blues, he thought, because only the Christian was concerned about sin and its punishment. The sinner is carefree—he doesn't worry, and so could not sing the Blues the right way. Therefore, Lacy thinks, the Blues are all right in church. In fact, he thinks that often the Blues are "more truth-ful" than conventional church hymns. He used as an example some lines from a song he used to sing:

> You never miss your water 'till your well runs dry,
> Never miss your good gal 'till she said "goodbye."

For Lacy, who had known days in Mississippi when the wells did run dry, that song had truth. But some church songs "tell lies" such as "When I take my vacation in heaven." A vacation, says Lacy, is some-thing that you come back from, and you do not come back from heaven. (Obviously, however, many people *have* felt that heaven is analogous to a vacation: Probably unknown to Lacy is a record cut by the Rev. D. C. Rice about the "Vacation in Heaven" on *Vocalion* Records [1502].) For at least as far as the Rev. Mr. Lacy is concerned, then, the church has something to learn from the secular world of Blues. I do not want to generalize from this one opinion, but I have found it typical. No one who has heard the "soul music" of Aretha Franklin (daughter of the Rev. C. L. Franklin), Dinah Washington, Sarah Vaughn, Nancy Wilson, or Stevie Wonder can doubt the easy exchange between gospel singing and that type of rock; even some "soul music" lyrics are taken from the church: "I Want To Testify." To the layman more familiar with psycho-logical than with ecclesiastical terms, there seems to be little difference, quantitatively, between the joyous hand-clapping of rock enthusiasts and ardent congregationalists.

McDowell or any other preacher is considered skillful when he has mastered several aspects of his craft, including singing. Most of the better men have good voices which enable them to sing many of the lines. The effect is aesthetically pleasing as well as spiritually moving. Lacy was a Blues singer; McDowell also sang professionally with small groups; and Brown sang in his church choir for many years. Others, like Freeman, are not accomplished singers but can do the next best thing, that is, chant on key. In Freeman's case it is good enough. C. L. Franklin hardly sings at all, but he has greater control over the tone, inflection, and timbre of his voice than most actors.

Timing is at least as important. Lacy knows intuitively when to sit down. He knows when he has reached a certain point in his sermon when to go on further will be to lose the high pitch to which he has brought the congregation. The skillful preacher develops his sermon with a certain care and with the emotions of the audience in mind. This is a test of the preacher's aesthetic sense; his timing—his development of ideas and sentiments—is part of the sermon's structure and it too must please in order to move.

Rhythm is perhaps the most important aspect of the preacher's musical art. Timing, in this immediate context, is concerned with the architecture of the entire sermon; rhythm is the property of the delivery of single lines. Rhythm is an on-going skill: it must be sustained and properly paced throughout the sermon to be truly effective. A few—but only a very few—of the most skillful preachers can sustain the rhythm of their lines regardless of the reaction of the congregation and regardless of whether they have a live audience before them or not. Jessup preaches more over radio these days than he does to a tent full of worshippers, and thus has had to develop his timing and rhythm without the response of an audience. It should be pointed out, however, that Jessup does not sing his sermon, and his lines are not easily divided into formulas. But a man like McDowell has enough presence of mind to maintain his rhythm and in so doing bring the congregation to his level rather than fall to theirs. In an art where the language is so intimately tied up with rhythm— where the language itself is determined by the meter of the line—a faulty rhythm causes various problems. When a preacher's rhythm is off, nearly everything he does will fail; in the 1968 sermon on the Twenty-third Psalm, Lacy reached out some distance thematically to use a theme on "The Four Horsemen" of whose rhythm he was sure. When that portion revived so did the rest of his performance.

The verbal skill of the preacher can be judged by his ability to compose formulas and the craft with which he manipulates them and his themes both for sense and for the emotional power they exert on his listeners. The manipulation of formulas is at least a twofold process; many are fitted spontaneously into the metrical pattern prevailing in the sermon of the moment whether the language so manipulated is being read, is known by heart, or is being used for the first time. And many "memorized" formulas to be used when he is behind the pulpit are no doubt conceived in privacy and peace of the pastor's home. Regardless of how the formulas are created, at the moment of the performance they must be fitted into the proper semantic and metrical mold. (The psycholinguistic process involved will be discussed later.) And the right lines must be used in the right places within the sermon, both in relation to other formulas and to themes; formulas often occur in a set order within the themes, and the themes have to be employed in proper relation to each other and to the sermon as a whole. In all this manipulation and usage, flexibility rather than rigidity must govern; there is no one proper or effective way to preach any given sermon. Everything is in flux: the congregation and its moods, the rhythms, diction, syntax, and the emotions of the preacher, and his message for the day. If the preacher is skillful he will take all, or nearly all, of these considerations into account, however unconsciously, and will mold his sermon accordingly. The end result should be the movement of the Spirit of God in the church.

When an audience is responsive the preacher catches its enthusiasm. The singing before a sermon begins is a sure indication of the congregation's emotional level. If the people are "high," the songs will be sung energetically and many of the verses will be repeated, with various improvisations by the piano player and lead soprano. (Brown's congregation is blessed with two fine gospel singers, his own wife and Mrs. Lucille Mukes.) When the congregation is "down," the preacher is likely to recite his sermon woodenly; only the most patient exploitation will bring them around. When they are "up" he gestures, he struts, he acts out the narrative, and he makes asides to various members of the congregation, the choir, or the visiting pastors.[5] A congregation must itself feel the urgency and truth of the sermon before it becomes involved in it. An "up" congregation punctuates the preacher's phrases, as already noted, with shouts, chants, and singing. At such moments they are filled with the "Spirit of God," as Lacy and Brown and the others say, yet it is the preacher's avowed purpose to tell the "truth of God," not merely to arouse the crowd. As William Butler Yeats once wrote about his own verse:

> The purpose of rhythm, it has always seemed to me, is to prolong the moment of contemplation, the moment when we are both asleep

and awake, which is the one moment of creation, by hushing us with an alluring monotony, while it holds us waking by variety, to keep us in that state of perhaps real trance, in which the mind liberated from the pressure of the will is unfolded in symbols.[6]

The Rev. Rubin Lacy says on the one hand that the idea is the most important part of the sermon, yet his diction is such, and the congregation's response is often such, that much of what he is saying is unintelligible. What is intelligible is his driving rhythm, his musical chanting, and the great passion he exudes through emphasis, expression, and gesture. As he says, "the people should be glad twice; glad when you get up and glad when you sit down." On the matter of making the audience glad when he sits down, Lacy intentionally makes his sermons short, about twenty minutes or less. He wants to get the people "home on time." And his build-up to an emotional climax is excellent—when his audience has empathy with him. He builds gradually and steadily from prose to chanting and then to singing, gradually getting louder and more dramatic, and then so as "not to go too far," he breaks off sharply. He catches himself, he says, so that he and the congregation can "come down" to "talkin' normal." Lacy can "feel" when he has gone too far and when he should stop, and his consciousness of it suggests more than a passing interest in his congregation's emotions and in the aesthetics of his own performance.

When Brown or Freeman or the Rev. Bennie C. Blair begin singing or chanting movingly, Lacy himself, from his position behind the pulpit with his fellow clergymen, responds much as does the rest of audience. On one such occasion Lacy kept calling out to Brown, "that's preachin'," and "you say it, preacher." Such moments are not common; they occur only when the tempo has increased, audience response is high, and the preacher is chanting, but they indicate that many preachers themselves understand the role of emotion in divine worship, by whatever terms they may happen to use to describe it.[7]

We have seen that the matter of emotion in church is a controversial one. To the visitor who goes to the Rev. Brown's church for the first time, the most important aspect of the service may seem to be the congregation's emotional expressiveness. The pastor and any visiting ministers at the same service would consider such emotion a manifestation of the "Spirit of God." To them the difference would not be semantic;

it is one thing to be emotional, quite another to be filled with the Spirit. Yet at least one clergyman who likes to stimulate his audience to a frenzy is not ashamed of it. A. A. Allen has attacked some Pentacostal Churches for playing down the roles of passion and glossalalia (speaking in tongues).[8] Referring to the Rev. Harry Faught's attempts to reduce the level of emotional reactions during services, Allen asserted that "the fact that there is no emotion is his [Faught's] church is a sure sign there is no revival!" Allen has long been disdainful of what he terms "dead, formal church organizations" which are "trying to get a little action back into their dead churches" through means Allen doesn't approve of.[9] We should not enter this controversy here, however; the point is that overt passionate expression is not shameful in certain circles, and has not been in the past: We have already cited George Whitefield who could wring tears from his listeners by enunciating "Mesopotamia"; the records of religious services, both black and white, following the Second Great Awakening are extensive and eloquent. Foreign visitors were especially intrigued by this unusual form of worship.

Contemporary white middle-class churches do not indulge themselves in emotion and seem embarrassed by the "passion" displayed in other more Fundamentalist, churches. The Rev. Mr. Robert Howland, Presbyterian, who shares this view, feels certain that his congregation would at first look on such a man as the Rev. Mr. Brown as a talented performer, but would soon tire of him. American middle-class society, for the most part, is ashamed of public emotion: we do not weep in public, and we do not shout in church. Howland's opinion is no doubt true, yet passionate sermons and weeping, howling congregations are quite old in Western traditions. Again, we can return to the Middle Ages and the preaching of the Dominicans and Franciscans: contemporaries describe the weeping, work coming to a standstill, and a steady flow of malefactors throwing themselves at the preacher's feet.[10]

I do not suggest that the preachers of the Missionary Baptist Church are counterparts of the medieval friars or that there is necessarily any similarity between their preaching styles, but that there are parallels and precedents that should not be ignored.

V

The Formulaic Quality of
the Chanted Sermon

When we try to learn in some detail how the preachers compose their sermons, we get little help from them in language that is meaningful to secularly oriented laymen. Whatever is to be learned must be from observation and by translating the preachers' remarks into secular terms. I have described the delivery of sermons without any manuscript and usually without notes of any kind except, perhaps, a Bible. However, most preachers do prefer to have some time to think about their sermons, though sometimes sermons are given (and hence composed) extemporaneously without any immediate preparation. Occasionally men are asked to say a prayer or a "few words" of one sort or another without prior warning, and in effect a short sermon is delivered. On one occasion a guest preacher delivered a sermon on a topic of which the host pastor had no prior knowledge; but the subject pleased the pastor so much that as soon as the guest had finished the host began preaching yet another sermon on the same topic, the Twenty-third Psalm. The second sermon was obviously composed spontaneously; it contained, naturally, language which the minister had been assimilating and arranging for many years (with his first words he said that he liked preaching on the Twenty-third Psalm because it was the topic of the first sermon he ever gave); yet the man was able to preach spontaneously for about fifteen minutes in the metrical style which characterizes the genre.

As with Yugoslav epic singers whom Parry and Lord investigated during the 'thirties and 'fifties, these compositions are put together with formulaic systems,[1] which are handled quite flexibly throughout the sermon, and of (nearly) memorized themes[2] which, if anything, are even more flexible than the themes of narrative epic poetry. It does not matter that the Parry-Lord singers composed narrative epics while the American preachers compose sermons: the modes of creation are similar and many comparisons may still be made. The sermons are hortatory, certainly, but even a superficial glance at the sermons collected in this volume will show that they are also largely narrative. Narrative and dramatic *exempla* are used throughout as are narrative stories from the Bible. Yet what is most important is that the language of the preachers is heavily formulaic in the sense that Parry meant,[3] and that their sermons are composed by using language that is largely formulaic.

For the spiritual preacher the moment of composition is the performance. Two sermons on the same subject or from the same text are never identical, though the bare structural skeleton may be the same. What is memorized is the sermon's basic outline and perhaps several themes, but the language itself with which the skeleton is fleshed in fluctuates substantially, even in the instance of two sermons delivered by the same man on the same subject. The preacher of sermons, then, is the composer of sermons.

I have already discussed briefly how the preacher learns: from his own pastor as a child, from hearing others in neighborhood churches, from radio and now television, and from reading religious matter. In the beginning he may sit passively and absorb the phrases of his (informal) masters, and just as importantly he may develop the sense of rhythm which will determine his own style later on. Eventually he may "preach to the trees and the birds" as Lacy did, recite the benediction in church while a deacon, give an occasional sermon as an assistant pastor, and then command a pulpit of his own.

All along, his basic problem is to fit the ideas of the sermon to the basic rhythmic pattern. As James Weldon Johnson observed long ago, the Negro preacher knows that the secret of oratory is a progression of rhythmic words.[4] The rhythm is the message; congregations have been moved to ecstasy by the rhythmic chanting of incoherencies. During many sermons it is physically impossible to hear what the preacher is saying—so loud is the singing, shouting, chanting, and humming of the audience—even if what he is saying is of some great import. Yet the congregation feels that it is receiving the truth of the gospel. Often the tapes, recorded with the microphone on the pulpit, are for many seconds blurred beyond distinction. Rousing the Spirit of God is the aim of these sermons, and rhythm best rouses that spirit.

As has been pointed out, the kind of meter spiritual preachers use is quantitive: the "line" depends upon the length of time required to pronounce the syllables, and is not usually determined by stress or accent. The rhythm—not only within but between lines—must proceed with the regularity and inexorability of a drumbeat. If the words or syllables within a given line are too few, they are drawn out to the required time value by singing, *recitivo*; if they are too many they are compressed so as to fit into the allotted space.[5] Not all preachers are consistent and not all have a fine ear for timing. Rhythms vary, not only from preacher to preacher, but from sermon to sermon and within the same sermon delivered by the same man. It may be occasionally necessary to fit the rhythm to the subject. And in an effective sermon it is always necessary to gradually increase the rhythm so as to inspire the congregation, and to build toward an emotional and spiritual peak through rhythm, whether that peak be at the end of the sermon or near its middle.[6]

To fit a group of words which would express a given idea to metrical conditions, a special mode of communication had to be developed, identical to the mode which Lord called formulaic. The formula must be identified, in this stage at least, as repetition, despite the inadequacy of the term. For instance, in one of the sermons collected below (D. J. McDowell's "The Christ of the Bible") one finds a striking repetition of certain phrases:

The Christ of the Bible	24 times
Am I right about it?	15 times
I know that's right	11 times
Amen (used as metrical line)	11 times
Keep your hand in God's hand	5 times

One would expect to find the phrase "The Christ of the Bible" in a sermon with that title and one whose subject matter is an attempted adumbration of the Christ of the Bible. But twenty-four times is far more than accidental, and a bit more than rhetorical. Furthermore, McDowell uses the same phrase (though not as frequently) in other sermons, just as many of the phrases—and entire sections or "themes"—are used elsewhere and in different contexts.

As a demonstration of the extent of the composition by formula of a spiritual sermon I shall cite a passage from the same source. Most of McDowell's work is heavily formulaic, it is true, and to that extent the use of his material does load the argument; however, many more heavily formulaic passages might have been used, either by McDowell or others. The most obvious examples have not been selected: the following passage is fairly typical of McDowell, and illustrative of oral preachers generally. The convention of designating verbatim formulas (solid underlining) and formulas from systems found in other performances (broken underlining) used by Parry, Lord, and Old English scholars, has been followed here for the sake of clarity.

Keep your hand in God's hand
And your eyes on the starposts in glory
Lord said he would fight your battles
If you'd only be still
5   You may not be a florist
Am I right about it?
But you must tell them, that He's the Rose of Sharon
I know that's right
You may not be a geologist
10 But you must tell them, that He's the Rock of Ages
I know that's right
You may not be a physician
But you must tell them, that He's the great Physician
You may not be a baker
15 But you must tell them, that He's the Bread of Life
Am I right about it?
You must tell them
That He's a friend
That stick close t'his brother
20 He said, I'll not cast ya out
In the sixth hour, and in the seventh hour
I didn't know I was turnin' ya out
If y'keep your hand in God's hand

The heavily repetitious quality of this passage is obvious on first reading. Of the twenty-three lines, nine (including 2 and 23) are repetitions of others within the same sermon. Eight lines are nearly identical: the syn-

tax is consistent, with the verb in the same relative position, though the
nouns are varied (florist, geologist, physician, baker). Four lines are syn-
tactically similar to phrases found outside this sermon, either commu-
nally or personally. At least twenty-one of the lines, then, are in effect
repetitions—or 91 per cent. The remaining lines (19 and 22) may also
have been repeated elsewhere in sermons not recorded or heard.

It should be stressed once more that these figures are illustrative and
not representative; a sampling of several other men showed that the percentage of those lines that we would underline on a formulaic chart,
with a solid line or a broken one, is somewhat lower. All the samples
were taken from the chanted portions of the sermons, when the prose of
the introductions had given way to metrics. When one hundred lines of
his sermon were sampled, McDowell was found to use repeated lines 19
per cent of the time and systemic formulas 67 per cent: total, 86 per
cent; the Rev. Rubin Lacy of Bakersfield had 32 per cent repeated formulas, 41 per cent systemic: total, 73 per cent; Brown used repeated
formulas 13 per cent of the time, systemic formulas 55 per cent: total,
68 per cent; and J. J. Freeman of Pixley had a relatively low 20 per cent
and 38 per cent (total: 58 per cent). For comparison, I also sampled a
professionally recorded sermon by Detroit's C. L. Franklin: 17.5 per
cent were repeats, 62.5 per cent were systemic. The total was, I think,
an atypically high 80 per cent.

The following passage is from a sermon by Lacy, "Dry Bones":

> Ezekiel come on the scene
> That great prophet of God
> Told him Ezekiel
> Go out yonder
> 5 Go an' pastor that land
> Save everybody
> Way they die out there
> By the millions
> Out yonder in the valley
> 10 Prophesy
> To the dry bones
> The Word
> The valley is white
> Bleached with dry bones

¹⁵ Go out yon
And prophesy to 'em
Tell 'em
To wake up
And hear the Word of God
²⁰ Ain't God all right?
God from Zion
Ezekiel went out there
Begin to prophesy
Dry bones
²⁵ Ezekiel said
I heard
A mighty rattlin'
The rattlin' of bones
Shakin' through the valley
³⁰ Hark Halelujah

Allowing for only the strictest interpretation of "repetition," there is still a high concentration of repeated material. Six of the thirty lines are repeated within the same sermon; one other line was used in other sermons; and twelve lines are near approximations of lines used here or elsewhere by Lacy. Near approximations are those lines in which only one word has been changed (in lines of two or more words), though two words may have been substituted for the deleted (or changed) word. For instance, this sermon has the lines, "Said prophesy" and "Prophesied again," close approximations to lines 10 ("Prophesy"), 16 ("And prophesy to 'em), and 23 ("Begin to prophesy"). Seven of the thirty lines are repeats, or 23 per cent; nineteen of the lines are either exact repeats or close approximations—63 per cent.[7]

Again, as with McDowell, passages could have been chosen from Lacy's sermons which would come quite close to being 100 per cent repetitious. If an exhaustive study of Lacy's style were ever to be made, I am sure that the percentage would rise beyond the 63 per cent in the above passage. But we are probably never going to find a sermon in which all the lines are traditional or memorized, if for no other reason than that they begin in prose and the prose of the preachers is too varied and too flexible to be formulaic in the Parry-Lord sense.

But it is only after we have examined several texts closely that we should return to Parry's original definition of the formula, for only then can we see that its utility is as a broad guideline; it will not stand close application to lines actually uttered during a performance. Objections are many; for instance, if mere repetition characterizes the formula, then any utterance I might make today that repeats one uttered several years ago, however coincidentally, would be a formula. Such utterances would be formulaic, but are not helpful in understanding oral composition. Donald K. Fry has recently shown[8] that the definition of formula depends entirely upon how broadly one wishes to interpret "a group of words which is regularly employed under the same metrical conditions to express a given essential idea," Parry's original conception.[9] Since Parry's initial pronouncement the idea of the "group of words" which is regularly employed has been expanded to mean "approximately repeated." And the original definition, "under the same metrical conditions," has been loosened in practice to become "under no metrical conditions."[10] As far as our immediate problems are concerned, in the American sermon, should we distinguish (formulaically) between McDowell's "Pray with me Church" and "Are you prayin' with me now?"; or between "Help me Lord Jesus tell your story" and "Help me tell God's story"?

As Fry has argued, the basis for understanding the composition of oral poetry (or oral narrative) is not the formula but the formulaic system, the verbal mold into which a variety of words are poured but which remains relatively consistent through similarities of diction, accent, or alliteration. Lord defined the system as "patterns that make adjustment of phrase and creation of phrases by analogy possible."[11] The Anglo-Saxon poet and the American spiritual preacher create formulas by analogies with others: the system creates nearly all formulas.

Fry was working with Anglo-Saxon poetry, and his definition of the formulaic system is applicable only to that language and that poetry: the Old-English system is "a group of half-lines, usually loosely related metrically and semantically, which are related in form by the identical relative placement of two elements, one a variable word or element of a compound usually supplying the alliteration, and the other a constant word or element of a compound, with approximately the same distribution of non-stressed elements."[12] It should be noted that each poetry which employs oral formulas must have its different kind of formulas and systems to meet the specific demands of the poetry. While Fry may be accurately describing Old English verse, it will not do for us: spiritual sermons seldom alliterate consciously; they almost never employ rhyme; but they are metrical. We might then modify his definition by saying that sermon systems are "groups of words, which, when recited, are metrically and semantically consistent, related in form by the repetition and identical relative placement of at least half the words in the group." Thus, "you may not be a geologist, but you must tell them, that He's the Rock of Ages," is of the same formulaic system as, "you may not be a florist, but you must tell them, that He's the Rose of Sharon." These groups of words, when recited, are metrically consistent, though when they are written and scanned they are not. But, "help me, Lord Jesus, tell your story," is not of the same formulaic system as, "help me tell God's story," though they are close enough for us to guess that one came, psycholinguistically, from the other.

Every preacher I have interviewed rejects the idea of the formulaic theory of composition, no matter how the idea is put to him. In an interview with Lacy I asked him if he ever repeated himself; he said that he definitely did not: once he said something "it's gone." He doesn't have time to repeat what he has said, and if the congregation doesn't get it the first time it will never come again. When the preacher is giving a sermon the words come to him directly from God. Sometimes, Lacy says, he receives words so fast that he does hum, but that is only to catch his breath. As the Rev. Rufus Hays (of Virginia) explained it to me, at such moments the preacher is merely the instrument for the Holy Ghost, who is really doing the speaking: the preacher is only lending Him his mouth and tongue and lips.

One time with Lacy when I played back a tape of his own recent performance and pointed out that he used phrases like "Hark Haleluja" and "God from Zion" several times each, he admitted that perhaps he did repeat himself, but that was because God was feeding him so fast at such moments that he needed time to sort out the proper thoughts. He even had a special word for such repeated phrases: "bywords" or "habitual words." But when I played a taped sermon by his friend, the Rev. Mr. Brown, and pointed out the repetitive language, Lacy said: "Oh, he's just stallin' for time." According to Lacy, Brown couldn't think of what to say next and so needed the stall to work out the next line. Lacy knew that other preachers repeated themselves, but he thought that he seldom did himself. When I questioned Brown on the matter he had a different response. Such language was a rest "on the highway, where you could pull off and regain your strength to drive on." The fact that he described the practice metaphorically suggests that he had long been thinking about it. He used certain formulas, in other words, to give him time to compose the next line; and all of his colleagues did the same. The formula was strictly for his own benefit, and even though he looked straight at the congregation at such moments he was actually "seeing" ahead "on the pages of the book" to what was to come next: he saw nothing of the faces before him, only the next line.

In all I have been able to identify five different kinds of memorized formulas, which have been classified according to their function within a particular sermon. The most popular, the most widely used, and the most stable are those which in some way resemble a refrain, yet do not function exactly as does a refrain within a ballad: refrain formulas do not advance the narrative or build the theme, yet they do not appear as regularly as ballad refrains. (To illustrate their positioning within a sermon I refer the reader to the works themselves, as it is impossible to reprint an entire sermon or even a large portion of one here for this purpose alone.) Lacy's refrains, as has been mentioned, include "Hark Haleluja" and "God from Zion." Brown prefers "Am I right this evening" (or ". . . morning," etc.) and "I want you to know." McDowell likes "I know that's right." Other typical refrain formulas may be listed briefly:

Do you know what I'm talkin' about (Brown and C. L. Franklin)
God from Glory (B. J. Blair)
I want to tell you (J. Charles Jessup)
Don't you know this evenin' (Brown)
I say unto you tonight (Neil Glasse)
I'm gonna tell you (Jessup)
I'm tryin' to tell you (Lacy)
I want you to know this evening (Brown)

Although I have attributed the above formulas to the men from whom I first heard them, none are unique to one man: the same phrases have been found in Virginia and North Carolina and one would be surprised not to find them throughout the South. Given the limited subject matrix from which they come and the common dependence on spirituals and Scripture, independent creation is the likely explanation.

The preacher prefers certain of these phrases for whatever semantic, psychological, and metrical reasons he may have, and then uses them verbatim repeatedly. Lacy, for instance, has only two or three; Brown has four or five; McDowell or Franklin have several; all of these men frequently use their refrain formulas without variation. Since it comes to mind automatically it is ideal for giving the preacher more time to think of what comes next. Some preachers use stalls not only to gain time but to establish their rhythm; since they can be as automatic as tapping one's feet, they are well-suited for this purpose. Other kinds of formulas, as we shall see below, are less stable because they are less frequently used (and thus do not get "memorized" as thoroughly), and because the metrical and semantic context in which they are used varies and causes the formula itself to vary accordingly. "I tell you" for instance, may be drawn out to "I want to tell you" or even "I want you to know this evening" according to the demands of moment. In the very strictest sense we may have two or three different formulas involved, one growing out of the other, and as shall be argued later such a difference in an analysis of formulas is not the most important element in understanding how the preacher composes; what should interest us is the psychological and linguistic process involved in phrase creation and in the relationship between basically similar phrases.

A second kind of formula functions as a stimulant on the congregation. Often the stimulant is difficult to distinguish from the refrain because many men use them both automatically. For example, the Rev. Mr. Franklin's question above, "Do you know what I'm talkin' about?" comes up frequently during a sermon, and the reaction it elicits from the congregation is neutral enough to suggest that it was not meant to get a response. Another of his formulas, the quite similar "I don't believe you know what I'm talkin' about" does seem to get some response, however. Lacy's question, "Ain't God all right?" is so rhetorical that no one responds to it as to a question: it is merely another formula, another line. But J. J. Freeman, for instance, timed his hortatory formulas so as to get a response, and he used them only when the congregation was in fact listless: "Gettin' quiet (in here) (again) isn't it?" The audience laughed and the intensity immediately picked up. When it let down again momentarily a little later, Freeman again chided them and again they picked up. To this very brief list of hortatory formulas one might add Franklin's "Listen if you please," which is probably the most effective of such exhortations.

Two other kinds of formulas may be distinguished which are involved intimately in storytelling within a sermon. One introduces dialogue and the other narrative. The manner of beginning a narrative is quite noticeable because we may think of it as a counterpart to "once upon a time." The preacher is likely to say, however,

Every now and then

or

I want to call your attention to the fact that . . .

The sermons also have characteristic phrases for advancing the narrative once it has begun:

After a while
I want you to know what he said
By and by

Characteristic of formulas in which dialogue is carried or introduced are the following:

The Bible said to me
I heard Jesus say the other day
Saint Peter said the other day

These formulas are very popular: any name can be substituted for "Saint Peter," giving the pattern a great flexibility within the structural framework. A slight variation of this—"I heard John say the other morning (night)" is also widely used and gives the immediacy of a face-to-face confrontation with sainted names that is dramatic, authoritative, and emotionally appealing. We might formulate this particular series of phrases thus:

(personal pronoun) said (message)

And I would include a version from the same mold:

David said to Saul, 'let me go'

We find also that the syntax as well as the incidence of enjambement present no surprises to anyone familiar either with English or with the oral style. The syntax is almost always straightforward subject-verb-object English with few inversions or convolutions. Most inverted sentences encountered resulted when the preacher stumbled over his words or couldn't quite think of what to say next; inversion was sometimes the result. This was to be expected in the pulpit where the subject matter could be expressed in simple language, a language, as it happens, of the everyday speech of the pastor and one by which he hopes to communicate with his congregation. Too many distractions get in the way of verbal communication as it is: singing, shouting, emotion, and the preacher's diction. If the syntax were not simple, much less would be communicated.

Enjambement also occurs quite frequently, as we would expect in an oral style. Long sentences are broken up to fit the meter of the sermon, so enjambement is inevitable. Even when the sentences are short the preacher is likely to break them into even shorter units, as in this passage from Lacy, composed mainly of brief sentences:

> And God
> Made the Father
> Son and Holy Ghost
> Ain't God all right?
> 5   And mister Hoyle
> Made a three-spot
> And called it a trey
> God from Zion
> In Matthew Mark
> 10   Luke and John
> Mister Hoyle
> Made a four-spot

One—but only one—of the reasons enjambement occurs is the frequent use of nouns, noun-compounds, and substantives in apposition.[13] The above passage does not provide any examples, though the closest is the lines "Made a three-spot/ And called it a trey." Whatever its effect on the audience such use of appositives gives the preacher more time to think about what is coming after. In the example above, once Lacy has mentioned the "three-spot" he associates it with "trey" which comes next. The narrative has not been advanced any by the second line, and since it comes "automatically" to the speaker he does not have to think about it, and so can use his time and mental energy to anticipate the line to come.

Periodic sentences almost never occur; this confirms Parry's findings with the Yugoslav *guslars*.[14] Again clarity is important for the congregation, and the conventional sentence is much easier for the preacher since its syntax comes to him intuitively. He does not have time to alter his syntax under the time pressure of his sermon and he does not utilize the poetic effects of such inversions. Occasionally a sentence such as the following does occur:

An' if we don't forgive nobody, we are hell-bound now.

This sentence, like nearly all of the periodic sentences encountered, came during the early parts of the sermon before the preacher had begun to chant. Those opening moments, we have already observed, are prosaic; metrics, and consequently the length and number of syllables in a line, are ignored. The preacher is often talking casually to the congregation, as in fact Lacy was when he uttered the sentence above. There is no rush to think of the next line and if periodic sentences do occur, they are most likely to be spoken at that time. In this most important aspect, syntax, the sermons of American spiritual preachers reinforce what we know generally to be characteristic of the oral style.

VI

The Theme

After listening to many spiritual sermons, one notices that particular descriptive formulas appear in clusters. In a hortatory art, however, such a cluster is likely to have great functional flexibility; so it does here. For instance, Brown is likely to say "so many times" in various nonnarrative contexts, or "I'm wonderin' . . . "—a phrase he shares with McDowell. An extended demonstration will better illustrate these phrases as they occur in clusters. In the following passages taken from various sermons of the Rev. Mr. Brown, the repetition, especially of "same man" always seems to be used in a characteristic way within the passage, and always with a similar galaxy of ideas and formulas around it. The first was recorded in June of 1967:

He left the church in the hands of a man
He left the gospel in the hands of a man
Am I right?
This same Jesus
This same One that stopped to walk at Bethlehem
This same One had concourse with the lawyers and doctors
This same man!
That had-gave-told 'em to fill up a pitcher with water
Same man gave sight to the blind
Same man!
Said I need somebody/To treat the world after I go home

Italicized words here were sung; half-lines indicate only a half pause
during which there was not the usual response from the audience. The
passage has to do with Jesus' miracles, and the descriptive "This same
man (Jesus/One)" comes up again and again in this particular context,
almost always related—in Brown's sermons—to the miracles. Lacy has
also used it, but simply as refrain. The following passage of Brown's
was recorded a month later:

Go now lawyers and talk to this man Jesus
We heard! We heard a man now heal the sick
We heard He give sight to the blind
Open up the dumb ears
He start the crippled to walkin'
Same man![1]

   .   .   .

Same man!
Same man!
Is comin' back one of these days
Same man this evenin'!

At another date in July, Brown recited the following:

Talkin' with the lawyers and doctors
Same man!
Same word!
He stopped over at the well of Samaria
Set down there at the well at Samaria
I want you to fill these water pots up . . .

And on August 6, 1967, Brown recited the following passage in a sermon on "Paradise:"

Same man
Same man
That got up off of the world Sunday mornin'
That said all powers
Inhabitin' the earth
Is in my hand

I want to tell you, ladies
Tell my brotheren

  .   .   .

Stayed here thirty-three long years
Same man got on the cross and got hung
Same man
Same man that . . .

A year after the above examples were recorded Brown was still reciting the same sequence of lines. The following passage was performed
in Corcoran, California (May 24, 1968) as part of a sermon entitled,
"He Is the Preparation":

 This same Jesus
 That was carried off in the wilderness
 Same man
 Is comin' back again
5 Same Jesus
 That walked the mile brotheren
 He walked the sandy deserts
 That many men believe in Him
 He healed the sick
10 And raised the dead
 Gave sight to the blind
 Ohh one day
 He went on home

One can say with certainty that Brown has associated the formula "Same
man" with particular events in the life of Jesus, and that this particular
descriptive passage intuitively calls this formula, and its variants, out of
Brown's word-hoard. In certain psycholinguistic situations the reverse
may be true: the formula calls forth the theme. When Brown wants to
describe the miracles or to emphasize Jesus' superiority to the "lawyers
and doctors"—the intelligentsia—this ready-made formula is immediately
available to him. And in Brown's case particularly I am sure that part of
the attraction of this formula is that its brevity allows him to sing it, to
draw it out and dramatize it, by putting his rich, deep voice on display.
 But if this is characteristic of Brown's descriptive language, it also

brings up another matter: where does the formula end and the theme begin? In the passages above one would not be likely to think of them as Lord thought of themes[2]—in terms of narrative events—but rather as linguistic entities, sets of formulas which are consistently used to describe certain events or scenes, such as the arming of a knight or of a horse, a council of war, or the description of a castle's battlements. We must again alter the definition to fit the demands of this particular literature: the sermon theme is a sequence of formulas, nearly memorized, used to describe recurrent scenes, ideas, or actions within the sermon. For illustrative purposes, Brown's passages are perhaps too brief and too disorganized. For a better example I turn to Lacy who discussed St. John in the same context at two different times; the first passage was taken from a sermon on "Dry Bones" delivered on July 16, 1967:

<blockquote>
¹ John was a young man
When he started out
About twenty some odd years old
Like him now, make a conclusion to the book of Revelation
⁵ Way up yonder, in his nineties
I said in his nineties
Fixin' to go home
But yet he had never sat down
And—uh—discharged his debt
¹⁰ He might have got to the place, brother pastors
Where he didn't shout as much as he used to
And do evangelistic work as he used to
But at this particular time
He was sitting down in the city of Ephesia
¹⁵ Pastoring a church
That Timothy—Bishop Timothy
Had founded a long time ago
Now I say to you we can't give up
As ministers of the gospel
</blockquote>

A week later, in a sermon on "Revelation," Lacy used the following series of formulas:

<blockquote>
¹ John was young then
But he's an old man now
</blockquote>

[3-line elaboration of his old age]
⁶ He's not doin' no evangelistic work 'mount to anything
He's the only 'postle livin' follow Jesus
Even the 'postle Paul came on the scene very late
After the death of Jesus Christ
¹⁰ 'Postle Paul has went and become beheaded yonder at Nero's
    choppin' block in Rome
And God rest the other 'postles; John was yet here
He's a old man
And at this particular time in this mornin's text
He's pastorin' now, not evangelistic work
¹⁵ But he's pastorin' the city of Ephesia
That's in Asia
Ephesia is the capitol of that country
He's pastorin' this church in Ephesia where this same Paul
Had organized the church long time ago
²⁰ And put his son Timothy there as bishop over that church

An intense reading would not be necesary to see that these are similar models from the same mold, yet that mold is twenty lines long. Lacy has not completely memorized the passage, though he nearly has, and in both versions he has gotten the essential points across: John was young man then/ but an old man now/ he's not doing evangelistic work/ he was in Ephesia/ as pastor of a church/ which had been founded a long time ago. The message is in the same order in both passages.

The sermon theme has a specific relationship to the formulas that comprise it; the theme is a series of related ideas, images, or actions, expressed by the relatively stable sequence of formulas. It is related to its formulas as is the entire edifice to its component bricks. Although the relationship between particular formulas and their order to the theme is often close, it is not inflexible: the same theme may be expressed in several (similar) ways since it is only as stable as the memory of the man who remembers it.

The difference between the two passages above can be explained most accurately by the relationship between preacher and audience during the different performances. At the time the first passage was recited, Lacy was breaking into a chant. The congregation was beginning to warm up, and its response to him aided Lacy in regularizing the lines. But he had not yet become fully metrical, and as can be seen from the text several lines are so hypermetric that they could not be compressed. Nevertheless, Lacy's pace is somewhat faster here than in the second passage, which was recited before a less responsive audience. In the latter section the pace is more conversational and unhurried, and because the tempo is slack, more details, especially descriptive details, creep in. This phenomenon is customary. The "basic" theme—the wording that is closest to Lacy's "ideal"—is the first illustration; the second is an elaboration of it, in this case an unfortunate elaboration because Lacy's wordiness cost him his rhythm and thus the opportunity to stimulate the congregation. And, sensing that the audience was not with him, he became self-conscious and stumbled over his words, and finally began to lose his conciseness. The idea expressed in four lines (14-17) in the first performance—that John was pastoring a church in Ephesia which Timothy had founded— in the second passage has taken seven lines (14-20).

Lacy did not, of course, realize that both passages would be transcribed and compared and so did not vary or try to keep stable the themes on my account; on another occasion I was able to get an even better illustration of the extent of memorization of themes. On July 9, 1967, Lacy delivered a sermon on the very popular Twenty-third Psalm during which, strangely enough, he suddenly recited a forty-seven-line descriptive theme of the Four Horsemen of the Apocalypse. Those lines are noted below in the left-hand column of the page. Several weeks later (August 6) I asked him if he knew the passage well enough to recite it to me by heart: my excuse was that I had not gotten it clearly on tape the first time. Lacy was willing, and recited the same theme to me while we sat at the kitchen table in his home; the "kitchen table" version appears to the right of the sermon performance:

They tell me	In the mornin'
In the mornin'	When the Saints of God shall rise
When the horses	When they all get together they'll
Begin to come out	be standin' lookin'
5 And the riders on the horses	Some'll be standin' lookin'
Want 'em to come out	5 For the general that they fought for
God from Zion	You know a general in the army's a
Riding a red horse	powerful man
There's somebody gonna say	They'll be standing looking for the

¹⁰ Is that the general
That I was fighting for
And I heard another cry
Saying no-oo
That's not the one
¹⁵ That you been fightin' for
Another one rode out
Riding a black horse
Is that the man
That I been fighting for
²⁰ I heard another voice say
No, no-oo
That's not the general
That you been fighting for
Another one rode out
²⁵ Riding a pale horse
Is that the general
That we been fighting for
A voice said No
That's not the one
³⁰ That you been fighting for
Another one came out
God from Zion
Riding a white horse
Rainbow round his shoulder
³⁵ Hark Haleluja
Dressed in raiment
White as driven as the snow
From his head down to his feet
God from Zion
⁴⁰ In his—from out of his mouth
Come a two-edge sword
Cuttin' sin
Both right an' left
I heard a cry
⁴⁵ Is that the man
That we been fightin' for
They said Yes

general that they been fighting
for
Out come a red horse
Somebody said
¹⁰ Is that the general I was fighting for

No that ain't the one
Out come a black horse
Is that the general I been fighting
for
Some say
¹⁵ No that's not the general you is
fighting for
Out come a pale horse
Is that the general I been fighting
for
No
That's not the general I been fight-
ing for
²⁰ Still standin' an' after a while he
looked to see one
Come out on a white horse
With the rainbow round his
shoulder
Out of his mouth

Come a two-edge sword
²⁵ Cuttin' sin
Both right and left
Dressed in raiment as white as snow
Head down to his feet
Eyes like balls of fire
³⁰ And his feet like polished brass

Somebody cried out
Is that the general I been fighting
for
Yes that's the man you been fighting for
I'm ready to go home in peace
³⁵ I seed the general that I been fighting for

To a certain extent the method of comparative transcription chosen here is visually misleading: the kitchen table recitation (to the right) appears to be twelve lines shorter, while actually it is somewhat longer. Many of the single lines ("Is that the general I been fighting for") are allotted two formulas during the actual performance. But without the pressure of having to come up with the next line in a hurry, Lacy could develop some descriptions in his kitchen which he forgot or didn't have time for during the sermon. "They tell me/ In the mornin'" gets elaborated into seven lines when the preacher is at ease, and several new ideas get added. Once into the business of the four horses "coming out," however, he is remarkably consistent, and adds nothing of note until the end when we have the sequence, "Eyes like balls of fire/ And feet like polished brass." Undoubtedly these descriptive elements, as well as the part about going home in peace now that the speaker has seen the "general," are part of the basic theme; they were, for reasons just mentioned, also left out. The description of the white horse's rider gets a bit jumbled in the church performance: at home it is (1) rainbow (2) sword (3) raiment (4) eyes (5) feet. But under the pressure of performance the "eyes" and "feet" formulas are left out and the order becomes: (1) rainbow (2) raiment (3) sword.[3] This last matter, the scrambling of descriptive formulas, happens quite often, as their order is usually unimportant; Lacy probably does not have any set pattern for the elements of this description, but does have five—in whatever order he happens to use them—at his command.

Also absent from the kitchen table version are the stall formulas. During the actual performance Lacy used "God from Zion" three times (lines 7, 32, and 39), and "Hark Haleluja" once (line 35). This was to be expected; since their function is solely for the preacher's benefit (to pause momentarily during the performance to decide what to say next), stall formulas would not appear when the conditions had been altered: there was no congregation and no press of time. In this particular theme, it should be noted, Lacy has made it easy for himself through a largely repetitive structure: the "red horse" sequence (lines 8-15) is nearly identical with the "black horse" section (lines 16-23); the "pale horse" part is "missing" one line (it runs from lines 24-30). Such repetition of the structure of sections undoubtedly also serves as a memory aid.

A close examination of the relative position of the stall formulas shows that their occurrence is not arbitrary and not without significance. Their purpose, we may recall, is to allow the preacher time to formulate the lines to come; they are a kind of automatic speech which can be uttered without hesitation while further speech, which will require thought to construct, is being planned. The stalls appear within Lacy's "Four Horsemen" theme just at the moments when one would expect him to be facing the widest choice of material with which to proceed. When the oral performer, like the conversational speaker, has to make a selection based on information content, he will pause. In a metrical sermon such a pause is unacceptable, so the preacher "fills in" the pause with a stall formula.

The seven- or eight-line section describing the emergence of each horse seems to be closely memorized, as we have seen; no stall formulas occur among them. But one does occur just before Lacy brings out the first horse (line 7). The three horses and their riders then "come out" faultlessly, but just before the final horseman emerges Lacy stalls again. Here, the theme's pattern has been disrupted and for the first time in several seconds (and over twenty lines) Lacy has to think about what to say next. His choice has been dictated by the necessity of having to think of new syntactical structures and new diction, and perhaps even new content. He can no longer merely repeat what has gone before and so he stalls: "God from Zion." Lacy mentions the "rainbow round his shoulder" but stalls again—descriptive themes not having a fixed order—until he decides to utter "Dressed in raiment/White as driven as the snow." When that simile is completed he pauses again, and again for the same reason: he cannot immediately decide what to say next. Further evidence of this appears in the next line, reproduced above as Lacy misspoke it: "In his—from out of his mouth."

Our conjectures above about the occurrence and frequency of stall formulas are confirmed by several experiments conducted about a decade ago on the relationship of hesitation pauses in speech to their context, to the length and transition probability of certain words preceding and following pauses, and to the information content of such words.[4] Professor Goldman-Eisler's experiments confirm that aside from psychological blocks which certain individuals might have regarding particular words, pauses in speech are related to word selection, choice of thought, and the framing of syntax. Hesitation occurs during situations of uncertainty, and usually that uncertainty is the result of too many rather than too few choices. Hence, pauses of this kind are of interest to us because of their relation to the sentences and formulas among which they appear. Hesitation is likely to occur before words of low transition probability when the possible choice of words to follow is great, and so is directly related to situations of potentially high information. Short words, especially articles and pronouns, often precede pauses while—again as would be expected—longer words tend to follow. We found these results borne out in the sermons.

Goldman-Eisler's experiments may also help us understand why the preacher prefers to use traditional themes in the construction of sermons. When a sermon is in the early stages of its development, the preacher has not yet formulated the best way of expressing its message. This weakness will be true of precise descriptions and even more so of abstractions. Generally speaking, the more concrete the utterance, the faster it will be learned and become automatic. Once a portion of a sermon—a theme— has been assimilated, it becomes ideal for the preacher's purposes: its automatic utterance allows him to recite it almost without flaw, that is, without pause, as well as allowing him to devote himself to dramatic action which will reinforce the effect of his words and, finally, will give him a chance to formulate the ideas and language to come. In the early portions of most sermons stall formulas and themes seldom occur: the pace of delivery, it should be recalled, is deliberate and leisurely, much as is conversation, thus giving the preacher time to encode his ideas fluently without the aid of stalls.

Now one of the interesting aspects of the recitation of this "Four Horsemen" theme is that it was performed as part of a sermon on the Twenty-third Psalm; it was, in other words, a thematic irrelevance. What makes it interesting is Lacy's reason for using it. The sermon on the Twenty-third Psalm was going badly: the congregation did not respond and soon became restless. Lacy detected their boredom quickly and tried several means to arouse them: he shouted, pounded his fists, exhorted the audience. A little past the middle he was able to get some response, but this soon faded. Just before the spark died out completely, Lacy then broke into his (nearly) memorized theme, the rhythm immediately caught on, and the sermon was "saved."

Later I asked Lacy why he had chosen these lines and he mumbled something about its "all being in the Bible." But on closer questioning he said he thought he used the passage so that he could pick up the rhythm. This answer may have been merely in response to my suggestion to that effect, but conscious or unconscious this theme's employ-

ment was purposeful. Because it was memorized he did not have to concentrate on what to think of next. All his mental energies could be put
to getting the theme across; his mind was released from the urgency of
composing and he concentrated on gesture, expression, intonation, and
perhaps most important, rhythm. Because in a passage of this nature the
diction and syntax were no problem, he was free to work on the other
aspects of his performance. It did not matter that the Four Horsemen
had little to do with the Twenty-third Psalm; what did matter was that
the Horsemen theme could be performed successfully and could save a
flagging sermon from failure and a lusterless congregation from boredom. The performance was the thing. When the same sermon was recited a year later to a livelier audience, the Four Horsemen theme was
not used.

There are at least five other themes in this particular sermon: David's
anointing, his fight with Goliath, his flight to the cave, the conversation
between David and his mother, and the recitation of the psalm itself.
Any could be used elsewhere if the need arose, just as the Horsemen
theme was used here. Once we realize this we can see something of the
nature of the composition of such sermons. The theme plays a large role
in their structure, thus making it easier for the preacher to compose them
spontaneously. In some sermons they may be the core of the entire composition, such as is the case with the "Deck of Cards" where all else is
prologue and epilogue to the one Cards theme. In the Twenty-third
Psalm sermon Lacy undoubtedly intended to use several relevant themes
before he started, but their placement within the sermon suggests that
the entire structure was not built around them. In other words, the use
of themes has great flexibility, and can be planned either as necessary or
ornamental elements within the structure; and they can be brought in
as the immediate situation demands.

On occasion a theme which has been almost entirely memorized will
be broken up and expanded. A sequence that would normally consume
about twenty lines may be dilated at certain times to three times that
number. In my own experience with spiritual preachers I found that
such expansion usually comes about as the result of the dramatic failure
of the preacher; one of the expected benefits of such dilation is the
arousal of the congregation by the lucid performance of fluent, metrical
lines. But on occasion the conditions are not right and even this does
not save the situation. When this happens it is hard to say why. The

preacher may have reached a point, in terms of subject, when a particular theme is called for. He has planned his sermon a certain way in his mind and for various reasons may not want to change his plans. But when that point is reached, the preacher may not have sufficiently excited his listeners, yet he goes ahead anyway. Why some preachers are not able at such a point to launch into a metrical theme is a problem I must leave to someone with more knowledge of psycholinguistics; I only know that it happens. Rubin Lacy has made such slips. The following theme on the "Four Beasts of Apocalypse" was taken from a sermon of his delivered on July 9, 1967:

    John said
    I . . . I . . . I saw four beasts
    One with a face
    Looked like a calf
5   Representin' patience
    And endurance
    'Nother beast I saw
    Had a head like a lion
    Representin' boldness
10 And confidence
    'Nother beast I saw
    A face like a man
    Representin' wisdom
    And he had knowledge
15 'Nother beast I saw
    Looked like a bald eagle
    Ain't God all right?

Three weeks later (July 30) Lacy used the same material, but the circumstances had changed considerably. The audience was not responsive the second time. Attendance was poor (less than fifteen), the morning was very hot, and the children were particularly restless. The sermon was going badly, but for some reason Lacy decided to use the Four Beasts theme anyway; this time not even a memorized passage could help. Lacy, whose timing had been poor all morning, continued to stumble:

I said Amen
One of those beasts had a face like a lion
Representing boldness and confidence
Ah, bold—Amen—as a lion
⁵ Harmless as a dove
Conquer anything you go up against
There be wars and rumors of wars
Tryin' to fight to get into—turnin' over in the hand of God
I heard God say to Moses, standing on the banks of the Red Sea
¹⁰ Tell the Israelites God will fight for you
And you just hold your peace
The next beast—Amen—face like a calf
Representin' patience and endurance
Every child of God oughta have patience
¹⁵ Be willin' to endure hardness as a good soldier
If you can't take nothin', you can't bear no—wear no—crown
If you can't bear no burden
Umm-hmm
You can't wear no crown
²⁰ God from Zion
I heard Jesus say the other day umm
If you wanna follow me
Amen
First thing you do
²⁵ Deny yourself, and then take up your cross
And follow me daily
Ain't God all right?
Seed him went on and said
The third beast
³⁰ Amen
Had a face, like a man
Representin' wisdom and knowledge
And understandin'
Heard Solomon talkin' with God
³⁵ When he was a young man

Occasionally one or two of the Four Beast theme lines will appear in
other sermons without the rest of the theme; they are, after all, formulas

which can be used separately as the occasion demands. But in the passage above Lacy remembered groups of lines rather than individual lines. As soon as he said "One of those beasts had a face like a lion" he immediately thought of the next one: "Representin' boldness and confidence." In the expanded theme several lines will intervene before he comes to the next animal, but when he does he will give all the lines "necessary" for its description—here, the calf, representing patience and endurance.

And (it may be significant to point out) Lacy also thinks in terms of grammatical units, not only metrical ones. Even though, in the expanded theme, the meter is quite different from the other theme recitation, certain diction is repeated. The words in this passage are what have made the deeper impression on Lacy.[5] When conditions are right he can break up the line "representing boldness and confidence" into two metrical lines:

Representin' boldness
And confidence

Again we see an aspect of the ability to compose metrically during performance; Lacy's genius lies in his flexibility.

And Lacy is by no means alone in this manner of using themes. The Rev. D. J. McDowell, whose sermon on "The Christ of the Bible" is included below, admitted that the series of lines beginning with "you may not be a geologist, but you must tell them that He's the Rock of Ages," is just such a device. In an interview the technical terms "formula" and "theme" were not used. But McDowell understood the principle involved, and said that he had recited this particular "theme" in other sermons: he used it in "The Christ of the Bible" because it "fit." McDowell is one of those men who relies on a note card, as I have already remarked; but I saw his card on this particular day and all it contained were the allusions to and epithets for Christ in various biblical passages: he had nothing in writing about the "geologist" theme. It came to him while he was performing, he thought that it would be effective, and so he used it. As it happens it was quite effective, though McDowell has so much ability that almost anything he did would "move the Spirit of God" within his congregation.

Like the words "formula" and "system," "theme" has acquired a connotation of something formal, rigid, and inflexible. But again, as the preachers use this device it is characterized by flexibility. Some themes may be largely memorized; most are not. As has been discussed, themes often occur in expanded form, and parts of them may be used in other contexts. Although they are primarily a mnemonic and histrionic device, they often fail in their purpose. They are seldom necessary to a sermon, and so often appear in seemingly irrelevant contexts; they float as freely as does the preacher's mind. The themes are probably the greatest of the preacher's memory aids; but because of their nature they also allow substantial variation. Themes give a great deal of coherence to the language in a sermon; the preacher depends on them to hold his sermon together and he uses them as a departure point. Without themes and a coherent narrative plot line, most sermons would be structurally (and probably semantically) chaotic; with them the sermon does not become inflexible, but rather just strong enough to cohere and just flexible enough to allow communication with the shifting moods of the congregation.

VII

The Making of a Chanted Sermon

After recording and interviewing the California preachers in 1967 I realized that additional sessions would be necessary later to discover the most important elements of oral composition. Lord had gone back to Yugoslavia many years after his first visit there to compare performances years apart, in order to determine which elements were memorized and which were entirely improvised, and to discover what effect time had upon the singer's performances. It was necessary for me to do the same. My return in 1968 clarified my theories and enabled me to observe the refinements of previously undeveloped sermon material. To a large extent much of what was learned on this second trip had been expected; but it was necessary that a demonstration be made. Consequently, if some material within this chapter has been anticipated by the reader, and the conclusions presented here are predictable, it is because the observations made throughout the rest of the book derived in part from the studies set forth below.

Early in July of 1967 the Rev. Lacy was asked to be the guest preacher at the Liberty Baptist Church in Bakersfield (the Rev. W. G. McRoy, pastor). But, for reasons which are not quite clear to me, Lacy did not prepare himself for the day's message; he obviously had not done his homework and had not in any noticeable way readied himself for the sermon. Not that excuses are relevant here, but Lacy had also been asked to preach on the previous Sunday, when at the last minute McRoy called upon another preacher who also happened to be in the church; Lacy may have anticipated yet another last-minute substitute, though if he did he was disappointed (or elated, depending upon how one looks at it). Although he had not done his homework, Lacy had been casually thumbing through a newly acquired *Master Sermon Outlines,* and he found one to his liking, probably because its theme was a favorite of his anyway: a eulogy of the Pastor.

This undistinguished sermon—carelessly prepared, poorly delivered, and tiredly received—does have significance for our understanding of the making of an oral sermon. Several days after Lacy's sermon I was able to purchase *Master Sermon Outlines* and so was able to compare Lacy's prose source with his metrical performance. This was interesting enough; yet eleven months later, when I returned to Bakersfield to rerecord Lacy and his colleagues, he used some of the same figures in another sermon, also on the importance of the pastor. This third version is relevant to any understanding of Lacy's art, for in it we can see language and idea as it is assimilated in the preacher's mind a year after he first conceived them. By comparing these three sermons we can see the preacher at first struggling with his source, and then mastering his material so that it becomes a part of his repertoire which he can recite without notes.[1] And we can also see how much outside material—language and ideas which the preacher has been absorbing for many years—finds its way into the performance. Finally, we can surmise how the preacher constructs the sermon—however unconsciously—by evaluating the relative position of formulas and metaphors in terms of their sources.

In this section we shall examine the process by which many oral sermons are composed, using Lacy's "God's Plowboy" sermons as a paradigm. Examples from the work of other men will be used also to illustrate certain techniques, for what we are trying to describe is the process of a tradition and not the exclusive property of one man.

We have already seen in an earlier section several passages from Scripture which the spiritual preacher uses to justify his style of preaching the Word. From Luke 24:49 he derives his most important lesson, that the apostles were to go to Jerusalem and wait there until the "power from on high" came to them. Nothing is mentioned in this passage about self-education, about biblical exegesis, or about seminary schooling of any kind. The spiritual preacher believes strictly in the literal Word of God; he is chosen from above and has no control himself over that choice, except, perhaps, to deny God. The reader should not think, however, that this passage from Luke can be used to justify sloth and ignorance. Sometimes that may be the way, but usually the spiritual preacher sincerely believes that God intended him to preach without a manuscript, straight from the soul, lending himself for the moment to the Holy Ghost. He will get these ideas from several people: his own pastor, his family and friends, or from preachers he has heard or seen as they ride through his town or appear on local radio. Spiritual preaching is the only way and that way rarely changes, no matter how much education the preacher may eventually receive.

The first thing the incipient chanting preacher learns that will influence his style is not language but rhythm. This hypothesis may be controversial, in part, because one cannot prove it; it rests, for the moment, as an article of faith. Any portrait of the preacher as a young child will show him in church on his mother's lap or by her side on the bench.[2] He will barely listen to the sermon because he can only distinguish a few words, and in any event their meaning is lost to him. But he does respond to the music. Seldom do young children in the churches I have visited bother with the sermons at all. When the preacher begins they get restless and fidgety, play silent games with the other children, and sometimes even sleep. But the singing usually elicits an active response, and very often the children sing along with the music and clap their hands to its beat. And there is often singing—even organized singing—in the home, but never any preaching there. We can see in such circumstances the beginning of "natural" rhythm; if the young child eventually becomes a preacher, his first schooling has been with the music of his church and with his culture.

The great importance of rhythm was demonstrated to me in Oklahoma City, where I encountered for the first time large numbers of preachers and evangelists who preached spontaneously but who did not chant and so produced quite a different kind of performance. As I have pointed out before, the nonrhythmical oral sermon produces syntactical units of greater flexibility than the chanted sermon, but is more repetitive than conversational speech; in this sense it is a kind of "transitional" performance. The nonrhythmical sermon has very few memorized formulas, and memorized narrative formulas are rare. Anaphoric passages do appear often enough to be noticeable, but they are by no means as frequent as in chanted performances. The following two examples, both taken

from a sermon by Dorance Manning of the Holiness Pentacostal Church
of Norman, Oklahoma (May 1968) will illustrate this point:

125 And so they moved their family and sold their land and
        headed for the land of Moab
  Now let's turn over to Jeremiah the forty-eighth
        chapter for just a moment
  And let's find out what the land of Moab is talking about
  What is the land of Moab
  In chapter forty-eight, if you have your Bible and
        would like to turn

45 And we find them doing something typical that most
        of us do in a like situation
  Instead of them examining the situation and then
        saying now what is the problem here
  Why do we not have rain
  Why do we not have a place of worship
  Why has our crops failed and why has this come upon us

The disinterest in rhythm has led to irregular sentence meters, and
formulaic language of the kind we have been discussing does not develop. As the line numbers indicate, the first passage is taken from late
in the sermon when Manning was far more emotionally involved in his
work than in the second. Yet the first passage is barely parallel in structure ("let's turn over"—"let's find out") and infrequently repetitive ("the
land of Moab"). The second passage, which seems to be more characteristic of the oral style, developed anaphorically more by chance. Manning
was not thinking about anaphora at the moment either, and his emotional involvement had little to do with the form of this passage. Thus,
as we have seen in more detail earlier, we cannot study closely the nonrhythmical sermon, even though spontaneously composed, for in it a
different set of rules apply. In this book we have to be concerned with
the man who chants and the effect of his chanting upon his sentence
formation.

The young preacher (we have already noted) develops in ways
roughly parallel to those described by Lord: he listens and learns (often
in ways unknown to him), he practices short prayers and testimonies,

and then, having mastered his material, steps to the pulpit and delivers his own sermon spontaneously. In the past year I have been able to record the sermons of two apprentice preachers; one of these sermons is included below. The Rev. W. L. Parker preached the other (May 28, 1968), and because Parker had been Brown's deacon for many years some interesting comparisons can be made.

One would expect Parker to have sounded like Brown, but actually, aside from one memorized formula, his style was nothing like his pastor's. The same was true of the Rev. Mr. Robinson in his independence of his pastor, C. Earl Williamson. Not only did the young preachers differ from their pastors in their first performances by not using formulas which they must have heard repeated thousands of times, but their rhythm was different; so was their inflection and the music of the few lines they did chant. It remains to be proved to what degree the young preacher reverts, with maturity, to the style of his "masters." But the performances of the young men are, in this respect, surprising, and I cannot account for it except to postulate the obvious: the desire to have an individual style while remaining within the tradition is strong, and the young men work to develop a sense of their own identity.

If the novices fail to use many of the formulas of their pastors, one is even more surprised to learn that they use few memorized formulas at all. Perhaps the reason lies in the fact that in the sermons by young preachers I have heard, the sense of rhythm is poorly developed; the trouble seems to be simply that during the first sermons of their lives too many problems intrude themselves: what to say and how to say it. Being so preoccupied with language, with both syntax and semantics, the rhythmical flow is interrupted and the sermon style nearly breaks down. Robinson has had a bit more experience than Parker, and this may explain why he was able to gain some rhythm toward the end of his sermon as he got more sure of himself and of his material. Also, with the finish in sight he could switch in a section which he had used before and knew well, knowing that it would carry him to the end. But not so with Parker; he was "teachin' not preachin'" as Deacon MacFaddin criticized it afterwards.

As the novice gains experience his style changes markedly. After several years—and of course this varies among men, depending upon their aptitude—the rhythm which was in them all along begins to show itself and to shape the language of the sermon. The Rev. D. J. McDowell is a good example: although in his forties, he was still considered a "young" preacher because he had only been preaching a few years. Mc-Dowell's supply of sermons is limited. He does not yet have enough experience to enable him to break away from prepared sermon structures and he works hard to develop new sermon ideas. Many years from now he will presumably be able to preach spontaneously (in the narrow sense of that word) by blending materials from many sources. But for now he works with established outlines. The curious feature of McDowell's style (and the style of most young men with his limited experience) is that he is heavily dependent upon "memorized" formulas. I assume this happens because after, say, five years, he fairly well knows what he wants to say and has sufficient mastery of his material to be able to say it rhythmically. The music is no longer a problem; what is of some difficulty is the phrasing of old ideas in new formulas. This may account for the young preacher's great repetitiveness: having learned to regularize the lines he has some difficulty thinking of what to say next and so must rely upon automatic formulas to give him a moment to think about the matter.

My theory is that this stage gives way to one in which both language and music are mastered: Brown, Lacy, Freeman, and nearly all of the other men interviewed and transcribed in this book are in that stage. They are rhythmical always. They have mastered their message techniques beyond the stage of preparing each sermon individually. Not that they may not think about each sermon, sometimes for several days, beforehand; but the experienced preacher has such control that he is able to create new sermons—message, language, structure, and rhythm—as he goes along. He continues to use verbatim formulas, as many of the men admit, and to use them to stall for time occasionally, but the experienced will not use them as frequently as younger men who have to think more often of what to say next. This stage of maturity seems to last the longest and in it the preacher is at the height of his creative powers. Only one further stage can be reached, and this does not seem to happen to all men: as the preacher becomes older many of his powers may deteriorate. The chanting may become irregular; he may have difficulty in converting prose to metrical verse during the performance; and most noticeable, he will once again rely more heavily on memorized formulas, as though to compensate for his failing faculties.

In Lacy's sermon on "God's Plowboy" we can observe two mental processes at work: the preacher's spontaneous conversion of prose to verse, and later, by comparing the resulting sermon with one recorded a year later, we can see what happens to the sermon after it has bounced around in his mind and has become fully assimilated in his repertoire. The former process has been described in some detail in the chapter on "Chanting." We saw Brown begin with a verbatim reading of St. John and turn to his own idiom. And we shall see Goins gradually change Genesis to his own music. For Lacy, on a very hot day in July of 1967, the following passage was part of his written source:

> II. GOD'S PLOWBOY MUST FEED HIS MASTER'S SHEEP
> The Lord said to Peter "Feed my lambs," and again He said "Feed my sheep." The Lord has no flocks or herds; He was talking about people. The lambs were the newborn babes in Christ and such as had not yet fully developed. He said to Peter twice, "Feed my sheep." He was referring to the fully developed and strong Christians.

But when transmuted through the alchemy of Lacy's brain the passage was recited somewhat differently:

¹⁴⁵ Let's go on a little further
God from Zion
God's plowboy
Must feed
We're goin' on to the feedin'
¹⁵⁰ I say God's plowboy
Must feed
His master's sheep
The Lord said to Peter
Feed, my lambs
¹⁵⁵ And then He said unto him
Feed, my sheep
The Lord
Didn't have no flock
No herd
¹⁶⁰ He was talkin' about
He was talkin' about the lambs
Of new-born babes

In <u>Jesus</u> <u>Christ</u>
<u>Such as had not yet,</u> fully developed
165 <u>He said to Peter twice feed my sheep</u>
Said to him the last time
Feed my lamb
Ain't God all right?
Feed my lamb

(I have used solid and broken underlining in this passage to show which lines were recited exactly and which approximately, with relation to Lacy's source text.)

Lacy's performance is faltering at best, and this section is typical of the entire performance. He did not know well the passage he was reading; perhaps he had glanced over it two or three times, but certainly not more. During the performance he obviously could not spend more than a fraction of a second looking for topics; his eye hit upon the capitalized title "GOD'S PLOWBOY MUST FEED HIS MASTER'S SHEEP" and he read, as metrically as he could, from that section. When he had gotten what he could from the heading he moved on to the next thing that caught his eye. A sure indication that this in fact is the way he composed this sermon is shown from Lacy's line 145, "Let's go on a little further." He had just finished talking about the preacher as burden-bearer, and having exhausted his source's ideas, moved on to the next one—on a little further. Sometimes he was able to regularize his meter, as in lines 156-160:

Feed, my sheep
The Lord
Didn't have no flock
No herd
He was talkin' about

But at other lines he is so dominated by the meter of his source that he repeats it exactly and ignores what he is trying to accomplish at the moment. In other words, some of the language can be assimilated into Lacy's style right away, but only a little at a time: it is hard mental work to make this assimilation, and after several lines his style breaks down. It may pick up again, but only for a moment, after which it collapses once more. Lines 164 and 165 are repeated without regard for meter:

Such as had not yet, fully developed
He said to Peter twice to feed my sheep

The following three passages are on the same subject; the first is from Lacy's source (*Master Sermon Outlines*), the second is Lacy's version during that first sermon in 1967, and the last is from a sermon by Lacy in May of 1968 after he had digested his thoughts and language.

> 1. TAKE HEED HOW YOU FEED THE FLOCK
> During a dearth, Elisha's servant set on the great pot and one went out into the field to gather herbs to feed the sons of the prophets. Not knowing the food properly, he gathered wild gourds; and when the food was served, death was found in the pot.

212 Let's see am I right about it
      God
      Went up on the mountain
215 The other day
      To pray
      And while He was up there prayin'
      Some of the
      Laborers
220 Said I'll be
      I'll go out an get some stuff
      And feed the people
      Because they're hungry
      Went out to pick vegetables
225 And got the wrong kind
      Brought 'em on back
      Put 'em in a pot
      Begin to boil green
      Had death in the pot
230 Ain't I right about it?

136 Pastor must know how to feed
      Just any old thing
      Throw in the trough
      Just won't do

140 Must know how to feed
Don't ya remember
When Moses went off that time
Up on the mountain
Left the boys down there
145 Somebody cried out I'm hungry
Went out there in the woods
Pulled up the wrong thing
Went on back there
Put it in the pot
150 Began to boil
Before Moses got back
Some of 'em was eatin' that stuff
Everybody began to die
I want you to know Moses
155 Umm-hmm
Somebody said Death
Was in the pot
Pastor must know
What kind of food
160 Is to give his children

The tapes would show far more clearly than does the transcription how Lacy's later performance is more uniform metrically. But something else has happened as well: the story has become amplified, the characters have changed, and the language has gotten further away from that of Lacy's source. All of these mutations (which are apparent and need not be repeated) have come about because the story is now Lacy's; with each new retelling he will change it more, though with diminishing variations, until its style and even its content are entirely his.

We can, however, profitably examine in some detail a few of the changes Lacy made from 1967 to 1968 to evaluate their quality, and should be able to decide about the effect of those changes on the sermon as oral art. Since the passage we have been discussing on the pastor feeding his master's sheep was selected for thematic reasons, so far as aesthetics are concerned its choice is random and it will do for our purposes here.

Lacy's major achievement with this sermon in the year's time was to blend the parable of the poisonous gourds into the texture of the sermon. In the 1967 version it is clumsily fitted into the exposition with abrupt transitions. A year later the story is more logically connected to the lines that come before and after it.[3] Although the earlier version begins with "Let's see am I right about it," the preceding lines had been jerry-built at best and appear to have been a stall while he groped for the next point in his text. In 1968 most of that has been boiled away: Lacy comes right to the point with "Pastor must know how to feed" and concludes the parable with the same message, "Pastor must know/ What kind of food/ Is to give his children."

The 1968 version of the parable is more interestingly and artfully told. Instead of the declarative (and dull) statement, "Had Death in the pot," we now have the slightly more vivid "somebody" who "said Death/ Was in the pot" drawn out over two lines, the first (enjambed) line ending with the dramatic word "Death." The 1968 version also gets a bit more action into the story by alternating its focus between Moses on the mountain (l. 142), the "boys down there" (l. 144), Moses getting back (l. 151), and the pot of Death (ll. 152 ff.). Instead of straight narrative as in 1967, the more recent version blends elements of conversation, narrative, and exposition.[4] Because the 1968 version contains direct dialogue, it has a greater vitality. This was the difference a year made.

Not all of the major structure elements of a sermon are altered. I was fortunate enough to record Lacy's performance of the Twenty-third Psalm on two separate occasions, also one year apart. Lacy's early version has already been discussed in the section on "The Theme." The sermon ended with a forty-five-line, memorized theme which was irrelevant to the subject of the sermon: a description of the Four Horsemen. I conjectured at that time that Lacy had used the Four Horsemen section just because it was memorized and thus could devote all of his energies to the various techniques necessary to revive a flagging audience. That hypothesis was proven a year later when Lacy fortuitously recited the same sermon without the Four Horsemen: a comparison was then possible. And while the language altered in this sermon much as it had in "God's Plowboy," the major structural elements of the narrative remained stable.

To facilitate a comparison of these two performances I have outlined both of them by subject. The 1968 sermon is on the left, the earlier, 1967, version is to the right:

Lines	Subject	Lines	Subject
1-4	Scripture	1-3	Scripture
5-10	Digression on experience	4-22	Digression on preaching
11-17	David as shepherd	23-55	Digression on self, fishing
18-19	Digression on self	36-44	Digression on liars
20-68	David's anointing	45-48	David's experience
69-100	Fight with Goliath	49-60	Digression on St. Paul
101-105	Transition	61-67	Description of David
106-143	David's flight to cave	68-81	David's anointing
144-167	Digression on dangers of being shepherd	82-107	Fight with Goliath
168-205	David saves lamb	108-140	David's flight to cave
206-213	Digression: Lord is shepherd	141-161	David as shepherd
214-222	Digression on personal experience and moral for day	162-218	David saves lamb and recitation of Twenty-third Psalm
223-235	Digression: warning to preachers	219-260	Digression on coming Judgment
		261-277	Digression on selfishness
		278-330	Four Horsemen

On the level of individual formulas, only the passages from Scripture and the stall formulas remained constant. But the structural elements that remained constant tell an interesting story. Both sermons contain the same four narrative elements presented in the same order: David's anointing, his fight with Goliath, his flight into the cave to avoid Saul's wrath, and the exemplum of David as the good shepherd. One can assume that so far as Lacy is concerned these four tales are essential to his sermon on the Twenty-third Psalm. That the narrative elements are most constant shows that they comprise the chassis upon which the vehicle is mounted. Various digressions are built around these four stories, and in the two versions before us we can see that Lacy used them with flexibility. He did not, however, always use them well, something that an analysis of the text will show.

The failure of the 1967 version and the somewhat warmer reception in 1968 can be explained by a simple line count. During the first performance Lacy took 330 lines to say practically the same thing about David he said in 235 lines a year later. The important statistic is not the 95 "extra" lines but the fact that they were spoken at the expense of the narrative stories from David's life—stories whose retention and repetition suggest that they were the chief elements in the sermon. In 1967 only 92 lines were devoted to these four episodes, while a year later Lacy spent 157 lines on them—and in a sermon 95 lines shorter overall. In 1968 only 78 lines, about one third of the entire performance, were used for exposition and other purposes; the year before 186 lines were so used, nearly two thirds (excluding the "Four Horsemen" which was a thematic excrescence). Including this last theme, 238 lines were not devoted to the four stories of David's life, three more lines than it took Lacy to preach the entire sermon a year later.

Digressions in themselves do not necessarily undermine a sermon; the important factor is the way in which they are used. The digressions in the successful 1968 version are few in number and are related, though often associationally, to the episodes. For instance, the digression on "experience as the best teacher" (lines 5-10 and 214 ff. in the 1968 sermon, lines 45-48 in 1967): I do not know whether C. L. Franklin of Detroit first thought of the idea or merely made it famous, but it is now a common *topos* for spiritual preachers to dwell upon David's face-to-face confrontation with God. David is alleged to have spoken so personally in the Twenty-third Psalm because he had had an experience with his Lord. Lacy thought enough of this *topos* to use it in both sermons, but its casual handling and the sparse time devoted to it in 1967 suggest that it was not central to the sermon, but was certainly something that Lacy was reminded of whenever he preached on this psalm. In 1968 it was deftly tied in with other digressions on self-experience, and its impact was not vitiated by the presence of several other digressions.

We can be nearly positive, then, that the four episodes from David's life comprise the core of this sermon around which the preacher established his message for the day. The episodes are the same in both sermons and they are related in the same order. Probably this comes about because the first three are taken chronologically from the biblical story of David's life; and the last, where David saves one of his lambs from the wild beasts, is important for showing the hero's devotion to his flock. And that, in turn, enables Lacy to move on to discuss the Lord as shepherd. He does not always take this course, however, and as in 1967 it was to his disadvantage. In any event, one can see in these four repeated episodes the core of the sermon which Lacy had mentally retained, and one can also see how much (and what) is extemporized. Preachers seem to retain the narrative; the morals are preached spontaneously.

As has been insisted on throughout this book, the key to understanding the composition of the oral sermon is an analysis of the preacher's psychological associations. In "God's Plowboy" Lacy retained certain images and ideas which he (apparently) found striking,[5] and added them to his repertoire, modifying their language and amplifying their details. In the Twenty-third Psalm Lacy had retained the core of the sermon from year to year by remembering just four episodes from David's life around which he could build sermons of from 235 to 330 lines in length. In the following analysis we return to "God's Plowboy" and analyze the entire sermon structurally. The version chosen is the more recent; here the language and images contained in that one sermon comprise a relatively small part of the entire performance. Several other sources intrude upon Lacy's mind so that the finished product is a very eclectic one indeed. As it happened this performance was smoothly delivered and was well received by a large congregation. As a guide, capital letters are used to represent the sermon's sources (if they could be identified): P, from a published sermon entitled "The Pastor"; O, original material as far as can be ascertained; G, "God's Plowboy"; B, material from Lacy's friend Brown; D, original and spontaneous digression; A, amplification of theme or subject; MP, from a published sermon on "Ministerial Promotion"; E, from the sermon delivered by Lacy in 1967 on Ezekiel's story of the "Dry Bones":

Lines	Brief Description	Source
4-15	Scripture	P
16-42	King of England	O (D)
43-69	Preacher's labors	G
70-84	Apostrophe to Rev. Henry	O (D)
85-102	Pastor as overseer	P
103-122	(Same)	P, A
123-133	Faults of present church	P (D)
134-157	Pastor as feeder	G, A
158-184	(Same)	P, G, A
185-197	Pastor as friend of congregation	P, A
198-211	Digression on Ezekiel, etc.	E
212-221	Preach the Word	B, A
222-239	The call to preach	P, A
240-253	(Same)	B, A
254-267	"Grievous Wolves"	P
268-286	(Same)	P, A
287-298	Boasters	O (D)
299-324	Joseph	MP
325-330	Closing	O

Lacy has retained the parts and consequently composed this sermon, as with his others, through associational clusters. The borrowings from "God's Plowboy" are within a third of the sermon; those from Brown (Lacy also chanted the lines with Brown's music), from Ezekiel, and from "Ministerial Promotion" are also bunched; the material from "The Pastor" runs throughout. Lacy seems to have had this last sermon most actively on his mind throughout the performance.

The subject, being one of Lacy's favorites, associationally attracts materials from other sermons to it. "God's Plowboy," "The Pastor," and "Ministerial Promotion" all deal with Lacy's profession. "Dry Bones" is also related: it is about the prophet in the desert, an image Lacy has used to describe himself before. All of them can be raided for materials and everything should fit; the resulting sermon does not have a formal structure, but this is to Lacy's advantage in that he can use each idea as it comes to him. He has several comparisons to make: the pastor as feeder, as burden bearer, as overseer, as friend, etc., but he need not make these comparisons in any particular order. If he just remembers most of the comparisons he will have enough to say for the morning. Unlike the sermon on the Twenty-third Psalm where Lacy was aided by the chronology of the story, he must rely on memory and association here. The pastor as overseer (I would guess) might remind him of the pastor as burden-bearer, and then possibly as feeder. Exactly how it is done will probably be Lacy's secret, perhaps unknown even to him; that it is done and done well we can see clearly.

Why a preacher retains a certain metaphor or exemplum only psychological analysis will determine for sure; I can only guess at the obvious, that it is for some reason appealing to him.[6] I have tried on several occasions to suggest metaphors and ideas to various preachers before their sermons, but always without success. On the way to a sermon which the Rev. Otis McAllister was to deliver in Delano, I intentionally suggested several ideas to him. Brown, who was also in the car, quite unconsciously suggested several others as we discussed, in rather general terms, McAllister's sermon for the night. McAllister used none of our ideas; but he did pick up a figure while talking to the host pastor and he used that. Brown has occasionally done the same. It would be interesting to learn whether either McAllister or Brown continues using the same figures after several months or a year. I see no reason why they should not, since there is nothing essentially ephemeral about spoken metaphors. We can conclude from this "experiment" that the preacher is continually open to suggestion from several sources, that his sermons can be altered, however slightly, at the very last minute. But what makes language memorable to any particular man, or to Lacy or Brown whose style I now know intimately, be it felicitous phrasing or soul-stirring idea, I cannot say.

One of the curious phenomena of chanted preaching is that two sermons on the same topic performed during the same day may not be very much more similar than two sermons delivered a year apart. The statement cannot be made with certainty since I have been able to record such a repetition only once. The Rev. T. J. Hurley, a white preacher, of the Oneness Pentacostal Church, Oklahoma City, spoke on "Perilous Times" on the morning of May 12, 1968, and that afternoon delivered a similar sermon over KBYE radio, Oklahoma City. I classify the sermons as "similar" and not "identical" because of the 483 lines in the (later) radio sermon, only thirty-one—or 7 per cent—would be underlined in a formulaic chart. Yet both sermons ostensibly dealt with the same topic and both contained long lamentations about the sinfulness of contemporary man and a discussion of recent mass murders—as evidence that we are living in the last days.

As we might by now well expect, the thirty-one lines which were repetitions appeared in the later sermon in four clusters: the first group of eleven appeared between lines 2 and 17; a cluster of two fell between lines 48 and 53; four consecutive lines followed line 180; and the last fourteen run from lines 429 to 442. Though Hurley remembered in clusters the words he had previously used, several ideas were repeated, and he occasionally used a word or two of the original expression. Several of the preacher's expressions return for the second sermon, but these involve a different sort of memory since they often come up in new contexts. Actually, aside from the opening lines and a well-developed theme which describes recent sensational crimes, the two sermons are hardly the same. Hurley does not rely on narrative particularly, and there is little that is necessary in his sermon. Consequently, we find much the same disorder as we found in other sermons of this kind; the surprising thing is that we should find such a disparity so soon after the first recitation.

Apparently Hurley knew in only a general way what it was he would communicate: he would talk about recent signs that the world was in its last days, but little else seems to have been planned. Only two passages have enough consistency to be thought of as themes. The first of these deals with the Scriptures on which the entire sermon is based, the admonition "that in the last days perilous times shall come" (from II Tim. 3.1). In the morning it took all of fifty-three lines to develop; in the afternoon sermon on radio the same idea was encompassed in the first seventeen lines. Several factors are involved in this compression. To begin with, any speaker with a modicum of self-awareness—be he actor, teacher, public speaker, or preacher—tries to improve his style in each succeeding performance. Hurley's morning performance was bloated with too many words; in the afternoon he disciplined himself and said the same thing in about one third the time and thus had more time for other subjects.

One of the reasons that led to the above conclusion was that in looking at the underlined typescript of the afternoon performance and comparing it with that of the morning, what immediately stands out is the spacing of the repeated lines. In the morning performance they are clustered in groups of three and four lines followed by three lines that are not retained, then three or four which are repeated, followed in turn by several that are not. In the afternoon these repeated lines are bunched, eleven of them falling within the first seventeen. Hurley had cut away much of the fat.

In general one should consider other possibilities, though they are not applicable here. The afternoon sermon was a radio performance, though recorded live in the church before the congregation, and radio sermons mean time limits. Although such limits can affect the length of sermons, such was not the case here, since Hurley actually finished preaching about ten minutes before his allotted time was up and had to have the rest of the program filled in with church music. However, his voice had begun to give out in the morning. T. J. Hurley is not the regular pastor and his voice was obviously not in shape for the demands two or more sermons a day makes on the throat. His father T. C. Hurley (the regular pastor) was called away rather suddenly and T. J. had to fill in at the last minute (his father's absence also evoked several minutes' harangue against "gossiping" on the part of his congregation, a totally irrelevant digression). On the air T. J.'s voice cracked constantly and that may have encouraged him to cut short the sermon, but it probably would not have affected the opening passage in any event, since his voice was strong for those lines. There are other possibilities, of course: that this passage was well known by him, got amplified in the morning and then cut back to its original shape later. I am not familiar enough with Hurley's style to know if this is actually the case; I can only guess that it is not, and conclude that in these performances at least, and in this particular passage, Hurley's style improved.

There will be more to say about the quality and character of repeated sermons shortly; meantime I want to conclude my observations on the tendency of preacher's minds to grasp ideas (and sometimes language) in vague clusters and to build sermons around these amorphous frames. Before Lacy first recited the "Deck of Cards" sermon he told me (as has been already related) that he could preface it with any remarks about "heart." And so he did:

3 . . . the fool, has said in his heart, there is no God
16 Therefore, the hearts of men are wrong . . .
23 The hearts of men is far from right
41 Whatever is in your heart
43 Tryin' to say I'm talkin' about heart
46 . . . after God's own heart
75 Some of us are too stout-hearted even to confess . . .
93 My heart is fixed
101 And know my heart
117 He's a heart-fixer

And so on. Now there is nothing central to the sermon on the "Deck of Cards" in these references to the heart. Admittedly, there is the slight though obvious connection between playing cards and "hearts," but that connection was lost on the several members of the congregation to whom I spoke. Lacy piled up references to "heart" in that first performance. The second time such allusions hardly appeared at all; after opening with the Psalmist's warning that "the fool hath said in his heart there is no God," he hardly refers to "heart" again. Lacy was sidetracked onto some other topic and never returned. The point is that he had demonstrated once that he could use an extensive cluster of references, but would not do it all the time.

We see very easily how even the simplest sermon structures are likely to vary by comparing the two following outlines of "Deck of Cards" performances by Lacy in 1967 and then in 1968. The structure here is so different from that of "God's Plowboy" that it is deserving of a few words by itself. The early sermon is outlined on the left, the more recent one on the right:

1-4 Scripture	1-6 Scripture
5-15 Messiah's coming	7-25 Noah and Messiah's coming
16-36 Man's selfishness	26-38 Digression: Elijah
37-46 Amplification of above	39-82 God is alive
47-69 David's selfishness and repentance; man's lack of same	83-91 God's return
	92-97 Noah's days
70-101 David's repentance; man's conscience	98-134 The end of the world
	135-139 Scripture; transition
102-118 Te Deum	140-205 Deck of Cards
119-249 Deck of cards	206-273 Conclusion
250-278 Conclusion	

What has remained the same is what Lacy predicted: the basic structure and the relative placement of the "Deck of Cards" theme near the end, where it would be most effective.

But much else has changed. Even the phrasing of the "Deck of Cards" theme, which Lacy must have known quite well, was varied somewhat. The passage on the left is, again, from the 1967 version; that on the right from 1968:

150 Ain't God all right?	162 And Mister Hoyle knew God had
And, God	two ways to go
Said there's two ways to go	Either heaven an'—or to Hell
Heaven	Mister Hoyle made a deuce
Or either Hell	165 God from Zion
155 Mister Hoyle	That—mmm—that meant either
Made a two-spot	heaven or hell
He called it a deuce	And Mister Hoyle knew there was
God from Zion	a three-Godheads
And put it in the deck	God the Father Son and the Holy
160 And God made the Father	Ghost
Son and Holy Ghost	And he made a trey
Ain't God all right?	170 God from Zion
And Mister Hoyle	
Made a three-spot	
165 And called it a trey	

Lacy's timing is poor in the second—the later—performance. He had poor musical rhythm that evening in 1968 and consequently his linguistic rhythm was thrown off. He should have alternated between God's actions and those of Mister Hoyle: God makes a heaven and a hell, Hoyle makes a two-spot, etc., and when Hoyle makes a three-spot the formulaic construction should be similar:

155 Mister Hoyle 163 And Mister Hoyle
    Made a two-spot   Made a three-spot
    He called it a deuce   And called it a trey

Both of these passages are from the 1967 version quoted just above; they demonstrate the regularity of phrasing that aids (or perhaps results from) a regularized meter. In 1968 there is neither.

    These characteristics of memory as well as the symbiotic relationship with the congregation must be accounted for in terms of the personal situations of the men at the times of performance. Lacy had good retention on the "Four Horsemen" theme when I asked him to recite it five weeks after its sermon performance. In his kitchen the meter was different, but he did have time to think about what he was going to say; the reader may recall that one sure sign of Lacy's calm was the absence of the stall formulas. Yet a year later, after three heart attacks and before an audience that did not inspire him, the "Deck of Cards" section was less "accurate." The fact that it is still more repetitive than the two sermons of T. J. Hurley is due, I feel, to the latter's youth and his failure to fully master any of his passages. Hurley simply did not compose sermons by the extensive use of traditional themes; he was more amorphous, and when he did use themes they were not as well retained. In the two lines below we can see two of Hurley's syntactical variations of a single day:

26 What is it that makes a man climb to the top of a tower and kill
    thirty-two people in one day

434 There's somethin' wrong
    When a man goes to the top of a tower
    In Austin Texas
    And murders thirty-two people in a matter of hours

The placement of these thematic lines has varied, the first example occurring near the beginning and the second near the end of the sermon. Typical of Hurley's use of metaphors is a traditional cluster which also appeared, as it happens, in the "Perilous Times" sermon on the afternoon of May 12; all have to do with the "Armor of God":

340 The armor of God
480 The girdle of truth
532 The breastplate of righteousness
570 The scandals of preparation for the gospel of peace
623 The shield of faith
632 The helmet of salvation

As the line references show, the individual metaphors are widely scattered throughout the sermon, evidence perhaps that Hurley knew this metaphor sequence well. This time he undoubtedly did. Unlike the "Texas Tower murder" theme which he had himself thought of recently, the "Armor of God" cluster is hundreds of years old and is likely to have been known by Hurley since he was a young boy. One is certain that it was memorized so thoroughly that it could be dissolved at Hurley's discretion and spread amidst 300 lines.

This rather detailed study of the fluctuations in the preacher's art over the course of a year may now conclude with a few remarks about the quality of repeated sermons. Unlike the ballad or the medieval romance, there seems to be no rule governing the length of the sermon in repeated versions. The Anglo-American ballad, we know, tends toward compression of episode; the romances frequently grow longer each time they are retold, owing to the inclination of medieval authors to amplify their stories with philosophical "matter." But whether a sermon will be compressed or enlarged depends entirely on the immediate circumstances of the performance. We have seen the Rev. Mr. Hurley shorten a theme by more than half in a second performance as though he were "perfecting" it, yet another traditional complex of metaphors, the "Armor of God," was widely scattered. Lacy and Brown have done the same things often: if their rhythm is erratic, or the audience dull, or the preacher uninspired, a brief theme may acquire a lot of fat and grow quite flabby.

And the immediate circumstances will also determine the aesthetic quality of the sermon; there is just no telling how well any particular sermon is going to be performed. Lacy's favorite sermon, the "Deck of Cards," was beautifully performed in 1967, but was mediocre a year later. On the other hand, "God's Plowboy" was a failure when first performed but a success later. If any principle can be drawn from this it is that while the preacher gradually improves the style of individual themes and sermons, he is subject to temporary failures and reversals at any time. These failures need not indicate a general trend; to determine that, we should have experience with a man's performances over the course of several years. During the course of several years, as a preacher improves, he will still have his poor days, just as a man whose powers are failing will have occasional outstanding performances. The folklore of the preacher never deteriorates, but his level of performance may be degenerate, as will be the case with a baseball player, an airline pilot, or an heroic baritone. Likewise, the texture of the preacher's folklore tends, if anything, to wax richer as he encounters and reflects upon more of the world, and this will be reflected in the richness of his sermon. But more noticeably, he will improve his techniques if he truly has the calling.

VIII
Conclusions

We have seen that the sermons of some American preachers are composed with the aid of syntactical units which resemble (in conception) the formulas and themes used by other oral performers. The oral tradition of composition, far from dying out under the relentless "disease" of literacy, actually flourishes alongside learning in one of the most highly literate countries in the world. In fact, in several ways this oral tradition exploits literacy. The ability to read and write does not seem to hinder the oral tradition at all, a finding that is at odds with Lord's conclusions. For instance, by far the most popular preachers are now in urban areas: C. L. Franklin's Detroit congregation (whose literacy is presumably higher than people in rural mountain regions) numbers over one thousand. More and more revivalists visit the major cities of the Northeast and Midwest more frequently each year. But specifically, literacy seems to have little to do with the sermon style of the men observed during this study. Lacy has not had more than a year or two of formal education. Brown got through grade school in Arkansas, Hanner in Virginia, and Ratliff in North Carolina. But the most heavily formulaic sermon recorded during the past several years was that of McDowell who has had college training, with two years at the Linda Vista Seminary in San Diego. McAllister has been to a seminary; and Manning attends classes at the University of Oklahoma.

The Rev. Mr. McDowell was born in Giddings, Texas, about 45 years ago, and had an extensive singing career which included stints with the

"Alabama Blind Boys." At one time he formed his own group, "The Southland Singers." These are the details of his life which are most relevant to his sermon style, as well as his early interest in and frequent attendance at church. Like nearly all the ministers interviewed, McDowell "fought" serving God, in his own case for seventeen years. At ten he wanted to be a singer; and, as I have said, his singing ability has not been wasted in the ministry. That McDowell writes, that his study is lined with books (which he reads), is irrelevant to his sermon style; it is irrelevant to his formulaic composition. What is pertinent is that Mc-Dowell's congregation demands that his sermons be metrical, that he has grown up amidst the chanted sermon tradition, and that this style not only comes "naturally" to him but he believes it to be the most effective way to communicate the Word of God.

Although literacy does not destroy this type of sermon, often when sermons or parts of them are read the results are poor. Almost always the rhythm is broken; the reading is usually poorly executed; the preacher's voice lacks conviction. Naturally enough, for most written matter is unconcerned with metrics. When a spiritual preacher reads during a sermon, he has to "translate" the prose on the page into the metrics of his delivery, and with all his other concerns of the moment, the translation is too difficult. We may profit by examining a portion of a sermon delivered by the Rev. Mr. Goins, unaffiliated, of Bakersfield (June 20, 1967) which begins with the preacher reading from the Bible—Genesis I ff.—preceded by apologies to the congregation because of Goin's poor eyesight, and which soon breaks into a chant:

> In the beginning God created the heaven and earth
> The earth was without form and void
> And the darkness was upon the face of the deep
> And there wasn't no light to be seen nowhere
> 5 And—uh—God said let there be light and—un—there was light
> And—uh—God saw the light and it was good
> And—uh—God divided light from the darkness
> And the light He called day/ and the darkness He called night
> And the evenin' and the mornin' were the first day
> 10 And God—God said let dry land appear
> And—uh—bent down and scooped up the mountain/ with His hand
> And—uh—thought of the sea

And—uh—gathered the water together/ in one place
And gathered the water together/ He called it the sea
¹⁵ Umm-hmm now now now now umm-humm
And God tooken this water together/ into one place
He made the great rivers and he made the fishes uhh-huh
And put them in the sea
And he made every living creature
²⁰ That creepéd upon the earth uhh-huh
He made the béastes of the forest uhh-huh that's right
He made green grass
And he made green trees
And all the beautiful flowers

After reading a few lines from the text, Goins prefers to tell the story
his own way, and so fits the words and the rhythm of Genesis to his own
metrical style, one that is in his case much like the camp and cornfield
"Hollers" on file at the Library of Congress.[1] In this passage we can see
Goins making formulas spontaneously. Goins can read, like nearly all of
his fellow pastors; but he cannot read well while preaching—like nearly
all of his fellow preachers. Lacy is an even better example of the way in
which the spiritual style deteriorates when the preacher tries to read his
sermon, or large parts of it, and I refer the reader to the section below
where his sermon on "God's Plowboy" is printed along with the text
from which it derived. The spiritual sermon, then, must be composed
spontaneously and is not effective when read; the spiritual preacher
cannot mix genres in the same performance effectively. The exception
is with written verse.

Literacy becomes a deterrent to oral recitation only when the preacher
tries to read his sermon; when this happens the effect is often discordant.
Almost always the preacher's rhythm within each line becomes erratic
and he loses metrical consistency. Spiritual preachers have been recorded
who can read aloud effectively, but for the most part such performances
fail: forced to rely on an established text, they cannot make the adjustment between stress for sound's sake and for the sake of meaning. Those
few spiritual preachers who occasionally use manuscripts do not write
their sentences to facilitate oral delivery, yet their thrust during performances is toward metrics. Hence the failure comes about because the
two modes have not been reconciled; literacy, *per se,* has nothing to do
with it.

When spiritual preachers have been recorded reading their sermons, only part of the performance comes from the prepared manuscript. The men eventually break away from the printed page and into their "natural" style; a man like Lacy who is uncomfortable with manuscripts will begin to extemporize early in the performance, while the Rev. T. R. Hanner, for example, who has had more practice with texts, will generally wait until he is well into the day's message. In both instances, however, the chanting emerges toward the end of the sermon for, again, rhythm, and not merely the words themselves, is necessary to "make the Spirit of God" move in the congregation. The point should be made clearly here that even within the same performance the preacher can both read and recite formulaically, that the reading is usually inferior metrically (but not necessarily so), but that there seems to be nothing in the preacher's literacy level to cause a poor reading performance. The trouble in such cases is always that the preacher does not know the text well enough to take liberties with conventional syntax so as to render it metrically. Some men can adapt well-known passages of Scripture to their own meter without any difficulty; but for the most part the preacher cannot even adapt his own written words simply because he does not know them well enough.

One final example on this point before moving on: so intuitive is the tendency toward rendering the sermon in metrics that in one instance, though the sermon had been written by the preacher himself for presentation to his congregation, before he had finished he had broken away from his own prose and had begun to chant. The man was the Rev. Theodore Roosevelt Hanner (of Proffit, Virginia), and though this instance has been found only once, I am certain that the same thing would happen if more spiritual preachers wrote out their material. To Hanner not even his own thoughts were inflexible, and since to him his medium was his message as much as his words, he could sacrifice his prose to the "Spirit of God." At his home he may have thought in prose, but behind the pulpit he conformed to his traditional metrics. The following prose is from Hanner's holograph:

> Then was Nebuchanezzer full of fury, and the form on his face was changed against the three men, so he ordered that they should heat the furnace seven times hotter. And he commanded the most mighty of his army to bind the three men, and cast them into the burning furnace.

Behind the pulpit, however, Hanner chanted these lines:

> I can see the old king when he ordered
> That their furnace be (heated?)
> Or heated seven times hotter
> They tell that he sent for the three strong men
> 5 The strongest men from his army
> He'd taken these men in and bound them
> Hand and feet

This tradition of which we have been speaking is a subtle chemistry of the art and the individual talent. As with Lord's epic singers, the tradition of spiritual preaching is kept alive by the constant re-creation of it. But unlike Lord's *guslars,* the preachers have some sacred texts which cannot be altered. That is not to say that Bible stories cannot be told in different ways—we have just seen quite an individual version of Genesis —but that David must always slay Goliath, Christ is always the Son of God, and always in the beginning God makes the heaven and the earth.

The tradition is also kept alive in its verbal aspects by the repeated use of shared, universal language. From the Bible the preacher gets not only his theology, not only his exemplum and narratives, but many of his formulas: "You shall know the truth/ And the truth shall make you free." Even "Amen" is used formulaically. Gospel songs and those from the Baptist hymnal, widely sung and long in the public domain, provide many another formula: "I'm glad about it," "After a while," "Am I right about it?" Still others come from the clichéd rhetoric of oratory: "I want to call your attention to the fact that . . . ," "I say unto you tonight," or "I want you to know this evenin'." These seem to me to be some of the most influential sources, though they by no means account for a majority of the preacher's formulas. All these sources function as agents of conformity of diction. Within the tradition—considered in the larger sense—there is a great deal of freedom and considerable liberty in the sermon's syntax.

For the source of most formulas is the everyday speech of the preacher and of his world: his family, his congregation, his friends, the preachers he hears on radio and in other sermons, and the songs he sings. Special diction provides only a very small part of the preacher's sermonizing vocabulary: Blair's favorite refrain formula, "God from Glory," for instance, is (so far as I know) peculiar to him. Lacy claims to have invented "Hark Halelujah," and Brown has his own preferences. Such language is not casual or conversational, while for the most part most of the refrains and stalls arise from everyday speech. McDowell admits that he has learned something from every man he has ever heard.

The special poetic diction, then, of the American spiritual preacher is derived from his own particular idiomatic dialect of American English. The diction is not as broad as is common usage in vocabulary, syntax, or flexibility. It is a specially ordered subgroup of southern American English, specially ordered because of its simplicity, its attention to meter, and its ecclesiastical vocabulary. It is, however, contained within the bounds of usage common to most of us.

Yet most of us could not stand up in front of one of the congregations in question and deliver an oral sermon for twenty minutes or half an hour. Showmanship aside, most of us do not "speak the language" though we know all the words and all the combinations of words. We do not know, in other words, the special poetic grammar.

To begin with, conversational speech is not concerned with metrics. That, more than any other factor, sets aside the grammar of the spiritual preacher. Lexical concentration on the Bible is heavy, as we have said and as would be expected; all the words themselves (some proper nouns aside) are of common usage, but some appear more frequently than would be the case in conversation: "church," "God," "preacher," "heaven." Curiously, "love" is seldom used; this is a faith among Negroes of endurance and of suffering, but not of love primarily. The gospel songs have contributed much, but again the words themselves are common; it is their combinations, and the frequent repetition of those combinations, that sets sermon diction aside: "every now and then," "I want to wear the crown," "I'm glad about it."

Periodic sentences are spoken often enough in English, but they appear to occur less frequently during sermons, because (as has been discussed) of the demands placed on the preacher of spontaneous matter. The preacher utters a line at a time; one is quite enough for him to handle, and in most periodic sentences a subordinate and a main clause are involved. In oral recitation governed by metrics the preacher is on safer ground with nonperiodic sentences. Among the men recorded the tendency was also away from Latinate words and polysyllables. In some instances the cause was quite simply a lack of vocabulary. One suspects this to be the case with Lacy, for instance, and even though such a word as "redemption" once in a while appears in his sermons we can feel certain that its importance as a doctrinal word has caused its retention. Polysyllables are avoided, again, not only because of a lack of vocabulary, but because such words are more difficult to handle in the metrical context. McDowell and Franklin (and many others) are well-educated and know —and use—polysyllables in conversation, but for the most part keep their language simple on the pulpit. If questioned about it, the preacher says that it is easier to communicate with his congregations in monosyllables since he has to speak the language of his flock.

For the spiritual preacher the ocean is the ocean, not the "swan's road" or the "linnet's bath." David is a king, not a "giver of rings." And Herod is a tyrant and not a "thrall-maker." Yet we can say that among the oral preachers the language is individual enough to speak of a special diction. There are no dawns painting the east with rosy fingers, but neither in Homer is there a Judas "crooked as a barrel of snakes."

As concerns the formula, whatever implications this study may have for other oral literatures, of this fact one may be certain: the great individual talent of the American spiritual preacher lies not in his memorization of a special diction or of thousands of formulaic systems, but in his ability to compose spontaneously the vocabulary at his command to fit his metrical pattern. The Bible, gospel songs, and the English of the American South provide most of the basic molds; the preacher fills them as the need arises. He relies, of course, on certain retained stall and stimulant formulas, and even on certain ways of introducing narrative and of carrying it along, but for the most part what he says is structured by the grammar of his community. Transformational grammarians can formulate the structure of English; a less complicated, but entirely compatible equation could be devised for the oral preacher. As for their vocabulary register, one begins again with the English language, and gradually reduces the register with successive overlays: southern dialect— Negro dialect (if applicable)—ministerial diction—and the limits imposed by meter.

In view of what has been said about the frequent repetition of refrain and other formulas, any theory about their spontaneous creation needs further clarification. Many such formulas as "Ain't God all right" and "I want you to know this evenin'" seem to be memorized; we have found that their function—that of allowing the preacher time to think of what he will say next—depends upon their easy delivery. Yet the vast majority of phrases within most sermons are not refrain formulas; are they automatic? McDowell uses a limited number of phrase-patterns, but Lacy, Brown, Freeman, and most of the others studied use far more. Often syntactical patterns are repeated but it is questionable whether the pattern as such is the unit repeated or whether what is "memorized" is an abstract pattern of English grammar. I have opted for the latter.

We should be skeptical of the argument that if many more of (say) Brown's sermons were available on tape, or on paper, and compared with a far greater sample of his preaching, that even seemingly unique phrases would be found to be "formulaic." This is hypothetically possible, of course, but what would such an exhaustive study prove? Only, I think, that the English language is limited in the possibilities of its syntactical structure, and that the preachers, because of their (often) limited education and the further limitation imposed on them by the metrics of their art, are thus limited in their syntactical possibilities.

However, since the field work in California was finished a convincing example has been recorded. Any formulas, which one claimed to be unique might be variants of systems which have not been collected: the theoretical possibility must be admitted. In the following passage the Rev. Rufus Hays of Virginia was preaching on the One Hundred and Sixteenth Psalm when he erred and said that the psalmist was David. He was able to correct himself without changing his meter or rhythm; I find it unbelievable that such self-correction of a spontaneous error could have been planned or that Hays had memorized formulas to cope with such a situation:

    David
    I gotta move on
    As he uttered these words
    He lay upon a sick bed
5   Oh I don't mean David I mean
    The psalmist
    If I don't make it correct me
    The Bible didn't say it was David
    I'm just sorta used 't
10 The greatest psalms of David
    When I get on the psalms I almost
    Go right on—carryin' on about David

But seventy-three psalms
Is credited by us to David
15 And many other psalms in the Samuels
And the other Scriptures about David
But this was just another psalmist

We have seen above an instance of the Rev. Mr. Goins "reading" from Genesis and we observed how he turned the "prose" of the Bible into metrical formulas as he read. Nearly all of the preachers can do the same with greater or lesser proficiency. The point is here that such ability is a further indication that formulas are creations of the moment to a great extent, and that the spiritual preacher's genius lies in the ability to intuitively render metrical lines. That ability is the most important lesson he learns about preaching.

The content of his preaching is stabilized because his text is sacred; the preacher's individual style, his preference for particular melodies, rhythms, formulas, and themes continually recreates the tradition within a Christian framework that is very much alive today.

We would be reasonably accurate in describing the services of spiritual preachers as antiphonal, but further refinement is possible. And while it is true that both preacher and congregation respond (often to each other) alternatively throughout the sermon, the latter's is not a wooden response to an aloof high priest, nor are the roles played by each party equal. In the ideal sermon both preacher and congregation are responding to each other and influencing each other, while ultimately they are identifying with the Spirit. In these sermons there is an intimate symbiotic relationship between the pastor and his flock: that he leads them—by selecting the subject of the sermon and to a certain extent by the proficiency of his performance—is obvious. What needs to be emphasized here is the active role of the audience in such performances. We have seen how they determine the length of the sermon: if they are bored it is likely to be cut short, and if they are caught up in the passion of the moment they may induce the preacher to extend his moments of ecstasy. Further, the congregation can improve the quality of the preacher's performance by their active participation in the service: they urge him on, encourage him, and infect him with their cries, their clapping, their tapping.

The situation is not quite the same as Melville Jacobs found among the Clackamas.[2] Brevity to the extent that he found is not desirable here; nearly all of the congregation know the stories from the Bible and the traditional exempla that the preacher is going to recite, and they are to a certain extent familiar with his sermons. Obviously they like hearing these stories over again, just as we have seen the preacher likes them and makes them the focus and the structural basis of his sermons, and they no doubt are comforted by the moral implicit (or explicit) in each tale. There is a great comfort not only in familiar and reassuring stories, but in familiar words ritually intoned and in well-known music as well. They all must immediately stimulate feelings of solace and release because of many years of association with such elements in the church. Repetition alone does not comfort, but repetition of the meaningful does. Often the congregation knows what words are coming next, or if they do not know precisely they are not surprised, as is the case with all oral literature. Occasionally they can anticipate, as I have pointed out, even the music of the line to come.

No doubt a great deal of the appeal of this kind of service is that it frees the minds of the audience from concern with what language, music, or story element is to come next, and so they are freer to involve themselves with the rhythm and the music and the emotion of the performance. Consequently, the audience is freer for active participation in the service, participation which is expressed in cries of joy, in clapping, in dancing, or whatever. Both the knowledge of the performance and the freedom to participate in it thus allows the congregation member to participate in the service and the sermon individually while he is expressing that individuality publicly; through his own singing, his own shouting, and his own clapping, the church member is to a certain degree creating his own service. Not only is he, by his active participation in the service, influencing the preacher in several ways, but he is creating a personal religious experience, and expressing it while the rest of the congregation are creating theirs. They are all a part of the sermon, and every bit as much as is the preacher. He leads, it is true, in providing the subject for the day, and is the most influential member in the church's rhythm, but often the music of his congregation is individual, as will be their cries of joy.

Self-expression aloud in public is always implicitly (and sometimes explicitly) encouraged; singing and toe-tapping are acknowledged as a sign that the worshipper is sincere and certainly "got the Spirit." Reticence, thoughtfulness, or emotional reserve is always somewhat suspect; the quiet person is not thought to be "moving with the Lord." The "good" sermon, then, is the effective one, the sermon that moves and that best allows the congregation to partake of the Spirit of the Lord with the preacher.

And as long as good sermons can be preached there is hope that the tradition can survive. After listening to spiritual preaching for several weeks, one can easily and without mental strain judge a good sermon and a bad. The congregation will also intuitively judge; they will "know" infallibly because in a sense they are the ultimate arbiters. If the congregation is not moved, the sermon has failed. It is almost as simple as that. And a congregation is moved, as most of us are, to great excitement by the gradually increasing rhythm and intensity of words movingly spoken. The response of a Negro congregation is the learned response of people who live with a rich heritage of rhythmic music and rhythmic sermons. They are a musical people because they have been brought up with music. As long as mothers bring their children to church each Sunday and bounce them on their knees in time with the preacher one would expect the heritage to perpetuate itself.

Repetition not only comforts, of course, but it adds to the mounting emotional intensity nearly as much as does rhythm. Lord has pointed out that the need to formulate the next line is upon the singer before he has finished the line of the moment;[3] thus he is more inclined to build his narrative in patterns of sequences, known as the parallelism of oral style. So it is from the preacher's point of view; the effect on the other side of the pulpit can be just as striking. Idea builds upon idea, image builds upon image as a series of incremental repetitions increases in emotional pitch.[4] As an illustration I quote first from a radio sermon by J. Charles Jessup on the crucifixion; his extremely rapid delivery persuades him towards parallel developments:

Oh my friends upon that cross of Calvary Jesus died for you and me
While blood flowed from his hands
While blood flowed from his feet
While blood flowed from his sword-pierced side
While blood flowed from his forehead
While blood flowed down upon that rocky crag of
      Golgotha's heel

            .   .   .

The sun hid His face
The moon blushed in kind of total darkness
The rocks were rent in twain
The veil in the temple was rent

And to give a better idea of the parallelism of the chanted sermons I would like to quote at length and in context a section from one of the Rev. C. L. Franklin's most famous sermons, "Moses at the Red Sea":

And here they were standing there on the brinks of the Red Sea
Here they were, when they looked behind them
They heard the rattling of the chariot wheels
Of Pharaoh who had regretted/ his decree of deliverence
⁵ And decided to recapture them/ and lead them back/ into the
      oppression of Egypt
When they looked on either side/ mountains prevented their escape
When they looked before them the Red Sea/ and its peril loomed
      large/ before their imagination
I don't believe you know what I'm talkin' about·
And the same folk who had praised Moses
¹⁰ For his valor and for his bravery
For his courage for his insight
For his great victory of deliverance
Began to complain
And Moses said to them stand still
¹⁵ And see the salvation of the Lord
I don't believe you know what I'm talkin' about
Stand still
Some time you know we can get in not only our own way
And everybody else's way
²⁰ But it seem sometime we can get in God's way
Stand still
My God I heard him say the thing that you need
Is in your hands
I don't believe you know what I'm talkin' about
²⁵ The instrument of deliverance
Is within your hands
It's within your possession

The-the-the way out
The powers that need to be brought into exertion
30 Is within you
Good God
What are ya cryin' about Moses
What are ya lookin' for
What do ya think that ya want
35 Why the rod of your deliverance is in your own hands
Stretch out the rod that's in your hands
I don't have a new rod to give ya
I don't have a new instrument to give ya
I don't have a new suggestion for ya
40 I do not have a new plan
Your course has already been charted by destiny

Parallelism appears in clusters. In line 32 Franklin asks Moses a rhetorical and expository question ("what are ya . . ."), then follows it with another question which uses the same syntax and the same first three words. The third question begins to break the pattern, retaining only the first word: "what do ya think . . ." Line 35 provides a transition though retaining the syntax and much of the diction of lines 25-26; the "questions" of the preceding three lines are answered and new elements are introduced: the "rod" and the fact that Moses has the power to deliver himself. Line 37 carries through on both of these new elements: "I don't have a new rod to give ya." The next two follow the same syntax, retain much of the diction, and convey very similar ideas. Line 40 begins to break the pattern, especially as concerns diction and syntax, and line 41 has broken completely and has moved on to a new idea. In this passage we can see the formation of parallelism and the creation of new formulas from extant systems. The oral tradition is alive so long as the preacher's imagination is alive, as long as he can continue to create within the existing limits of that tradition.

The passage from the Rev. C. L. Franklin just cited can serve as an excellent illustration of the method of oral composition, that at least as important as the formula and the theme is the phenomenon of association, of creating new formulas by adjusting the patterns of the old. The tendency in Old English scholarship is away from concentration on the formula to an understanding of the formulaic system, the "mold" from which various related formulas are formed. The results of this study suggest that by no means are all lines within sermons formulaic,[5] but may actually be recreated anew for each performance. To be specific, I would like to repeat three lines from Franklin's sermon on "Moses at the Red Sea":

[25] The instrument of deliverance
    Is within your hands
    It's within your possession

Now the line, "It's within your possession" is formed by analogy, and there can be little doubt that its use at this particular moment in this particular sermon, its diction and syntax, in a word the distinct qualities of its creation, were largely dictated by the context and especially by the preceding line. Semantically it is similar to (though a generalization of) the line before it, "Is within your hands." It is very hard to believe that once Franklin had uttered line 26, which in turn merely completes the sentence begun in line 25, that he had not paved the way, in however slight the microsecond, for line 27. Even supposing that line 27 was a memorized formula, it is hard to think of it in its relative position isolated from the preceding line which is so similar.

What is at work here is the psychological association of many factors: diction, syntax, and the logic of the sermon. In these lines Franklin tells us that Moses holds the power of his own deliverance; the next three lines in the sermon say nearly the identical thing—that the necessary powers are within Moses:

[28] The-the-the way out
    The powers that need to be brought into exertion
    Is within you

The associative link between these three lines and those that preceded it is thematic: they express the same idea. But Franklin has used different language in saying it. I do not believe that he did so simply in order to vary his phrasing and so please his congregation. Rather, I suspect that his mind, like those of other men of whatever genius, is nevertheless finite and could not advance at once along every front: semantic, syntactical, lexical. Rather, by retaining the meaning of the preceding three lines, he is more easily able to "concentrate" on changing syntax and diction. In this instance meaning provides a bridge. Thus the oral style moves at a leisurely pace as much to ensure the listener's comprehension as to aid the preacher.

In Franklin's construction of the above passage there is the key to spontaneous oral composition, a principle to which our theories of formula and system—the broad syntactical pattern from which closely related utterances are extracted—may be subordinated. To understand oral composition we shall have to go beyond the level of formula creation and somewhat beyond the Parry-Lord theory. Once more, the experiments of Professor Goldman-Eisler on the context of spontaneous speech are helpful.[6] To begin with, we must distinguish between "subjective" speech in which thoughts are encoded into words, and the planning of the content, grammar, and diction in the physical utterance of "objective" speech.

The context of the oral performance bears upon the speaker—be he preacher or otherwise—in at least two ways, for while he is objectively uttering sounds, he not only has recall of what he has already said, but he is subjectively forming the ideas, and though somewhat vaguely, perhaps the syntax and the diction of what is to come. This subjective preparation of the lines yet to be spoken may not be very precise—one has no way of testing how vague or how specific such subjective composition may be, but certainly the speaker has at least a general idea of what he intends to utter shortly. Goldman-Eisler conducted predictability tests on both forward and reverse guessing; and while all the guessers thought that forward guessing would be easier, guessing in both directions was found to be about equally accurate. Many words of poor predictability were readily predictable when the following context was known, even though their predictability was poor when the subjects had knowledge of the previous context. The speaker's subjective anticipation of the utterance to come is, then, at least as important to his construction of the moment as is what he has already said.

Given the subjective as well as the objective nature of speech, we can understand how the future context is being conceived at the moment objective speech is being uttered. Thus the preacher can anticipate himself by using immediately some words and constructions which he will also utter later. In literary texts such devices are the author's intentional signals to the reader to prepare him for the action to come, but such anticipation also occurs in oral performances though for these quite different reasons. Since the relationship of context to the lines of the moment works both forward and backward, we can also see how formulas derive from systems already uttered, yet form the basis of those which are several minutes away from utterance.

Only in this light can we understand the frequency and relative placement of stalls, and most important, of the symbiotic relationship of formula and context. It is fragmentary and ultimately fruitless to think merely of the formation of single lines. Without that single line's context we really do not know very much about the way oral narrative is composed and nothing of the way by which it progresses from line to line. Oral literature is, after all, a sequence of interrelated lines, and not the mere amassing of individual and discrete formulas. Ultimately, what does the Parry-Lord theory—as significant as it is—tell us about the way in which a single line is formed? Unless we are familiar with the particular performance and the context of that single line, one thinks of formulas as memorized or analogously manipulated entities—which was not Lord's idea—and instead of creativity we have an analogue computer.

We are, unfortunately, as was mentioned earlier, stuck with the nouns "formula" and "system," whose connotation is that of something precise, mechanical, and above all autonomous. One suspects that such an attitude is a concomitant with that philosophy which has been given us by the New Criticism, which held that finished works of literature were not the personal products of human authors intimately related to those works, but autonomous artifacts of eternity which the critic knew as much about as did their creator. An analogue is to be found in the prevailing attitude toward the formula and the system; we have not tried to see their creation as related to the other formulas within the same composition (except in terms of memorization), nor as something closely related to the life of the singer. This way of thinking produces a concept of the formula that is rigid, "memorized," and somehow apart from the forgetful, sometimes careless, occasionally faltering, and altogether creative human singer who composes them.

From the preacher's point of view, however, this is not the way his sermon is composed at all. Everything comes from God. The entire sermon is divinely inspired and everything in it is an expression of God's will; the preacher simply lends his voice to God at those moments so that He may express Himself. If the preacher has been "reading up" on a particular passage in order to prepare himself for a sermon, God has given him the thought in the first place. When the preacher thinks about several passages in the Bible which may be relevant to his main idea, or if he marks several passages in Scripture for use in a sermon, God will come to him at the moment of performance and select for him the proper passages. Association and context in the psycholinguistic sense has no meaning to a spiritual preacher. Lacy said that he could begin his "Deck of Cards" sermon with any biblical passage having to do with "heart"; but he would deny that his eventual choice was inspired by less than the Divine. This process has been described to me by the Rev. Rufus Hays:

> You don't always have the time to use the access of Scripture that you have referred to in your particular study, simply because at the time of your communication of preparation of sermon material where the spirit of inspiration might relate to you certain passages of Scripture that would blend in with the text verse that has been given to you. You don't always have the time to refer to this in particular simply because of the lack of time here, but at any normal time for sermon material, or sermon for instance in your church, at the time that you would enlight upon any particular passage of Scripture or a number of passages of Scripture, there is an outburst of spiritual inspiration that is spurred by the edification of the Spirit of God at that particular time; in other words this is the—in the unknown—unbeknownst to us inspiration of God that He would have related to the congregation at this time. I certainly believe, distinctively believe, that any time that the ordained minister—the appointed minister of God is administering, it is God actually doing the speaking—we are only vessels: our lips, our tongue, our mouths, our mind, our thoughts, and if we will be submissive to this leading and this guiding, God can use us. If we be contrary or stubborn or resistant in any way, He would not be able to get His point over to the congregation.

I have given this quotation at length not only to present the preacher's point of view on why he chooses a particular passage from Scripture for his text—a summary might have done just as well for that—but also to show how the repetitive, adding style appears even in his conversation. Now, it must be remarked that this was not conversation of the market-place; the situation was something like that of preaching in that he was trying to educate me. It was a quasi-formal public situation. Nouns get repeated ("ordained minister—the appointed minister") though little new has been added because "appointed minister" is in apposition. The syntax of the phrase has been repeated; sentence patterns recur: "you don't always have the time to . . ." Word leads to word, phrase to phrase, sentence to sentence, all the while that idea leads to idea. The basis, as Hays himself suggests, may be in Isaiah 28:10-11: "For precept must be upon precept, precept upon precept; line upon line, line upon line; here a little, and there a little. For with stammering lips and another tongue will he speak to his people. " Nevertheless, Hays's conversation is not repetitive to the degree of his preaching.

Ultimately, we may be encouraged to inquire more deeply into the concept of a "special poetic diction." I have tried to argue that in the case of the preachers interviewed, the most "special" part of their diction is that it is a limited register of English. Within such a register, of course, certain words and phrases are likely to appear more often than outside, thus giving the appearance of a special diction. In Old English, however, the situation is somewhat different, as those compound nouns, the kennings, do not appear in the prose. But whether the kennings developed as magical word-avoidance synonyms or as a language to be used only in poetry (for whatever reason), further examination of special diction could be fruitful. Lacy does not use "ain't God all right?" when sipping his breakfast coffee, yet there is nothing mysterious, exclusive, or special about each word in the expression.

We can see in most of our own communities that this tradition survives and is available to those who wish to study it; but what can we learn about those oral literatures which are moribund, the Old English and the Yugoslav? Or those which are not available, in Central Asia? The principles that apply to one may be applicable to the others, but we must be careful about using the principles of one art, however similar, to try and explain another which existed in an altogether different climate, time, and place. The American preacher's art is not narrative in the same way as was that of *Beowulf* poet: one suspects that the Old English *scops* were not as free metrically and had a greater inherited selection of formulaic metaphors—the kennings. On the other hand much of the contemporary sermon is narrative and, more importantly, the techniques of composition appear to be similar. Hopefully, then, a close analysis of the sermons should reveal points of contrast and similarity, and should ultimately reveal more of the techniques of oral composition.

Lord argued that illiteracy was one of the essential requisites of the oral singer: "there seem to be two things that all our singers have in common: illiteracy and the desire to attain proficiency in singing epic poetry . . . it is the first, namely their illiteracy, which determines the particular form that their composition takes, and which thus distinguishes them from the literary poet."[7] In the American tradition literacy is not a factor in sermon style; and though the few singers whom Lord interviewed could not write a poem as fluently as they could recite the same piece, further interviews might have uncovered other men who could. More important for a comparison with Old English verse, Lord was not looking for a literate singer who had been impressed with the desirability to write metrically or who had been trained to do so. As most Old English scholars now believe, there is little reason to think that the *Beowulf* poet or any of his colleagues was necessarily illiterate; the evidence from the text suggests just the opposite,[8] and analyses of modern sermon formulas support the view that our oldest English epic was composed by a literate man writing in the traditional, formulaic style. On the basis of sermon analysis, one should have no difficulty believing that the authors of Old English lyrical and narrative poems were learned men, since their education would not necessarily interfere with their "oral" style.

While the comparative study of oral composition reveals much that is similar, it also shows subtle variations. We have seen in detail how the preacher allows himself time to formulate future lines by the use of stall formulas. And we have seen that although stalls are occasionally used in Yugoslavia they are not pleasing to the audience and so the singer tries to limit their use. Nevertheless, the *guslar* (as well as his central Asian counterpart, the *akyn*) also needs time for his composition. We get an idea of the *guslar's* "stall" in his leisurely pace and especially in his incrementally "adding" style. The following selection is from song No. 8 of Parry's collection:

> When Mujo was a shepherd, he used to tend cattle with the shepherds; he used to go out with the shepherds. He was weak and the shepherds beat him; they beat him and tormented him. The unhappy Mujo was walking along the mountainside and he found the young of a Vila, the little children of a white Vila, in a thicket on the mountain.[9]

Not only are key words carried over from line to line, but many phrases merely repeat the previous phrase without advancing the narrative: "he used to go out with the shepherds" is a rephrasing of "he used to tend cattle with the shepherds," thus giving the singer time to think of "he was weak and the shepherds beat him," a new idea.

And we find much the same technique used by those fascinating and little-known (to the West) oral epic singers of central Asia, the *akyn,* Kirghiz traditional performers:

> When he grew to be a prince, he overthrew princely dwellings;
> Sixty stallions, a hundred horses,
> He drove thither from Kokand;
> Eighty mares, a thousand kymkar
> He brought from Bokhara;
> The Chinese settled in Kashgar
> He drove away to Turfan;
> The Chinese settled in Turfan
> He drove yet farther to Aksu.[10]

Stall formulas as the American preacher knows them do not appear in these oral epics, so the *guslar* and the *akyn* construct their poems in other ways in order to effect the same result. The *guslar* may occasionally use a stall just as the preacher resorts to the adding style, but for the most part each device is characteristic of its own literature, which has in turn derived from the demands of the audience and the singer. This incremental adding will be retained to a large degree when the *guslar* and the *akyn* write down their texts, as Lord has observed, even when the performance is in other ways substantially changed.[11] But the preacher's stalls do not occur except during performance; thus, in at least this one aspect, what is paramount is the performance and not merely its transcription from a casual interview.

As concerns the printed text of *Beowulf,* we may see oral residue in this poem, but we cannot treat it entirely as oral art. That *Beowulf* is "formulaic" is without doubt, but as we know all language is formulaic in that it is grammatical. An analysis of the sermons suggest, however obliquely, that *Beowulf's* formulas are not all memorized, but that certain repetitions were likely to occur given the structure of Old English grammar and the further restrictions placed on that grammar by meter and alliteration. These restrictions do not rule out the possibility—I would think the likelihood—that most of the half-lines were recreated rather than memorized during performance.[12] The findings of Russian ethnologists in their study of the central Asian epics supports this view: "yet it is not a case of passive memorizing and mechanic reproduction of verses learned by heart, but of a creative memory which, in the process of recital, reproduces anew and recreates the contents of a poem already familiar in its outlines to the singer."[13]

If one may be allowed to end on a further note of speculation, I think it possible that more intensive study of the American oral sermon tradition may reveal yet more about the oral (or recorded oral) literature of the past than has concerned Lord. For instance, my preliminary study suggests that the theme of the oral performer may have some functional relation to those catalogues of trees, foods, weapons, or names which appear so often in medieval romances. The catalogues are usually condemned as tedious excrescences, but their frequent employment within the romances is strong indication of their popularity. Is it possible that they, like themes, are (almost) memorized so that the reader or performer may devote his energies to making the performance more lively? One is hard put to think of a minstrel listing a score of dishes at a royal banquet in a bored monotone; that would be little more entertaining than reading a grocery list. A bored audience would not pay him very much. But if all the dishes were recited with a sensual intonation and inflection, with appropriate gestures and expressions, one can easily imagine that such a catalogue would be among the more interesting parts of the narrative. It is irrelevant that the catalogue had quite another rhetorical and possibly didactic function in the epics of Homer and Virgil, or that they had become schoolboys' exercises in the late Middle Ages; the important thing is that they could be used to good dramatic advantage during a performance and that such good dramatic advantage explains the catalogue's obvious popularity.

F. Scott Fitzgerald made up a guest list for Gatsby's first party that is one of the novel's unsuccessful passages because it is a meaningless list. But fresh and succulent beef, pork, lamb, and venison are not meaningless to a society without refrigeration, a society which evolved rich sauces to conceal the taste of sour meat. And it is now hard for me, at least, to imagine any minstrel worth his salt going over such a list without describing the succulence of the dishes with some delicious gesture—perhaps running his tongue over his lips. But this is, as I acknowledged before, pure speculation. I suggest it only as a possibility of the results of studying the oral sermon tradition.

This project began with the idea of studying the chanted sermon in America for what light it could shed upon the principles of oral-formulaic techniques of composition, and I feel that it has added to what we know about such methods. But I now believe, as do many others who are familiar with these performances, that the chanted sermon is an art form worthy of study in its own right. At one time it was ridiculed and contemptuously parodied, but many intelligent people are coming to recognize that it is a composition of dignity and artistic merit.

Faulkner recognized this: one suspects that the Rev. Mr. Shegog's sermon in *The Sound and the Fury* was created not only for its realism, not only as a thematic and philosophical epitome, but for its emotional and artistic impact as well. The spiritual sermon can be a moving experience: among the congregation ecstatic trances are common, tears flow and laughter rolls and the air is often charged with the "Spirit of the Lord." This emotional impact, gained in part through the gradually increasing rhythms and intensified tone as well as incrementally accumulated language, has been obvious on sophisticated academics who have never been to such services, but who respond emotionally even to the tape recordings of live performances. This aspect—aesthetic, dramatic, emotional—may well have been Faulkner's first thought in using an "authentic" oral sermon. We would do well to be guided by his taste.

PART TWO

PART TWO

Formulas of J. Charles Jessup

The following illustrations of the use of formulas in characteristic semantic contexts were taken from several sermons of J. Charles Jessup at
various times during the summer of 1967:

1.

I'll tell ya a lot of these seminary preachers
A lot of these big-wig intellectuals
That stand up on Sunday mornin'
And depend on their literary education
To lead people
I want you to know
They need some more prayer and fastin'

2.

Brother let me tell ya this
Not many high and mighty
Not many intellectual big-wigs
Not many money people
Are willing to pay the price
And order themselves and go to heaven
But I'm gonna tell ya

3.

The altars have been taken out of the churches

And with sugar-coated and white-washed and bargain-countered and
  streamlined and wholesaled and bargain-counter religion
To the public today

4.

How many of you will stand by a preacher
That won't compromise or sugar-coat the gospel

5.

We're livin' in a compromisin' age
When religion's been put on the bargain counter
When the altars have been taken out of the churches
When 'do the best you can' has been our modern theme

6.

I want you to know that there are some people in this good old United
  States of America and our sister countries
That's still appreciate a man that'll roll up his sleeves
And preach the Bible and the truth of God's holy Bible without fear or
  favor of man
If you want a compromisin' sugar-coated and bargain-counter gospel
Then you don't need to hear J. Charles Jessup of Gulfport, Mississippi
There's been some of these intellectual big-wigs and some of these
  modernists
Have been writing to me and saying that you make God a monster

7.

An' if preachers that go to rollin' up their sleeve
An' preachin' sin black hell hot
There's certain judgment shoulda'
An eternity long
We'd save this generation

8.

No it's not what I say
It's not what you say
It's what God's black-back holy Bible teaches
I'm gonna tell you the Bible said
Ye shall know the truth

9.

How many of you people out there listenin' to God's humble servant
Are still sincere enough
That you love to hear the old-fashioned black-back Bible preached

10.

You keep writing to me you hypocrites
You keep writing to me you fault-finders
I'm gonna preach the truth whether you like it or lump it
You can take it or leave it
The Bible said Ye shall know the truth

11.

Praise Allmighty God
Like it or lump it
Take it or leave it
Get in or get out
Put up or shut up
We've got a bominstic modernistic hand-shakin' jack-jawin' world today

12.

But do you know that in all the cities of Sodom and Gomorrah and the
    plain
They couldn't find ten holy dedicated separated, consecrated people
That were walkin' before God and living a holy life

13.

God will call
His separated dedicated (unintelligible) Christian people

14.

How many of you are willin' to live a holy consecrated life

15.

We've got to get the power of God in our lives
The spirit of God in our hearts
And it can only come
Through the medium of consecration and dedication and separation
From the world

16.

Brother let me tell you
You've got to live a holy consecrated dedicated life
If you wanna get to heaven
You can't drink on Monday
And gamble on Tuesday
You can't play cards on Wednesday
You can't commit adultery on Thursday
You can't paint the town red on Friday and Saturday
And go out to church and have the kind of religion
That's a holy religion

17.

It's gonna take a clean holy consecrated sanctified dedicated separated
     life
Hidden away with Christ in God
To be among that number

The Sermons

A word will be necessary to explain the principle used in transcribing the sermons. Since punctuation is a subtle and effective form of editorializing, the first principle I tried to observe was to punctuate as little as possible. That, of course, is editorializing also, but in this case it was deemed a less offensive course. In a major part of most of the sermons the congregation and the minister himself do the punctuating. They regularly call out exclamations of piety and joy (such as "Amen," "that's right," "you tell it," "Lord, Lord") and the preacher pauses at the same time. These pauses regulate his meter and his formulas; but he also uses the pause to gasp for breath, and with most preachers recorded this gasp is clearly audible. When the congregation is not punctuating, usually the minister is. At other times I have had to rely on my own judgment by taking account of the meaning of the words spoken, the intonation, and any other pauses in the preacher's speech.

The sermons have been printed with one formula or sentence to a line to facilitate comparison and to convey the sermon's rhythm; this arrangement also allows the reader to see at a glance whether any given passage is metrical.

However, some punctuation was necessary; in a very few cases I was not certain whether a group of words should be rendered as one formula or two; I then used a virgule between groups (/). More often, a preacher stumbled over his words by beginning a sentence that he really did not want to say, and he had to change his words in mid-thought. Usually, however, he was able to change ideas without pausing excessively, so that some mark was necessary to help the reader: a dash is used (—). Often a sound is uttered which fills enough of a space within a line to be quantitatively significant; most preachers think of such sounds as flaws, but since they do become part of the meter they are rendered: ah, ahh, uhh, etc. "Amen" is often used as a formula and is shown as such; usually when it is used this way it is sung so as to draw it out, or else it is spoken briskly and slightly off the established rhythm, thus syncopating the line.

These particular sermons were selected for inclusion for several reasons. The most popular topics should be made available both because they were more representative of this subculture and because their popularity with other preachers would make comparison easier: "The Eagle Stirreth Up Its Nest," "Dry Bones," "The Twenty-third Psalm," and "Preach the Word" are examples here. But also included are sermons that are typical of delivery style as well as of subject: hence Brown's "Mindful of Man." "God's Plowboy" is printed here because the Rev. Rubin Lacy read such a large part of it, and since I was able to get his source one could easily determine what he had done with it. Assistant Pastor William Robinson of Santa Barbara is represented because his performance shows an apprentice at work; in subsequent years I would hope to record him when his sermon style has matured; for now, a meaningful comparison can be made with those of his more experienced colleagues, if made with caution. And I have included the Rev. J. J. Freeman's sermon "The Postage Stamp" for its novelty and its excellence (as well as for frequent enjambement), and the Rev. D. J. McDowell's "The Christ of the Bible" for its beauty, piety, and formulaic content.

I have tried to avoid reproducing the dialect of the preachers for obvious reasons, the most important of which for me is that such dialect presents other problems in transcription and imposes an additional burden on the reader. In some cases, however, I deemed it essential; usually dialect is reproduced when the preacher slurs words or otherwise compresses them: "I'm gonna tell ya" is shorter than "I am going to tell you," which is not what the preacher said in the first place. The former gives more of a sense of the compression actually used in the performance, and on that basis was felt to be justified.

THE DECK OF CARDS

Recited by the Rev. Rubin Lacy, June 20, 1967, in Bakersfield, California, this sermon was well received; the congregation responded readily and consequently a good portion of the text is metrical. Lacy told me earlier in the day that the sermon could begin in a number of ways so long as it had something to do with "heart." Hence line 2: "the fool, has said in his heart, there is no God"; line 16: "the hearts of men are wrong"; line 22: "peace come when the hearts of men is right"; and lines 37, 39, 40, 41, 42, 43, etc. With "heart" in mind, Lacy was able to stock his sermon with its frequent use. Otherwise the structural plan was simple: to dwell on man's sins and on his conscience, and when the time was right—when the congregation was "up"—to bring in the "Deck of Cards" theme (Thompson Type 1613). A partial chant begins at line 77; by line 83 music has taken over the rhythm and meter completely, which is sustained until line 249. At this point sung lines, spoken lines, and lamented lines are juxtaposed arbitrarily. Lacy ends by singing "Jesus," lines 275-77.

We're gonna talk short tonight, if we can

Watching, watching, close to the psalms

Now, it read like this: the fool, has said in his heart, there is no God

All right, the fool has said in his heart, there is no God

5 Book says right here, they haven't got the strength—history repeats itself

That has been said before Christ come

Your, prophets had said He was comin'

Men wiser than the prophets had said He wasn't comin'

Been sayin' that for years, for hundreds of years—got to see it yet —sayin' He's not comin'

10 They're saying the same thing now

First Jesus died, they say He's not coming back, been dead yet two thousand years and hasn't got back yet

He'll be back but they don't believe He's comin' yet

That's natural—history repeats itself people had the same mind today that they had in those days

Jesus said when I came back, just like it was in the old days

15 So it will be when I come again

Therefore, the hearts of men are wrong, have a wrong heart

How can men get peace in the world

We are the men goin' around here
    talkin' about peace that ain't
    even been born yet
Runnin' from seaport to seaport,
    flyin' through the air at two
    thousand miles an hour
20 Talk about peace
But Jesus said there shall be no
    peace
I'm trying to say to you peace come
    when the hearts of men is right
The hearts of men is far from right
We're selfish, every man is for him-
    self
25 I think every man should be named
    Ahab
Because the word Ahab means selfish
Everybody is for himself
Nobody looks after the things of his
    friend
Ahh—ahh—and as long as we's self-
    ish we can't get no friends
30 I don't care how you boot[?], how
    you grow, how good you say
    you are, nearly everybody else
    is sayin' nothin'
In the eyesight of God
I heard Jesus say the other day,
    when you think you're some-
    thing you're nothing
I heard him say that
He who exalts himself shall be
    abased
35 I heard Him say that too
We have to be mindful along these
    lines
David here says the fool has said in
    his heart

There is no God
I'm tryin' to say to you this evenin',
    that out of the heart pours the
    issues of life
40 Don't let nobody fool ya, that your
    heart can one thing and your
    life another
Whatever is in your heart
I heard Jesus say the other day
    where your treasure is, there is
    your heart
Tryin' to say I'm talkin' about heart
    —in your heart
This same David Amen
45 Was born and God's only man in
    the world ever was born by a
    woman an'—was near and was
    after God's own heart
Only man, that was ever born by a
    woman, after God's own heart
And goin' up the road, after he be-
    come king hmm?
He got selfish
And wanted everything he saw
50 That that belonged to him and that
    that didn't belong to him
And he committed the crime of
    murder
To accomplish his deeds
Hmm?
But one thing I like about David
55 He didn't get too high to fall on his
    knees
And call out all of his servants
And close the door of his office
Got on his knees and asked
    God to forgive him for it
The trouble about some of our bad

hearts these days

60 We do these things but we're too
stout-hearted—Amen—to ask
somebody to forgive

We just don't need to askin' God, unless you ask the one that you
ain't done wrong to

So many of us tries to go to God,
to straighten up our heart

Amen, and then give our brother or
our sister Hail Columbus

Am I right? But you can't cut no
air away [other way?]

65 You got to come by God first, Amen

He said the other day ahh—in the
prayer—he said give us our
debts, as we forgive those, that
we are indebted to

Amen

An' if we don't forgive nobody, we
are hell-bound now

Think I know what I'm talkin'
about

70 Ahh—we must fix our heart—the
same David—Amen—after he
had done so badly wrong

Uhh-huh and after he'd been to
God

God had forgive his other sins

Heard God say the other day If you
confess your sins, you don't have
none

That's another thing wrong with us

75 Some of us are too stout-hearted
even to confess that we done
wrong

Ahh—David went to God

Just to be satisfied

As long as that sin was resting upon
him

You heard me talk about your conscience condemning you

80 Paul say when your conscience condemn ya, you is condemned
already

When your conscience's condemned,
don't care what nobody say
about ya

No man is condemned, unless his
conscience condemn him

An' when your conscience condemn
you

You better go in bed

85 Oh yes he is

An' after David, had went to God

This same David

I said this same David

After he'd went to God

90 Got up one mornin'

An' walked out in the breeze

Said my heart is fixed

My heart is fixed

Uhh-huh, my mind is made up

95 My heart is fixed

Umm-hmm, ya know why?

Nobody tells somebody

Heard it said one day

Be sure that you're on the right
road

100 Said to God search me

And know my heart

God got a search-warrant

God from Zion

These days are searchers

105 Search all day and all night

Know all about you

Seed everything you do
Hear everything you say
I heard him say the other day
110 I heard it before you opened your
     mouth
Get ready to come back to God
When you done done wrong
God sees you
When ya get t'get ready
115 He knows ya mind
He's a mind regulator
He's a heart fixer
God from Zion
Mister Hoyle
120 Tryin' his best
To compare with God
Look this evenin'
God made a heaven
And God made a world
125 Mister Hoyle decided
That he here
Could compete with God
That he might draw
Disciples from God
130 Look this evenin'
Men are always
Tryin' t'equalize God
So God
Made a earth
135 A world
With three hundred and sixty-five
     days
In the year
Mister Hoyle
Made a deck of cards
140 With three hundred and sixty-five
     spots
In the cards

Ain't I right about it?
And God
Made a year
145 With fifty-two weeks in the year
Mister Hoyle
Made a deck of cards
With fifty-two
Cards in the deck
150 Ain't God all right?
And, God
Said there's two ways to go
Heaven
Or either hell
155 Mister Hoyle
Made a two-spot
He called it a deuce
God from Zion
And put it in the deck
160 And God
Made the Father
Son and the Holy Ghost
Ain't God all right?
And Mister Hoyle
165 Made a three-spot
And called it a trey
God from Zion
In Matthew Mark
An' Luke and John
170 Mister Hoyle
Made a four-spot
Put it in the deck
God from Zion
Jesus, the lamb of God
175 Dyin' on the cross
Dyin' of wounds
In His body
Two in His hands
One in His side

180 And two in His feet
Mister Hoyle
Made a five-spot
Placed it in the deck
Ain't God all right?
185 Mister Hoyle
'Membered it took
Six days
To make the earth
Heaven and the earth
190 Mister Hoyle
Put a six-spot in the deck
An' he remembered
That God rested on the seventh day
Mister Hoyle
195 Made a seven-spot
And placed it in the deck
God from Zion
Then God
Saved Noah
200 And his bretheren
In the ark
Eight people
Saved in the ark
Mister Hoyle
205 Put a eight-spot in the deck
God from Zion
And then
They put a nine-spot in the deck
Representin'
210 Hangin' from the sixth
To the ninth hour
Hangin' on His cross
God from Zion
And then he put
215 A ten-spot in the deck
Representin'
The ten commandments

God from Zion
Thou shalt not steal
220 Thou shalt not commit adultery
Thou shalt not bear false witness
God from Zion
Not over yet
And Mister Hoyle
225 Put a Queen in the deck
Representin'
The Queen of Sheba
Ain't this a good story?
One day
230 Lookin' over God's children
Not only that
Said the half had never been told
Ain't God all right?
Mister Hoyle
235 Put a King in the deck
Representin'
King Solomon
Wisest man that ever lived
And Mister Hoyle
240 Put a Jack in the deck
Representin' black horse—that death
That rides from home to home
And from house to house
Then ya see what he did then
245 After a while
He put a ace in the deck
Representin' the high card
The Lord Himself
Ain't God all right?
250 Ohh, He's my friend
I say He's my friend
He's my company-keeper
When I get lonesome
He keeps me company
255 All night long

You know what I'm talkin' about
He's a good friend
I said He's a good friend
He's closer than m'brother
260 Sometimes a friend
Will put ya down
Yes he will
Sometime
Ya don't want to be around
265 Every hour in the day
(Singing)

I got my hand, in God's hand
He scoop down, and pick me up
God from Zion
I don't want you to see me fall
270 But you can't see me get up
Sometime I get up
Feignin' dead
Flat on my back
All alone by myself
275 Jesus!
Jesus!
Jesus!

THE DECK OF CARDS

Recited by the Rev. Rubin Lacy, May 19, 1968, in Corcoran, California, this is Lacy's favorite sermon, although on this occasion it was poorly delivered and badly received. But it is interesting for several reasons: it shows how flexible the form is and how different messages can be attached to the same "story"; comparison with the earlier version shows the flexibility of structure in oral literature (discussed in Section VII); and we get an excellent example of how metrics affects even memorized passages. The 1967 "Cards" portion was metrically performed, but notice the difference in 1968 when Lacy's meter failed. Only those lines which appeared in 1967 are underlined.

In the Fifty-third psalms and the
    first verse it reads like this
The fool has said in his heart there
    is no God
The fool has said within his heart
    there is no God
I repeat that
5 Fifty-third psalm and part of the
    first verse
The fool has said there is no God
We living in the last days
In Noah's days people didn't believe

there was any God or at least
    they didn't believe there was
    any savior coming
To redeem the world—the people
    they didn't believe that
10 That thing had been heard ever
    since Adam broke the law
And nations and generations had
    come on the scene
And people were still listening to
    their prophesy
First one thing and another about

the messiah would come to redeem the world
They had heard it so long until
didn't anybody believe it
¹⁵ Fact of it they heard that thing four
thousand years
And didn't nobody believe it
When you hear a thing so long it
goes in one ear and come out
another
If you ain't got mighty strong faith
For about four hundred years there
even the prophets stopped talking about it
²⁰ Hmm? yeah the prophets stopped
talkin' about it
But there was somebody among the
Israelites that didn't—that still
believed that He was coming
There was somebody I said among
the Israelites was still looking
for this messiah
But the majority of the people had
forgot about Him
Because they didn't believe what
they had heard
²⁵ Didn't read the prophets—fact of it
they had murdered all of the
prophets just about it
Elijah said one day to God said
they've killed all of the prophets
And I am left here only one
And they're seeking my life to take
here
It was a great mistake that a greater
prophet as that would make is
to tell God that he was the only
one

³⁰ God has always had somebody else
If I'm called today from this rostrum
there is somebody to take my
place
Is to carry on
You may not know who they are
But there's somebody to carry on
³⁵ God said to Elijah that day I have
seven—several thousand
That's walkin' around you every day
You see with your own eyes
Have never bowed to Baal
I'm tryin' to say to you this evenin'
that God is not dead
⁴⁰ As you hear them say
These days the people has got a
great rumor
All over the world/about a dead
God
They don't realize the things that
whispers within a man's heart
Even when he's on the job
⁴⁵ He hears a voice that talks with him
even when they are on the job
They don't realize the lightnin' and
the thunder
They don't realize the shaking of
the earth
What we call earthquakes
It takes a God to do these things
⁵⁰ Science is not able to do it and they
are not able to stop it
Fact of it they're not able to tell
when it's comin' on
Science has been studying for years
trying to find out when a earth-
quake and where will it occur
But they're not able to do it

God has that secret hid
55 Man learns so much and He lets
    him know so much because he
    can know too much
And if he do he'll know much as
    God knows
The devil lied in the garden of
    Eden
When he said you'll just become
    wise
And know as much as God
60 Uhh-huh man never has knowed as
    much as God
And never will know
As much as God
He search the earth and now he's
    searchin' the heaven
He's tryin' to search the moon and
    the stars
65 But he never will know much as
    God know about it
But I want to tell you today that
    He's not dead
An' they're ain't nobody says He's
    dead but a fool
The wise man never says God is
    dead
I don't care how much education
    you've got
70 How great a science you is
If you say God's dead you's a fool
You're not wise
Solomon said a wise man will
    change
And a fool will continue
75 Nobody says—Amen—that God's
    dead that's got good sense
We know that God is alive

An' He always will
I think I heard Him say out yonder
    to Moses on Mount Hebron
    one day
You tell them that I am Alpha and
    I am Omega
80 That means that I am the beginning
    and the ending
I am He that liveth—told John on
    the island—I am He that liveth
    and was dead but behold I am
    alive forever more
Tryin to say to ya this evenin' God
    is still alive
An' on his way back—the reason I
    know He's on His way back I
    see a great falling away from
    the church
People don't have time with the
    church
85 Nobody can't tell nobody nothin'
Everybody has his own law
Everybody has his own way
Everybody got his own religion
An' nobody can tell the other when
    things get like that
90 It's in a bad condition
Tryin' to say to ya that He's on His
    way back
He said so it was in Noah's days
So shall it be when I come again
In those days nobody would listen
    to the Word of God
95 He preached—I think the history
    said—every time the hammer
    would hit on the head of a nail
The sound of the hammer would
    . . . and men would laugh at

old man Noah
But after a while that rain did come
I wanna tell you it's on its way back
again
But it won't be rainin' water
100 It will be rainin' fire 'n brimstone
He said I won't come with water
the next time—but I'll come
with fire
This fire will burn up the roofs and
the stairways
All sin shall be burned out of this
world
Then I think John said I looked and
I saw a new heaven
105 And a new earth
Comin' down from God
A new heaven
This old heaven
Will pass away
110 This old earth
Will be passed away
I saw a new heaven
And a new earth
Comin' down with God—you're
talkin' about the King
115 Amen—that's the time, that Jesus,
will take His kingship
Jesus in the miraculous name of
God
Will come down on this new earth
Amen—and set up His kingdom
On this earth
120 His kingdom means a government
I mean a Christian government
Where there will be no more dark
Umm-hmm no more sickness
No more pain

125 No more heartbreaks
An' no more cryin'
An' every day
Will be Sunday
And every month
130 The month of May
You heard the song about the
flowers
Blooming forever
Amen
That's the time when these things
will happen
135 Said in the language of the text—
Amen
The fool, has said within his heart
That there is no God
I wanna tell you today again
That there is a God
140 Mister Hoyle
Amen—the man that made the fifty-
two cards
Tried to equalize with God
Amen God had made a heaven and
made a earth
And had made—Amen—the earth
with fifty-two weeks in the
earth
145 And three hundred and sixty-five
days in the year
Mister Hoyle went on about his
business
Said that I will equalize with God
Hark Halelujah
Made a deck of cards
150 With fifty-two cards in the deck
Representin' the fifty-two weeks in
the year
And the three hundred and sixty-

five spots on the cards
Represented the three hundred and
   sixty-five days in the year
Mister Hoyle
155 Remembered that there was some-
   times extra games played in
   these cards
An' he thought about the leap year
That had sixty-nine days—twenty-
   nine days every fourth year
An' Mister Hoyle put a Joker in the
   deck of cards
That you could play—extra card
160 Every now and then
God from Zion
And Mister Hoyle knew God had
   two ways to go
Either heaven an'—or to hell
Mister Hoyle made a deuce
165 God from Zion
That—hmm—that meant either
   heaven or hell
And Mister Hoyle knew there was a
   three-Godheads
God the Father Son and the Holy
   Ghost
And he made a trey
170 God from Zion
And Mister Hoyle knew that it was
   Matthew Mark Luke and John
Three—four gospel writers that
   wrote the gospel of our Lord
   and Savior Jesus Christ
He made a four-spot representin'
   the four gospel writers
An' he made a five-spot representin'
   the five wounds that was in the
   Savior's side—body

175 Two in His hands, one in His side,
   two in His feet
An' Mister Hoyle made a six-spot
   representin' the six days man
   shall labor
An' he made a seven-spot representin' the seventh day—was
   the day of rest
An' he made an eight-spot representin' the eight that was saved
   in Noah's ark
An' he represented and made a
   nine-spot
180 Which represented
Hung from the sixth to the ninth
   hour
Out yonder on Mount Calvary
And he made a ten-spot which
   represented the ten command-
   ments
Hmm-mm
185 That was handed down from Moses
Out yonder on Mount Sinai
An' he made a Queen which repre-
   sented the Queen of Sheba
Came all the way
From Africa
190 To meet King Solomon
And told him I heard about you
But the half had never been told
Ain't God all right
Well on then
195 He made a King
Which represented Jesus
The King of the world
Then he made a Jack
Representin' the black horse death
200 That rides to every man's door

That's been born in the world
God from Zion
Then he made a ace which repre-
    sents the highest order
God—that sets high in glory
205 Looks down on a sin-tired world
I'm tryin' to say to you
In my conclusion
That God
Is not dead
210 God
Is still alive
He's alive
In my soul
He's alive
215 In my everyday walks
He's alive
In my home
He's alive
On my job
220 I'm tryin' to say to ya
He's a teacher to me
He's a guide
An' He's a company-keeper for me
I wonder do ya know what I'm
    talkin' about
225 That same God
Same God
I say that same God
Is a way-provider
When ya don't have a way
230 When ya can't make your own way
He's a way-provider
He's a rock
In the weary land
And a shelter
235 In the time of a storm
That same God

That met me one mornin'
In the state of Mississippi
I shall never forget the day
240 I shall never forget the time
An' I shall never forget the place
One Monday mornin'
That same God
Met me that mornin'
245 And said Lacy
If you don't go
If you don't go
This is your last chance
I never shall forget the word I said
250 I said to Him that mornin' I'll go
Where ya want me to go
If it's to California I'll go
If it's to Nebraska I'll go
All the way
255 Ever since that day
I been on the job
I been into many cities
But that same God
Has been along with me
260 I been into many state
But that same God
Has walked by my side
I been into many dangerous places
And many dangers and unseen
    dangers
265 That same God
Has been on my side
Has walked along by me
An' I thank Him this mornin'
I wonder is you able to thank Him
270 I thank Him
Pretty good things He's done me
I thank Him for keeping me alive
Door of the church is open

TWENTY-THIRD PSALM

Recited by the Rev. Rubin Lacy, July 9, 1967, in Bakersfield, California, this sermon was nearly a complete failure, but Lacy managed to pull it out of its nose dive at the last minute. He started off badly because he did not know what he was going to say. Probably it was a matter of relying too heavily on divine intervention and not enough on preparation. The first twenty lines have little coherence; then he got sidetracked on a reminiscence of his childhood, triggered by the metaphor of God as a fisher of men (line 20). Lacy allowed himself to get carried away because the congregation was enjoying the story. But he was not establishing any rhythmical pattern and it soon cost him the attention of the audience. When he tried to get back to the subject he had nothing to work with. The biblical allusions skip around somewhat: line 70 appears to be from 1 Samuel 16:10 ff., but after that the stories of David are known. The parable of David and the spider is very popular among Baptist preachers; Lacy has probably memorized it. At line 169 he attempts to salvage the sermon by beginning a theme, but that soon fades. At line 193 he begins a second theme, that of the Psalm proper, and this is slightly more successful though at line 230 the congregation is still rather listless. Somewhere around this point he must have decided to use a theme which he could master, that of the four horsemen of the Apocalypse: line 241 anticipates the opening of the four horsemen theme ("But in the mornin' ") which is repeated in line 278. From that point on until the end Lacy was able to devote himself to all the histrionics necessary to getting the "message" across; the audience responded warmly and Lacy finished strongly.

I'm gonna talk today about the
    Twenty-third psalm of David
The Lord is my shepherd
The Lord is my shepherd, I shall
    not want
I likes that
5 When I was pastoring I uses that
    every Sunday morning for the
    opening of my service: the

Lord is my shepherd
And every now and then I preaches
    it—and I wouldn't preach this
    if I didn't believe it
I noticed the deacon prayin' a while
    ago, and I noticed when the
    tears just broke out of his eye,
    settin' there thinkin'
You know when people fight you

'bout righteousness it make you
cry sometime
But people have always fought folks
about righteousness
10 When you hear everybody on a
man, or on a woman, they
pretty well standin' up for
what's right
Paul ain't look like he got all that
many friends, among his kind
Hmmm?
I know what I'm talkin' about, he
ain't got all that many friends
among his kind, he should have
Ain't nobody give him his, Amen?
15 You work hard, sacrifice, get anything for it?
But somebody don't like him
Somebody is stealin', if they could
steal your very best members
they'd do it
I done heard some of them say so
Hmmm?
20 But I think if you wanta do what's
right, God said if you want to
'come fishermen of men, why
don't you get out there and get
the right kind of bait, and fish,
catch ya some
If ya ain't got the right kind of bait
ya jus' can't catch a fish
Hmm?
Some people fish all day—another
thing you gotta move about to
fish, just sitting in one place all
day, sitting there in the same
spot, thinkin' the fish's gonna
come to you—he goes in schools

in droves
You don't move about to catch the
droves you don't catch no fish
25 But it's the truth
My mother—I used to go to fish
with my mother, she carry me
to fishin', all the time—all the
rest of the children at home
but she carry me to fishin,' I
love to fish
But why did she carry me and both
of us was scared of snakes
I couldn't understand that, both of
us scared of snakes, and she
carried me
As I get older I get a lot more ways
like my mother
30 If you noticed me whenever I sit
down in the pulpit at home
anywhere I'm shakin' that leg
all the time
That's a gift from my—I mean a
birthmark
As I get older my head give me
trouble like my mother
And one mornin' it took her away
from me, jus' after . . .
Couldn't 'a told her, son-in-law . . .
where she's goin',
35 So I'm no better than she was, it
may take me
But I—if it takes me I want to be
a truthful man, not a liar,
'cause God hate all sin but He
abominates a liar
I don't think it says He abominates
anything else but a liar
But He hates all sin

Hmm?

40 But I think people oughta tell the truth, especially leaders

If I'd 'a told a man I was gonna be here I'd 'a been here

I don't care who come to offer me fifty dollars I'd say I gotta go to Blair's if I promised to go

Just like I told a man I'd be back there tonight—he know I don't wanna go out here tonight, but I'm goin'

'Cause I said that I'd be here

45 David said The Lord is my shepherd, I shall not want

And he couldn't say this until he got to be up in age

Nobody can talk about God until he 'come experienced enough to talk Him

Hmm?

Paul couldn't talk about Him, he didn't know nothin' about Him

50 Amen, but after he was stricken down on the road to Damascus

He said, in Damascus, I heard a voice

He never did forget that

When he was talking to Festus he told Festus I heard a voice

He was talkin' to Felix he told Felix I heard a voice

55 When he's talkin' to King Agrippa he said—I heard a voice I saw a light

He said the men that was with me saw a light but they didn't hear a voice

He said the light blinded me

The King said ya gotta take 'im outta here

Said if ya don't take him outta here he'll convert me

60 Paul said not only you, but I wish every man under the sound of my voice would be converted

David said—after he got up—ahh— an' he said the Lord is shepherd

I shall not want

He began to think about—like you and I—how God had taken care of him in his young days —in his hard days

David was a lover of feeding things

65 A lover of watching things

From a bird on down

Hmm?

And the other brother was rich, loved dressing

Hmm?

70 That's how come Samuel was fooled when he went t'honor a king

All them big robust and dressed-up boys come walkin' out seven of 'em dressed to death, say I just know that was king

But when he drew the oil horn it didn't flow

Old man begin to get worried, said to Jesse, is you got another son?

I know God sent me here, and I came but the horn ain't holdin' no oil

75 Is you got another son—Jesse say

yes, the David boy
Said he's the little red-headed thing
down yonder in the hot sun,
watchin' the sheep, said but I
can't sit down 'til ya bring 'em
here
Talkin' about?
I can't sit down until ya bring him
And they brought him on—oh yes
it's in the Bible—brought him
on down there, and brought
him there, and David . . .
80 And you laugh and little David had
been anointed—a little shepherd
boy, been anointed king
Hmm?
Oh my
They had a man from the Philis-
tines over there, he was a giant,
a great big tall giant
And every morning he's walk out,
with his war clothes on
85 And holler somebody send me a
man
They couldn't get nobody to go
David said one morning I'll go
Say we love you but to go David
said we want you to dress up
in some of our army clothes
Put the things on David that didn't
fit
90 Hmm?
What you put on somebody else
doesn't fit him, use what ya
got
God want ya to use what ya got
You can't preach like me—Amen—
God want you to preach with

the gift that He gave you
Hmm?
95 Ahh, David told to put off these
things
An', ah, give me my little shepherd-
boy clothes
An', an' ah, give me my sling shot
Went on down there and picked
him up five rocks
Just five
100 Goin' against a giant
He comes laughin' at him saw
David comin', he comes
laughin'
Ha ha ha I'm goin' to give your
body to the so-an-so today
David, he was walkin' up on him,
he done this, one! in the name
of the Father, 'nother! in the
name of the Son, now! in the
name of the Holy Ghost, and
then he really slinged
Walked on up there cut his head
off, and took it on, away—began
to show it
105 And the women come as braggin'—
women I say come as braggin'
Don't let the women brag on ya
Amen! women do as they brag,
sayin' Saul has killed his thousands, but David has killed his
ten thousands
Then the news went out
The news went out about David,
and from that day on, the devil
got behind that boy
110 Amen he had to run for his life
But if he run God run with him

He run when his friends would tell
him sometime why don't you
stop and fight?

David kept running, don't tell me
he ain't got nothin', somebody
said what you gonna do run all
your life yeah he said if it's
necessary

Hmm? God'll stop me in time

115 Now while he was running and—ah
—Saul was hunting him, and
he was running and running
in, a cave

And—ah—Saul was so close behind,
and was searching every nook
and corner

And God made a protection out of
a black widow spider

Ah—David ran in the cave, God had
the spider to web up the hole

He put a web there he'll know that
you're not in here

120 'Cause you're not far up ahead of 'em

He'll know that the spider web has
been broken, you not in that
cave

David lay in that cave

Ain't God all right?

I heard somebody praying a few
minutes ago said God will
make a way

125 He'll do that

Ahh-David lay there

Well, I said in the cave

Saul there in the other end

Said let's rest a while, lay down and
went to sleep

130 When he lay down and went to
sleep God woke up David, and
his servant

The servant said looka here, we got
him now, the Lord has de-
livered him into our hands

Watch this closely, the Lord has
delivered your enemy into our
hands

David had been like some of us
would of said sure did

He said let me go up there and cut
his head off

135 David said no don't do that

Said go up there cut off a piece of
his garment

And back up—come on back here

And then when he wakes up and
starts down the road, I'll have
ya show him that, and that will
let him know that you had a
chance to take his life

And just didn't do it

140 Hot dog, just did that

David had something to thank God
for

I said as a boy—ahh—a little shepherd
boy

He loved his sheep

And he had a hundred sheep and
one would go astray he would
risk his life to find that lamb

145 That means that he had the staff
with the crook in the end

If that lamb was down in the gutter

He would take the crooked end of
that staff and reach down and
pick him up

Go on up and put up on his
shoulder

Carry him on to the fold
150 He was a lover of the lamb
And he was a feeder
He would lead his lambs—I said—
    into green pastures
By the still waters
By the pretty grass
155 I said he was a feeder
Ahh, he knew what kind of food
    to give those sheep
Ahh, he knew what time to take 'em
    into the fold
And he knew—Amen—who to leave
    at the door of the fold
He knew about that
160 Ahh, I'm tryin' to say to ya he said
    after he got home the
Lord is my shepherd
One day as he was out there
    watchin' his sheep, ahh, ya
    know the devil is big
He's always tryin' to throw a rock
    in some good place
Amen—the wolf slipped up and
    caught a lamb but David risked
    his life to take that lamb from
    the wolf
165 Oh yes he did I say he risked his
    life to take—and—ahh—he went
    on and killed—Amen—that lion,
    overpowered that lion, takin'
    that little lamb and carryin'
    him on back to the fold
Comin' on home that night, he was a
    travelin' musician
Playing something—Amen—on a
    twelve-string harp
That night sitting out in his room

Mother—Amen—tipping across the
    floor
170 David was sitting there
Playing on his harp
The Lord is the strength of my life
Then whom shall I fear
Mother kept tipping 'cross the floor
175 Wondering in her mind
What had happened that day
Managed to tip back and said to
    him son
What's happened today?
He said a lion
180 Got in among my sheep
And taking a lot of my little lambs
And God enabled me to overpower
    him
And then replaced the lamb back
    in the flock again
I heard a fellow Oh Lord
185 Is the strength of my life
Then whom shall I fear?
And the Lord is my shepherd
If He hadn't 'a been my shepherd
I'd 'a been gone a long time ago
190 If He hadn't 'a been my shepherd
Door would be closed in my face
But now it's open in my face
But Lord God
Lead me
195 By the side of still waters
I heard Him say
God from Zion
He leadeth me
In the path of righteousness
200 For His namesake
Yea though
I walk through the valley

Of the shadow of death
I fear no evil
205 For Thou art with me
Thy rod
And Thy staff
It comforts me
Thou preparest a table
210 Before me
There in the presence of my
    enemies
Thou anointest my head with oil
And my cup runneth over
Surely
215 Goodness and mercy
Shall follow me all the days of my
    life
And I shall dwell
In the house of the Lord
I wonder do ya believe me
220 You that been home again
You that burd—bear the burden
In the heat of the day
You
That know
225 That ya met Jesus
One mornin'
Somebody said in Mississippi
Some said in Arkansas
Somebody been in Tennessee
230 Everywhere you go—that same Jesus
Is right here today
I said that same Jesus
Is right here today
He's on your barn over there
235 He's on your barn here
But some of us forget about that
We got up—for get up in the world
And get a suit of clothes
And able to get a car
240 And said we don't need Jesus
But in the mornin'
We gonna need him
I said in the mornin'
When money won't do ya no good
245 In the mornin'
When clothes won't do ya no good
Oh in the mornin'
When fine home won't do ya no
    good
Oh in the mornin'
250 When good-lookin' furniture don't
    do ya no good
Ya gonna need
Ya gonna need
By and by
I will see Jesus
255 By and by
I will see Jesus
By and by
I will see Jesus
Oh, in that . . .
260 Over there . . .
I don't care what ya say I got
Ya know some people got a lotta
    clothes, don't think about
    nothin'
But whata ya gonna get—he's selfish
I say he oughta be named Ahab
265 Because we got so many selfish
    people
And the big assembly in the church
Umm-hmm
They got that way in the world
If a gambler break his buddy
270 He won't let him go home to his
    wife broke

He'll give him a dollar or two
But a church member umm-hmm
Can break you
And then he'll laugh about it
275 They oughta have sense enough
To save some
Ain't I right about it?
But in the mornin'
I wanna be looking
280 For the man that I been fighting for
Umm-if you sold him
You gonna be looking for him
God from Zion
They tell me
285 In the mornin'
When the horses
Begin to come out
And the riders on the horses
Want 'em to come out
290 God from Zion
Riding a red horse
There's somebody gonna say
Is that the general
That I was fighting for
295 And I heard another cry
Saying no-ooo
That's not the one
That you been fighting for
Another one rode out
300 Riding a black horse

Is that the man
That I been fighting for
I heard another voice say
No, no-oo
305 That's not the general
That you been fighting for
Another one rode out
Riding a pale horse
Is that the general
310 That we been fighting for?
A voice said no
That's not the one
That you been fighting for
Another one came out
315 God from Zion
Riding a white horse
Rainbow round his shoulder
Hark Halelujah
Dressed in Raiment
320 White as driven as the snow
From his head down to his feet
God from Zion
In his—from out of his mouth
Come a two-edge sword
325 Cuttin' sin
Both right and left
I heard a cry
Is that the man
That we been fightin' for
330 They said yes

THE TWENTY-THIRD PSALM

This sermon was recited by the Rev. Rubin Lacy, May 5, 1968, in Corcoran, California. Because this is a repeat of a sermon on the same topic
as a performance of Lacy's a year earlier, it has great value for the study
of variation in structure and language over a year's time. A detailed comparison is made in Section VII. Most interesting is the absence of the

"Four Horsemen" theme which Lacy used a year earlier. When that sermon was first delivered (in 1967) I could only guess that the "Four Horsemen' theme was out of place and was inserted by Lacy to arouse his audience. This speculation was borne out in 1968 when Lacy recited the same sermon but omitted the "Four Horsemen." Only those lines which appear in the 1967 performance are underlined (solid or broken) here. This performance was well received though the congregation numbered only about fifteen. Lacy begins to chant near line 87.

Twenty-third psalms of David
Since it's so late
The Lord is my shepherd, I shall
    not want
The Lord is my shepherd, I shall
    not want
5 We're talkin' tonight from a man
    that is experienced
You know experience is your best
    teacher
I don't care what you learn in books,
    it's fine—don't understand me
    say it isn't fine, but don't let
    books carry you away
Hmm? experience is your best
    teacher
David here knew what he was
    talkin' about
10 Because he was experienced
From his youth he had—he had—
    been a shepherd boy
He wasn't like his other fine rich
    brothers
That didn't believe in nothin' but
    dressin' fine in the very finest
    of linen
And waiting on the servants as they
    wait on them
15 But David loved the sheep

And he cared for the sheep
I'm tryin' to say to you that David
    was a leader from his youth
Sometime you see a little boy run-
    ning around your home
And you watch his appearance and
    somebody will say that boy is
    a preacher
20 I don't know I don't think Samuel
    was able to see that about his
    son—I mean Jesse was able to
    see that 'bout his son David
Ah, he rather thought that some of
    the boys—other boys—was more
    dressed fine—an'—ah—stayed in
    among the big people would
    come nearer makin' a great man
    than David
Because David stayed in the field
All the time—'fact he stayed there
    so much until his color—ah—
    wasn't like his other brothers
He was sun-burnt
25 An'—ah—his color 'count of this
    didn't favor his other brothers
But we see here that he was God's
    chosen man
From the Jews
When the time come—ah—for the

second king to be anointed for
Israel
God told Samuel to go to Jesse's
house
30 An'—ah—anoint a king
Now listen—God didn't tell Jesse
who t'anoint
Jesse had eight boys
You go there an anoint a king
Ah—among those boys
35 God fools Samuel too
Jesse wasn't the only man fooled
But Samuel was fooled too
Because these men—no wonder the
writer said the other day
Ah—God looks at the inward and
man looks on the outer appearance
40 Samuel and also the father of David
were looking on the outside
Looking at the high—robustest boy
That dressed in fine clothes
They wasn't thinkin' about that boy
in the field
But when Samuel begin to draw
the horn
45 It failed to pour
And they passed through until seven
boys had went under the horn
And then old man Samuel began to
get all uneasy
I know that God don't make mistakes
Samuel—listen to Samuel talkin' to
himself—I know that God don't
make mistakes
50 But there's something wrong—all
seven of these boys that went

under the horn and the oil had
failed to pour
He asked the father didn't he have
another son
He said oh yes I got another little
boy but he's in the field
Goodness sake I know he's not the
one
But Samuel knowin' God and believed in God said I won't set
down/don't offer me a chair
55 I won't set down until ya bring him
here
And they had to hurry to the field
and found David around his
sheep
Found little David with the staff in
his hand
Found David with his light layin'
on the altar for his sheep
Found David standin' between the
lions and the bears
60 Guarding his sheep
And they said the prophet wants
you at the house
David went on up there with his
little bushy head
See him in my mind
And ah sun-burnt face
65 Went on up there
But when he walked under the horn
the oil began to pour
Listen—and the news went out
That little David is anointed king
What I'm tryin' to say to ya as long
David was in the field watchin'
sheep he didn't have no
trouble

70 Nobody wasn't payin' him no attention
But when the news went out
That David is anointed king
Saul got in behind
I hope you see what I'm talkin' about
75 The devil got in behind
Yes they tried to get him killed
Put him up—Amen—before that great giant
And he trusted God
King sent for him and dressed him up in a suit of clothes
80 David looked at the clothes and said it don't fit me
Ahh—gimme my little clothes what I had on
And then the sword is not the right kind
Gimme my little sling
And my bag
85 David went on and this king looked at him
Begin to make fun of him
Talkin' about how he would give him the fowl of the air
David just stood there
Reached down and got one of his little rocks
90 Placed it in his sling shot
He made three swings
Representin' God the Father
God the Son
And God the Holy Ghost
95 And direct it between/the two eyes
Ohh the giant fell
And David walked up and cut his head off

And the news went out
That Saul has killed his thousands
100 But David has killed ten thousand
Ain't God all right?
No wonder
David in his old age
Can say the Lord is my shepherd
105 I shall not want
Devil kept on runnin' after David
They run him so tired
Sometime he was hungry
He had to eat the short bread
110 He didn't have time to go to the store
He had to eat the bread
That the trees issued
God from Zion
They kept on runnin' him
115 They runned him so fast
'Til one day
They was so close behind
God said to David
Run in the cave
120 David didn't argue with God
Went on in the cave
A widow spider
Crept up the cave
Behind little David
125 Saul come by
Looked and saw the web
And said I know
He can't be in here
Went on down the road
130 And went in the cave
And went to sleep
And God
Called David
To go in the other end of the cave

135 And found his enemies asleep
His <u>servant</u> said to 'im
The <u>Lord has delivered</u> 'em
<u>Into your hands</u>
But David said
140 He's God's anointed
No wonder he said
The Lord is my shepherd
He was experienced with that
There can't nobody say that
145 But people that's experienced
David was experienced
And then a shepherd must lay his
        life on the altar
A shepherd don't just drink the milk
And eat the flock
150 But he lay his life on the altar
In those days
It was dangerous to be a shepherd
Because the wolves
The bears
155 The lions
The bobcats
The panthers/and all those things/
        were dangerous
And it was an open range
And men had to stay out there
160 Both night and day
I wonder are ya goin' with me
That's what the men were doin'
The night when Jesus was born
Out yonder on the plains
165 Watching the sheep
David was one of these men
He were out there
One day he was out there
And a lion got among his sheep
170 Come along and grabbed a lamb

You know the Devil always hits the
        weakest spot
The weakest thing he can find
He don't bother the strong things
So the lion come in the flock
175 And saw this little lamb
Hadn't been long born
And he couldn't run
Like a old sheep
And the Devil got after the lamb
180 And caught the lamb
Little David
Laid his life on the altar
Taken his sword
And walked up there
185 And taken the lamb
Out of the lion's paws
Went on home
Sit down that night
<u>Playin' on his harp</u>
190 <u>The Lord is the strength of my life</u>
<u>And whom shall I fear</u>
<u>Mama tippin' across the floor</u>
Listen' at his new song
A song she had never heard before
195 Jesus
Here come the strain
She said to him son
What happened today
He said mama
200 A lamb
Was got in the lion's paw
And God
Delivered the lamb
Back into my hands
205 Ain't God all right?
I said it takes a man of experience
To say the Lord is my shepherd

Oh anybody can say it
You've heard it so much it has become common
210 For people to say the word
I read it to ya every Sunday morning
The Lord is my shepherd—people
   don't pay that no attention
But it takes somebody with experience to know that God has
   been your shepherd
I remember once some time in my
   life
215 Guns were throwed in my face
By men that was no . . . kin
But they couldn't pull the trigger
Because the Lord was my shepherd
God bless ya/hope you got something out of this/the Lord is
   my shepherd
220 And if He's your shepherd there's
   no need to worry

You know some of us worry 'cause
   people don't go to church
There's no need to worry
If the Lord is your shepherd preach
   on
Preachers, preach on
225 Singers, sing on
You gonna get your reward
God has given you that gift
You sing on
And God will give you your reward
230 Preach if you don't have but three
   to preach to Preachers, don't be
   shamed to preach—I preach just
   as hard to this—bunch like this
   as I would a church full
Because I think that's the church
I'm through
I think that's the church
235 Whoever be's here I think it's the
   church

THE POSTAGE STAMP

Recited by the Rev. J. J. Freeman (of Pixley), July 23, 1967, in Bakersfield, California, this sermon appears to be a favorite of Freeman's, and
he has prepared it well. The congregation responded cordially and Freeman was in control of his material at all times. He was giving a guest
sermon in the Rev. Elihue H. Brown's Union Baptist Church and was
to be followed by a lecture from a local prison officer, the Captain Medlock mentioned in line 8. The reference to a (hypothetical) police captain in line 33 was provoked by Medlock's presence, as my presence
induced the remarks about the "collector" in lines 8 and 35. Freeman
does not sing well but his sense of rhythm is impeccable. He breaks into
a chant at line 58; and the congregation is receptive. This early start
gives him a good deal of time to work with them—to get his message
across. At line 173 he reverts to a more normal speech, but at line 193

he breaks into singing, which carries the sermon to its conclusion. The
text for the day, "Go ye into all the world and preach the gospel to every
creature," is the most popular Scriptural passage among the preachers
interviewed.

And He said unto them, Go ye into
    all the world and preach the
    gospel to every creature
He that believeth and is baptised
    shall be saved; he that believeth
    not shall be damned
From the sixteenth chapter of the
    book of Saint Mark, fifteenth
    and sixteenth verse
We're going to use the latter part of
    the first verse, ahh, go ye into
    all the world
5 And our thought will be, be like a
    postal stamp
And down a way you'll find why
    I'm choosing the stamp
Amen
Giving thanks to God and honor to
    Pastor Brown and to all to of
    my co-workers in the ministry,
    to Captain Medlock, this fine
    recording gentleman, and to
    Union Baptist as a whole, and
    to all our friends and visitors
    we thank God for the privi-
    lege—we deem it honor that
    out of all the fine ministers
    here you chose me for this hour
Thinking as I received the invitation
    said the professional program,
    and I thought of everything in
    the world to bring to you today
10 And I wound up with the gospel of

    the Lord and Savior Jesus
    Christ
I'm using the stamp because my,
    follow-up for the subject would
    be stay in your place
Amen
I believe it's a mighty fine thing to
    have a profession
It's better when you have this
    profession to stay in your place
15 Amen
We find that most professions
    seemly to stand their ground
    and wait, until we get to the
    church
Gettin' a little quiet now
Amen
Ahh, the doctor knows his profes-
    sion, and one thing about the
    doctor, when you go to him and
    he diagnose your case, unless
    it's your wife or some close
    relative, he won't tell you a
    thing
20 That right?
Because he's your doctor 'n this is an
    oath, that whatever is wrong
    with you I'm gonna keep your
    secret
Likewise—Amen—every attorney
    knows his field
I call them the liars
'Cause most attorneys have to lie if

he's gonna free you 'specially if
you're guilty of a crime

25 Amen, but he's a profession in his
field

So he goes about it in an intelligent
way

Sometime he make folk lie that
wouldn't lie ordinarily

But he is after winning the case

But he knows his profession

30 Amen

I believe that—ahh—in the church
we ought to know our
profession

We ought to know how to stay in
our place

Ahh, if the captain should leave his
post

Try to walk the beat, Amen he's
getting out of his place if he
have man on the beat he oughta
give him his order 'n leave him
alone

35 Ahh, I'm comin' to you now Amen

You're not gonna be quiet after a
while

Ahh, an' every profession seem to
be able to make a mark

But when it comes to our profession

The preacher

40 The highest office that's in the world

The lowest-paid office in the world

The most talked-about man

Amen, everybody knows his
profession better than he does

Don't nobody know how to stay in
their place

45 When it comes to the church

Brother Pastor, if I was you

Ha ha—I'd do this and I would do
that

Brother Pastor if I was you I
wouldn't let this go on

And I wouldn't let that—but have
you ever stopped to think that
have you done your duty

50 Have you stood in your profession

Just as a member in the church

God Almighty I'm sick of folks tellin'
me what I oughta do

And then leaving their job undone

Have somebody that don't live right

55 Amen, Lord God, you run to the
Pastor and say turn him out

I'm not big enough to turn anybody
out

If you do your job you—ahh—make
the first trip

I believe this is your Bible

Say if you overtake you in the fall

60 You go to the—you can't get
reconcile

You go back and get another one

And you go the third time

They feel they hear you—then they
bring them before the church

We don't bring nobody before the
church

65 There hasn't nobody turned out of
the church in the last twenty
years

Amen?

Gettin' quiet in here isn't it?

We—we're—we ought to know our
profession

Reason why, that I chose the postal
stamp

70 Ahh, the minister is like a stamp
He's a messenger bearer
He's an ambassador to God
Ahh and Jesus gave him a
   commission
Said Go ye
75 In—all over the world
And preach the gospel
Yeah?
Sometime they bring us sad news
Sometime he's meddlin'
80 Sometimes makes you mad
Sometimes he makes you glad
But ohh
You oughta listen sometime
Yeah the stamp
85 Around your home
Sometime a stamp'll get lost
Lay around and get a little dirty
And lose the glue power
We throw it away
90 But you can use it
If you just try
To help it along a little bit
You clean it up a little
Put a little glue on
95 And put it on the envelope
Oh yeah
And drop it in the box
The post man
Will stamp his approval
100 And send you on your way
A five-cent stamp
That will take this message
Over into Philadelphia
Your mother's dead
105 Ahh—the airmail stamp
Will take the same message

Your mother's dead
A special delivery
Will take the same message
110 Your mother's dead
Oh Lord
I see the three stamps
Standing together
I have heard one say
115 How come you're like you are?
I heard that stamp say
You did a good job
You carried the message
And I brought the same message
120 Stamp didn't say well I'm better
   than you are
But it said well
I got a job to do
The five-cent stamp
Will do as much as a special
   delivery
125 In its own category
Say you oughta stay in your place
Ohh Lord
If somebody
Was to say to the stamp
130 I don't like your look
The stamp say well
I tell ya what you oughta do
Take it up with my maker
I did not make myself
135 Ohh Lord
Want you to pray with me
Ahh yeah
I see a preacher
On his way
140 Carryin' God's word
Somebody
Say I don't like it

Don't like the way you look
I don't like what you say
145 This is what you oughta tell him
If you don't like me
Take it up with my maker
He made me
Just like I am
150 The stamp
Never stands still
Till it got its approval from
    Washington
Then if it's OK
Before it carry the message
155 The preacher
Ohh yeah
Got to get a OK from God
Ohh yeah
I heard a poet sang it a song the
    other day
160 I been sealed
Till the day of redemption
I don't care what happens
The storm cloud may rise
But I been sealed till the day of
    redemption
165 Don't make me 'posin' my faith
But I been sealed till the day of
    redemption
Jesus said go ye to all the world
And preach the gospel
To every creature
170 He that believe, shall be saved
He that believeth not, shall be
    damned
I'm here to tell you, you oughta save
    your place
Those, young man, he was good at
    doing his job

He built him a little boat
175 Storm came and the little boat got
    lost in the storm
Went down town, saw his little boat
    in the window
Went inside and said looka here
    mister, is that boat for sale
The man said yes
Give me fifty cents and you can
    have it
180 Took the boat and walked outside
Began to look at it and say, yeah,
    you mine
Cause I know my handwork
And now I wanna tell ya somethin'
I own you twice
185 I made you
Now I bought you
And I got a thought from that
Jesus
Yeah, Jesus
190 Say I made you
Went to the cross of Calvary for
    you
How can you say I'm my own boss
I heard Paul say the other day
I'm a prisoner of Jesus Christ
195 Ohh Lord
I can't do like I want any more
Since I been regenerated—born
    again
Holy Ghost got a hold 'o me
Every once in a while
200 Gonna turn around
But the Holy Ghost say you can't
    turn around
Ohh Lord
Ohh this evening

Lord be my home at evening
205 And walk along with God
Walk and look-a-here
I said look-a-here
Your pump is so sweet
I just can't turn it down
210 Walk another hundred years
Said I've come too far
Just can't go back
Walk another hundred years
They kissed him and . . .

215 Am I right about it?
If you stay in your place
God can use you to serve
Oh what is this
I can feel
220 Deep down inside
What is this
Set my poor, soul on fire
With an ever ready heat
Ohh it won't let me
          (dissolves in singing)

THE EAGLE STIRRETH UP ITS NEST

The sermon was recited by the Rev. Rubin Lacy, July 9, 1967, in Bakersfield, California. This popular theme was fairly successful in Lacy's version, despite the preacher's very poor diction and almost incoherent structure. His diction was so garbled, and the response of the congregation so heated, that several lines are inaudible and cannot be clarified even after repeated tape runs (lines 72, 88, and 178). One of the interesting aspects of this sermon is that when it was over Lacy remarked to me that he had forgotten to come back to the main point of the image of the eagle stirring its nest. The preacher jumps around here from passage to passage, one Bible story reminding him of another which he then proceeds to tell without attribution. Toward the end he uses a favorite theme of his about "the eagle bird" (lines 230 to 301); the relation to the main theme is obvious, just as it is superficial. He then begins another of his favorite themes, on the four beasts of the apocalypse (lines 326 ff.), comes back to dreams (lines 354 ff.), then reverts to the story of Daniel's dream which he had used earlier; Daniel's function reminds Lacy of the functions of various members of the clergy in Ephesians 4:11, and on that note he closes. As in few other sermons can we so clearly observe the preacher's mind traveling from idea to idea and phrase to phrase through association, possibly because so much material came to mind when he used this old favorite. The chanting begins on line 84 and continues until line 351, where he begins to speak more conversationally. The mention of "a desert land" in line 7 reminded Lacy of Bakersfield.

Reading today from the book of
Deuteronomy, chapter thirty-
two

Remember the days of old, consider
the years of many generations:
ask the father, and he will
show you, the elders and they
will tell you

When the most high God divided
nations—their inheritance separation of the sons of Adam

He set the bounds of the people
according to the number of the
children of Israel

5 For the Lord's portion in His people

Jacob is the lot of his inheritance

He found them—watch this—in a
desert land

In the waste howling land

He led him about and he instructed
him

10 He kept him as an apple of his eye

Eleventh verse said

And as an eagle stirreth up the nest

Fluttereth over her young

Spreadeth abroad her wings

15 Taketh them, beareth them, on her
wings

Twelfth verse said

So the Lord alone did lead them,
there was no strange god with
them

Bible says—our text says—eleventh
verse

As an eagle stirreth the nest

20 I have to jump down to the twelfth
verse

He said that there were no strange
gods

I don't care where Jacob went

How much God stirred him up

You know he stirred him up a
whole lot of times

25 When he was a boy—nothin' but a
boy

His mother might have been the
cause of some of it, but it was
the will of God that he be
stirred up

It could have been through
encouragement of his mother

Because he didn't know or didn't
desire to do some of the things
that his mother insisted that he
ought to do

What belonged to him I believe he
'ventually would have got it
anyway should she waited on
him

30 But she couldn't see it like that

Jacob was her favorite son

Hangin' around the kitchen—uhh—
in the house

Practicin'—he made himself a good
cook

He made hisself such a cook until
he could—when his brother
came in hungry one day

35 And there wasn't nothin' to eat
down, he told him—said—I'll
make you some lentil soup if
you give me your birthright

All these things was comin' upon
Jacob that he might become
stirred up

So one day he stole his brother's
birthright . . . his mother

The thing got so bilious and so
dangerous until his mother
then had to lose her son for a
while, hafta' lose him
Cause he had to go to her brother's
home
⁴⁰ A distant land from that particular
place
And as he went on, runnin' away
from his brother, in a strange
desert land
He lied down one night and went
to sleep, and his pillow was a
rock
And as he was sleeping that night
he saw a ladder let down from
heaven
⁴⁵ An angel descending on that ladder
From earth to heaven
He's asleep
An' he woke up the next mornin'
and said, surely the Lord is in
this place
He said and this rock that I made
for a pillow I set over here
⁵⁰ It shall be the gate therein
The house of God
I'm tryin' to say that was long time
'fore Jericho were built
Amen! That was long time 'fore
Bethlehem was thought of
Long time before Jerusalem—Amen
—was built
⁵⁵ But keptin' still, Jacob was able to
see these things
That's God—God was with him
though he had done wrong
Amen! A man does wrong don't let

nobody fool ya, he's got to reap
what he sows
Ahh, Paul had to reap what he
sowed
I don't care how much God forgives
you, you got to reap what you
sow
⁶⁰ When a man's forgiven for his sins
looks like it ought to be all over
But hear, he's got to reap what he
sows
Jacob was stirred up and had to
leave home
Went on over there an' married
Um-hm
⁶⁵ An' he stayed over there—let's see,
I think he worked for seven
years for a younger girl
And then, after he worked seven
years for a younger girl
Old man Laban told him, he said
this, you have got to work now
for seven more years because
the oldest girl was married first
And there so he worked seven more
years
That mean he worked fourteen
years—Amen!—for those two
wives
⁷⁰ Then when he had to work for six
or seven more years which
made it twenty or twenty-one
years—Amen
In order to get a . . . of cattle—a
herd—Amen
One day, Amen
God had always been with old man
Jacob

But he had to reap what he sowed
75 He went on from there and God
    stirred him up over there
Things got bad, he had to pull up
    and leave there
He's on his way back to meet his
    brother Esau
Want to hear this treaty, but he was
    rich man then
Had a lot of cattle, a lot of herd, lot
    of sheep and all these different
    things, lot of camels—Amen—
80 Camels worth a whole lot of money
Amen—started out on his journey
Makin' his way back to meet his
    brother
Shows ya how God kept him stirred
    up
Umm-hmm
85 He went on back home
Stayed around there a long time
And, his brother's son was born
Benjamin and Joseph an . . .
Amen! and Joseph got up to be a
    seventeen year old boy
90 He was loved very much by his
    father
One day he was sold—Amen—
    to the Ishmaelites
Down in the land of Egypt
They take him down there—Amen—
    and make a slave out of him
God begin to stir Jacob up again
95 After a while the well got dry
Nobody could make no wheat,
    nobody could raise no corn
And this uh—butler—down in that
    country

Told the king, said, I know about
    Pharaoh this mornin'
Said, uh, there was a little Israelite
    boy
100 Go down in jails
That interpreted my dreams
Nigh on two years ago
An' I promise that I will tell you
To let the little boy out a free man
105 That hadn't done nobody no harm
But this day said the king
Had dreamed a dream
God from Zion
He said to 'em, tonight I know my
    fall
110 And the king
Told 'em to go get the boy
Had him a shave
Amen! and put on a clean raiment
Amen!
115 Put a necklace around his neck
Bring him on up here
Brought him on up there
And get him to interpretate the
    king's dream
He called it the seventh lean years
    gone
120 He saw the dream/ meaning seven
    years of poordom of no
    prosperity
And the seven fat years of corn/
    mean seven good years
And you know about the cows
I said was seven poor cows
Ate up the seven fat cows
125 And they was still poor
God from Zion
The king said to Joseph

If you all that wise
What shall I do about it
130 Joseph said to him
Get a man
God from Zion
To go around
And get all the people in the land
of Egypt
135 Get 'em more bonds
Ain't I right about it?
Store up their food
Get ready for preparin'
For seven years of famine
140 Went on down there
Ain't God all right?
King said to him
You shall ride
In the second chariot
145 God from Zion
King got the job
Of doin' all these things
I'm tryin' to say to you this evenin'
Joseph dreamed
150 Aggrigated [sic] to come true
When he was a little boy
He dreamed
That his mother 'n father
And his twelve brothers
155 His eleven brothers
Would bow and receive
Ain't God all right
And then he dreamed another
dream
God from Zion
160 About the sheaf
In the field
But all these sheaves/stood upright
All the rest of boys' sheaves

Bowed down to him
165 And Joseph here
Was thirty years old
Before he saw his dream
Comin' true
Hark Halelujah
170 God from Zion
Riding in the chariot
Gettin' ready
To do business
Down yonder in Egypt
175 I saw
A dream give out in Israel
Old man Jacob
. . . .
Been down in Egypt's cell
180 All those boys together one day
Goin' over the news
Get your sights in your hand
And bring some money out
Put money in your pocket
185 And get on down to Egypt
And bring some food on here
That the people here don't starve
And Egypt's cattle don't starve
I saw the boys
190 Gettin' ready to go to Egypt
You know the story
God was gettin' ready
To stir old man Jacob up again
God said to him
195 As the text says tonight
As the eagle stirs the nest
Gotta go over yon
So God
Stirred up Jacob
200 Every land
That Jacob went alone

God was on his side
He didn't accept no strange gods
God said to Jacob
205 God had told him
Thou shalt have no other gods
Before me
God from Zion
He held on to
210 That thing that he was raised up
        with
Held on to it
Some many of us today
God from Zion
Don't even have a culture
215 Am I right about it?
But Jacob held on to
His old culture
Ain't God all right
Goin' on from there—goin'
220 I saw Jacob
Gettin' ready
To stir himself again
Went on down there
God sent him
225 As an Eagle stirs the nest
So was he further over yon
God from Zion
About a eagle bird
Now let's go on
230 Eagle bird
Is a mighty wise bird
Sets out yon
Only fit for the mountain
He don't allow
235 No clouds
No dangerous clouds
To get between him and the sun
God from Zion

Eagle has got an eye
240 Look at the sun
The beams of the sun
All day long
Don't have to bat his eyes
He don't turn his body around
245 Jes set there in one place
Turn his neck around
And watch the sun
As she rise
There as she go down
250 Behind the western drum [?]
Ain't God all right
That eagle bird
Is far-sighted
He seed a long way
255 Seed the end
Before he makes it around
I saw the eagle
Settin' down on the mountain
Lookin' out yonder
260 Watchin' the sun
As it traveled
He saw
The 'mensions of a tornado
Make its way to him
265 Three days
Before the tornado arrive
I saw that Eagle
Gettin' ready
To get on its wing
270 Dive down
In the water
Bathe itself
In the water
Fly back to the mountain
275 Shrug itself
Look around at its body

Seed if it have any false feathers
If he saw a false feather on him
Take his bill
280 And pull the feather out
I'm back again
Revelatin' God the Father
Son and the Holy Ghost
If he didn't see a false feather
285 On his first flight
He set there and looked
And after a while
He begin to get up
To get on his way
290 Every travlin'
That eagle make
He would go higher 'n higher
Where ya goin' eagle?
How come ya pull the feathers?
295 Out o' your wing
I don't want no trouble
When I get on the wing
I don't want no false feathers
I don't want no trouble when I get
    on the wing
300 I wonder do you know what I'm
    talkin's about?
God from Zion
Look today
In the church of God
We got so many
305 False prophets
So many
False feathers
In the church
So many green trees
310 Don't bear no fruit
In God's church
That eagle was set on the wing

Where ya goin' now?
I'm gettin' on the wing
315 I'm gettin' higher 'n higher
Higher 'n higher
And after a while
Get above the clouds
See you down there
320 Storms overblowin'
Come on back
To these dips [?] in the mountain
Ain't God all right
Let's see what John said about it
325 John said
I . . . I
I saw four beasts
One with a face
Looked like a calf
330 Representin' patience/
    and endurance
'Nother beast I saw
Had a head like a lion
Representin' boldness
And confidence
335 'Nother beast I saw
A face like a man
Representin' wisdom
An' he had knowledge
'Nother beast I saw
340 Looked like a bald eagle
Ain't God all right?/Yeah, Yeah
I know He's all right!
Any time a boy
Oughta be wise
345 B'able to see trouble
Know when he comes to it
Any true-born child
Ought be able . . .
If ya can't see trouble

350 There's somethin' wrong
Don't tell me that you—God don't
    have nothin' to loan ya
Some time ya don't what it's all
    about
But you know what something's to
    happen
Some folks say well, I don't believe
    in dreams,
355 I don't belive in visions
Let me tell ya one thing, there's
    somethin' to both of 'em
Just got to be talkin' about dreams
Father said young men would
    dream dreams
Old men would see visions
360 I think I'm right about it
Umm-hmm
I know you're all right
Kings have dreamed dreams
I said kings have dreamed dreams
365 All the wise men
One day they couldn't interpretated
When they send for the guard man
    [God man?]
That guard man to tell them about
    it
I heard 'vangelist say the other day
370 All kings
Don't look to me to interpretate
    your dreams
Look at Daniel
Ohh, I heard

You able to give me to interpretate
    your dreams
375 And I heard
Umm-hmm
Daniel said that
When they had to send—Daniel to
    interpretate the king's dreams
He told him
380 I can't do it
I heard you talkin' 'bout healin'
Some—God got somebody to heal
Everybody can't do it
I say everybody can't do it
385 I heard it said the other day there's
    some to heal
Umm-hmm
Some to pastor
Some for evangelist
But everybody nowadays
390 Will do what they want to do
It just won't work
In the end   (song)
I want to take, take my rest
Lord, in the end
395 When I have done
Done my best
I want to smile
When I have no-thing to hide
Ohh, ohh, Lord, in the end
400 Lord will not grow
On this old battle-field
I want to rest
    (dissolves in humming)

GOD IS MINDFUL OF MAN

Recited by the Rev. Elihue H. Brown, June 11, 1967, in Bakersfield,
California, this sermon was a success, as are nearly all of Brown's. He is

quite popular in his community and his sermons are almost always well attended. Brown's style is somewhat different from those of the other men collected in this volume; he has a good rich voice whose plaintive tone is quite appealing. And he uses his voice to good advantage, singing nearly all of the sermon. The chanting begins here on line 24 and very quickly becomes singing; it would be very difficult to say exactly when. Because nearly all the lines are sung, the transcription may be deceptive in that some lines appear to be short because few words are spoken in them: "He told him" (line 76), for instance. But when this line is sung it is drawn out and may take four or five seconds to recite. Brown's lines are slowly delivered, his over-all pace is methodical and deliberate, and more than half are sung. His sermons are almost entirely lyrical, which more than makes up for his poor sense of timing: he has no emotional build-up as such, hits a high point fairly early and sustains it throughout; there is no denouement. This sermon includes one of his favorite themes, that of Jesus and the miracles, lines 191 ff.

But one in a certain place testifies
    saying, what is man that thou
    are mindful of him, or the son
    of man that thou visit him
Hebrew two and six
God's concern about man
The text is a quotation of the
    position of the Eighth psalm
5 The Psalmist in the third and part
    of fourth verses sayest
When I consider thy heavens, the
    works of thy fingers, the moon
    and the stars which thou hast
    ordained what is man that thou
    art mindful of him?
I want you to know my bretherens
    and sisters that God's concern
    for man is very great
And I never can get myself adjusted
    to why that man's concern is
    so limited for God

Considerin' thy greatness and the
    handiwork of the omnipotent
    God, who by His own fingers
    made the heavens the moon
    and the stars
10 The psalmist could not understand
    how or why He be in unlimited
    ability the power and authority
    which noticed such a low being
    as man
Man is a low order of creation but
    is the greatest that God placed
    here on the earth
Why is the man is a little lower
    creation because he is a little
    lower than the angels
But then he is the greatest created
    thing that ever creeped this soil
God is mindful of man because He
    know how He made him
15 And He's still mindful of man

today/as He was in the days
that He made—that He created
Adam

Men are born now with the same
heart/the same mind and the
same instruments [?]

They are developed in human flesh

They have the same activities of the
limbs we use to lean against

When he is developed according to
the adoption of conditions—
physically conditions in good
condition then he's found with
nine gallons of warm blood
that run through his veins

20 God is mindful of man because He
gave man a little more brains

That you may think how to carry
on and operate what my fingers
have written

As we read in the Scripture they
said that as God written with
His fingers the stars they came
/and the moon it came in
existence

And the sun came according to how
God ordered it

But He said now listen I want you
man to rule every creeping
thing that creeped upon the
earth

25 I want you to take care of the cows

Then I want you to be mindful how
you go in and out before me

Because I made you in my own
likeness

I don't have anything else to get
glory out of except you

But I'm gonna make somebody for
your glory

30 Then He placed man in—out of
sleep

And taken from his side a rib

And made woman

And this woman was made for the
glory and honor of man

I want you to know dear hearts you
has your glory

35 Whatever you do my bretheren this
mornin' I want you to give God
the glory

And after God had made—created
man in His own likeness and
image

Then He provided a home for him

Over in a little old garden they call
garden of Eden

And placed man in that home

40 And placed his wife in there with
him

He said now after I have given you
the dominion over everything

I want you to still know

I want you to know my brotheren
if you don't be strong in the
Lord

Satan will ease upon you

45 And get you to accept him a little
easier with no faith

Am I right this mornin'

What I'm talkin' about you're not
able to rule your own house

If you don't let the Lord lead you

But I said He provided a home for
Adam

50 Out in the garden

Told Adam I want you to rule and
   rule well
'Long came the devil, began to
   whisper to Adam's wife
And she began to get close to old
   man Adam
Well I want you to know this eve'
   —this mornin'
55 The Lord wants you to hear Him
Obey and do what He says
And he'll make everything all right
After listen' to and obeyin' his wife
He obeyed the voice of the devil
60 Well I want you to know this
   mornin'
Only way that Satan can get in
   Union Baptist Church
He must come through by
   somebody
If I was you
I wouldn't be so weak
65 That I would let Satan crawl inside
   by me
I would stand on everlastin' courage
And hold to God's judgment
I say God is concerned about man
He trusted a lot of things into his
   hands
70 He gave a man the knowledge
How to go in and out in this world
And till the soil for a living
He gave man dominion and opinion
How that they could come together
   and make all of these habits[?]
75 Am I right this evenin'—mornin'
He told him
Why're you so disobedient
You're gonna have to till the soil

You're gonna have to live by the
   sweat of your own brow
80 I want you to know
He said to the woman why're you're
   disobedient
You're gonna have to bring forth
   fruit
We find now—every now and then
Somebody began to try to bring
   something to tell us
85 The constitution don't give no life
Some way [highway?] we cut out
   what God said
You must bring forth fruit
Tell me he said He's all right
O women that take these kind of
   pills
90 That will not bring forth fruit
But I want you to know this morn-
   ing God is mindful of you
In every walk of life
Don't you know the Lord is so
   mindful of man
He wanted man to have everything
   that he need
95 He gave him five thinking
   capacities
One that he could smell
One that he could see
One that he could hear
One that he can taste
100 One that he can feel
Say now I want you to go through
   the land and country
I want you to see all the good things
I want you to hear all the bad things
   said

That you may be able to turn with
    your life
105 And just listen to my voice
One thing I want you to know
    brotherens
You can't serve the Lord unless you
    let the Lord guide you
Am I right this mornin'
You can't serve the Lord five days
    a week/ and try to serve the
    Lord on the day Sunday
110 You're gonna have to live the thing
    y'say on Sunday
To save your soul
Am I right this mornin'
Jesus
Jesus was so concerned about man
115 Until He left His richness and glad
    glory
Came down here in this old sin-
    cussed world
Stepped on the train of nature with
    a virgin woman
And brought Himself out an infant
    baby
On the train of nature nine months
120 Stepped off the train at a little old
    station called Bethlehem
Wrapped over there in swaddlin'
    clothes
Stayed right there
'Till God told His father Joseph
I want you to carry the baby over
    to Galilee
125 Keep it right there 'till I bring the
    Word
God was always concerned for man
Proved His concern for man so

I tell you what brought Him here
    as a little baby
Grew up on a man's stature
130 And began to get acquainted out on
    the field of acquaintance
At His first stop bretheren He made
    after He started out on His
    father's journey
They stopped in the midst of law-
    yers and doctors
I see in her mind she's gonna get
    worried
She got worried about her son
135 As any mother do these days
One thing I want you to know
Mothers love children
Doesn't matter what the world may
    say about the child
Mother say the child is mine
140 One thing between a mother and
    father
Father will do the best he can
But mother will understand
Yes she will this mornin'
Same Jesus
145 That stopped over at Bethlehem and
    got off the train of nature
He pull off the detour road
I can hear the mother begin to
    worry about her son
She said where is my son
Who had followed me and be with
    me all of his days
150 Now I can't seem to find my son
I see mother and father
They're down to pick up . . .
They go back and see what hap-
    pened to the son

They found Him in the midst of
the lawyers and doctors
155 Askin' questions askin' questions
I can hear the mother say to the son
Why you gotten so far behind now
He said Mother I must go about my
Father's business
That may prove God's concern
160 How much God is concerned a'man
God is so mindful a'man
I better skip along now bretheren
Bring it to a close now
I'll tell that to the judge
165 That I left you at twelve years old
See Jesus now
Walkin' out on the field one
mornin'
Stopped over there at the old place
they call Cana
There was a wedding goin' on at
Cana
170 Oh hear what He said to the servants
around there
Whatever He said to do I want you
to do what He said
See Jesus
He walked on right through—
He said fill up a pitcher with water
175 Somebody said Jesus turn around
that water to wine
But I want you to know this
brotheren He said fill it up
with water
Fill it up to the brim
I could hear the priests sayin' out
there
Oh you save the best for the last
180 God is still mindful of man

He said—gave them water to put
it in
That they may have to carry on the
way to the feast
Then He started on out on His
journey
Heard Jesus say
185 I'm so concerned about Man now
I'm goin' home some of these days
I must leave the church with man
He left the church with us in the
hands of a man
He left the gospel in the hands of
a man
190 Am I right?
This same Jesus
This same one that stopped over at
Bethlehem
The same one that had concourse
with the lawyers and doctors
The same man
195 That had—gave—told 'em to fill up
a pitcher with water
Same man gave sight to the blind
Same man
Said I'll need somebody
To treat the world after I go home
200 Walked out along the seashore
Noticed—saw Andrew
Simon Peter
Told Andrew
Simon Peter
205 Lay down your nets now
Come and follow me
I will make you become fishers of
men
Same man
Still talkin' 'bout the gospel

210 Walkin' on down the river
     brotheren
Looked out there they saw old man
     Zebedee's son
Ohh John now
Ohh James
Drop your nets come follow me
215 I'm talkin' 'bout Jesus' concern 'bout
     man
God is mindful of you this evenin'
     brotheren
He'll follow you
I'd walk a little closer
I started to singin'
220 If you can't sing so well
Just use the words
Use me Lord
In thy service
Well, by the river
225 Every day
God an' man
Has to run
Run all the way
Serve on
230 The Lord is mindful this evenin'
Of how we go in and out with
     others
I want to say to the deacon board
     I want you to be mindful
I want you to be mindful how you
     serve as a deacon
Because the Lord doesn't have to
     use you
235 I want to say to you brother preach-
     ers be careful how you preach
Because the Lord didn't have to
     have you to preach
Am I right this evenin'?

I'm so glad this evenin'
Cause I know the Lord'll do right
240 Am I right this evenin'
Have you tried the man/ on this old
     journey
Do you know He's a doctor
In a sickroom
Ahh, he carry me on a stretcher
245 When I be worried
Some time I get tired on the journey
He is my strength
He is my prop
When I try to lag on the journey
250 There is somthin' to lift me up
Keep on brotheren
Few more days
Few more days
This journey gonna be ended
255 Not how fast you run Brother
     Brown
But how long
But how long you run
Not to the swift not to the strong,
     but he that hold out to the end
I want you to know that I know
     my brotherens it's not what you
     been doin' but it's what you be
     doin' when Jesus comes
260 It's not how you have lived, but
     how you be livin' when the
     roll is called
Ohh when the roll is called
     brotheren
I'll be there
I want you to know that God is
     mindful, He trusted something
     in my hand
When He trusted His Word to go

into all the world and preach the gospel
265 Whosoever shall believe and be baptised shall be saved
Doesn't matter with me how you may feel about what I say
When I know I'm right I'll tell it all, I'm in your care
Ohh Lord
Ohh I'm in your care
270 Told me every now and then I'll be in your care
It's all right children
Tell the Lord sometime I'm in your care
I don't know about you

But I'm gonna see the Lord for myself
275 Well one year
When I can see the Lord brotheren
I'm gonna have to see the Lord for myself
Ohh in the mornin'
When every belief should bow before the judgment bar
280 My mother can't bow down for me
Ohh I got a tongue
I'll have to confess with my tongue
By and by
I will see Jesus
285 By and by
(singing)

THOU SHALT HAVE NO OTHER GODS BEFORE ME

Nearly a year after the sermon above was recited, Brown used a similar theme in a sermon, delivered in Bakersfield on May 19, 1968.

Same Jesus
Same Jesus this evenin'
Was concerned about us so much so
Until He left glad glory
5 Came out of glory to this old sinful world
Got on the train of nature
Stayed there nine months
Stepped off at the station one mornin'
Early one mornin'
10 Stepped off at the station of Bethlehem
Wrapped up in swaddlin' clothes
Way down in an oxen manger
Stayed right there

Until God wanted Him to come on out
15 Stayed right there
Until God wanted Him what to do
Stayed right there
And time began to move on
I'm talkin' about thou shalt have no other God before Me
20 God was so concerned brotheren
Till He came all the way to this sinful world
That you an' I may have a right to tree of life
Came in the shape of a baby
Wrapped Himself in human blood
25 Dwelled here thirty-three long years

To facilitate comparison with the earlier performance of this theme I
have underlined only those verses which are repeated from the 1967 version: other lines may be repetitions from other versions of Brown's but
are not marked. See lines 114-180 of the 1967 sermon for a comparison
with lines 1-11 and 23-24 of the above passage; lines 13 and 17 (above)
are marked as they repeat each other.

GOD'S PLOWBOY

This sermon was recited by the Rev. Rubin Lacy, July 2, 1967, in
Bakersfield, California. The idea and a good deal of the language for
this performance was taken from a printed sermon, "God's Plowboy."
Clearly Lacy does not read well and the sermon was not successful.
When he tried to follow the text closely he could not establish a consistent rhythm. The material was unfamiliar to him, and that further
caused him to stumble; but he used it because it eulogizes the role of the
preacher. Lacy was able to regain his rhythm only when he broke away
from the manuscript (lines 138 ff.). From that point on his eye caught
only an occasional word of print and he elaborated spontaneously on
those few words; that was the only way he could gain momentum. A few
lines are taken from the written material (147-48, 168, 190, 241-42)
and are then expanded with the material from the preacher's word-
hoard. The chant breaks down at line 311, but resumes again at 320 and
continues until the end. Lacy's source, from *Sermon Outlines* (Atlanta,
n.d.), pp. 24-29, is printed first.

> . . . *For our sakes, no doubt, this is written: that he that ploweth*
> *should plow in hope.* . . . ,
>
> 1 Cor. 9:10.

INTRODUCTION: The text is taken from Paul's letter to the Corinthian church. The plowman mentioned is God's minister of the
gospel. It seems fitting here to call him "God's plowboy." The man
who plows has many duties other than walking in the furrow behind
the plow. God's plowboy likewise has many responsibilities other
than standing in the pulpit.

In this message we will consider the minister under three topics:
first, as a burden bearer; second, as a feeder of the flock; third, as a
plowman of hope.

I. THE PREACHER BEARS THE BURDENS OF THE PEOPLE AND PULLS
THE LOAD FOR THE CHURCH.

*For it is written in the law of Moses, Thou shalt not muzzle the
mouth of the ox that treadeth out the corn. Doth God take care
for oxen?*

1 *Cor. 9:9*

The minister is here referred to as an ox. The ox is a very strong
beast, stands a great deal of abuse and hard labor. He never complains in his suffering or holds any ill will against his punishers.

1. *The Ox Worked at the Will of Others.*

The old ox was not a freewill agent. He worked at the will of his
master. He never stopped in the shade when he was tired; he
stopped when his master said to stop. He did not eat when he was
hungry; he ate when his master fed him. He did not eat what he
wanted; he ate what he could get and had time to eat.

2. *The Ox Was a Plowman but at the Reverse End of the Plow.*

The minister usually gets the end where the hard work is to be
done. The task of the ox was to plow one-half acre a day. The
minister has a job to do and it will require his best and full time
to complete his task.

3. *The Ox Was Hitched to Heavy Loads.*

The ox was very stout and his master knew it; therefore, he got
little sympathy or mercy. The minister is called upon by his Master,
and of necessity by the church, to pull. The true preacher will pull.
The minister must never get it in his mind that he is being mis-
treated or that unnecessary loads are required of him. He must not
sympathize with himself or solicit the sympathy of others. The
minister has no time to feel sorry for himself.

4. *The Ox Was Used as a Burden Bearer.*

Being strong, very heavy burdens were often laid upon the faithful old ox. He may grunt and groan under the load but must not
complain. The church may lay upon their pastor unnecessary burdens but there is not much left for him to do but carry them.

II. GOD'S PLOWBOY MUST FEED HIS MASTER'S SHEEP.

The Lord said to Peter "Feed my lambs," and again He said,
"Feed my sheep." The Lord has no flocks or herds; He was talking
about people. The lambs were the newborn babes in Christ and
such as had not yet fully developed. He said to Peter twice, "Feed
my sheep." He was referring to the fully developed and strong
Christians.

Take heed therefore unto yourselves, and to all the flock, over the

*which the Holy Ghost hath made you overseers, to feed the
church of God, which he hath purchased with his own blood,*

Acts 20:28.

Paul was speaking to pastors who were feeders of the flock of
God. Every pastor must not only feed, but properly feed the flock.
1. *Take Heed How You Feed the Flock.*

During a dearth, Elisha's servant set on the great pot and one
went out into the field to gather herbs to feed the sons of the prophets. Not knowing the food properly, he gathered wild gourds; and
when the food was served, death was found in the pot.

*And one went out into the field to gather herbs, and found a wild
vine, and gathered thereof wild gourds his lap full, and came
and shred them into the pot of pottage: for they knew them
not.*

*So they poured out for the men to eat. And it came to pass, as
they were eating of the pottage, that they cried out, and said, O
thou man of God, there is death in the pot. And they could not
eat thereof,*

2 Kings 4:39, 40.

The pastor must know his flock, understand the food (the Word),
and know what they need. Many flocks have been poisoned and
some have died because of improper feeding.
2. *The Babes in Christ and Weaklings Must Have Milk. As new-
born babes, desire the sincere milk of the word, that ye may
grow thereby,*

1 Peter 2:2.

New converts may be considered babes, newly born of the Spirit.
They must not be fed strong meat. The pastor must know how to
start them off on the sincere milk of the Word.

*I have fed you with milk, and not with meat: for hitherto ye were
not able to bear it, neither yet now are ye able,*

1 Cor. 3:2.

The Corinthians to whom Paul was writing were evidently not
babes in Christ. Paul had been feeding them, possibly for some time,
but they had not properly developed; they were still weaklings. They
seemed to be spiritually diseased and still needed to be fed on milk.

It is no honor for the pastor to boast that he has no bottles for any
member of his flock. He must have bottles; if he doesn't have, many
of his flock will die for the lack of good care.
3. *The Strong Must Have Meat.*

But strong meat belongeth to them that are of full age, even those who by reason of use have their senses exercised to discern both good and evil,

Heb. 5:14.

All members of the family of God do not eat the same diet. Strong meat that would be required for some might kill others; likewise would the strong become weak if they were continually fed milk.

The pastor must know his flock; equally so, he must know his Bible from which he feeds them.

Study to shew thyself approved unto God, a workman that needeth not to be ashamed, rightly dividing the word of truth,

2 Tim. 2:15.

He must know his Bible well enough that he may gather from its contents the very food each member of the flock may require.

III. GOD'S PLOWBOY HAS A RIGHT TO PLOW IN HOPE.

Notice the text, "He that ploweth should plow in hope." It is only right and fair that the pastor should hope to share in the carnal things of his members.

Who goeth a warfare any time at his own charges? who planteth a vineyard, and eateth not of the fruit thereof? or who feedeth a flock, and eateth not of the milk of the flock?

1 Cor. 9:7.

In this one verse Paul impresses upon the Corinthians in duplicate forms the righteousness of the minister being supported from the products of his labors. As a soldier he is supported; as a planter he eats of the fruit; as a shepherd he drinks of the milk. Let us consider separately the pastor under each of these three headings.

1. *The Minister as a Soldier Is Dependent for His Expenses.*

No soldier goes to war at his own expense. His government pays the bill. Likewise must the soldier of God who takes up the sword in warfare depend upon God who through the church supplies all his needs, which would be from a reasonable way of thinking the necessary expenses of normal living.

2. *As a Planter, the Minister May Eat of the Fruit.*

It is not reasonable to expect a man to prepare the ground and plant a vineyard without hope of enjoying the fruit thereof. Neither does God expect His servant to go out into the world, break up the fallow ground, sow the seed of the gospel and plant a vineyard and not enjoy the fruit. The pastor certainly has a right to share in the fruits of his labors.

3. *As a Shepherd the Pastor Eateth of the Milk of the Flock.*

The pastor is a shepherd of the spiritual flock, and God expects him to share in their earnings, just as much as the farmer would expect to milk his herd. He who feeds has a right to milk.

CONCLUSION: God's plowboy has a big job and many responsibilities. He must be ready and willing to work at either end of the plow. He must carry the burdens, pull the loads, stay sweet, conceal his feelings, and go straight ahead with his work.

For our sakes, no doubt, this was written: that he that ploweth should plow in hope
For our sakes, no doubt, this was written: that he that ploweth should plow in hope
First Corinthians ninth, and tenth
The text is written—taken from Paul's letter to the Corinthian Church
5 The plowman mentioned here is God's minister of the gospel
It seems fitting to call him God's plowboy, or plowman
The man who plows has many duties other than walking in the furrow behind the plow
God's plowboy likewise has many responsibilities other than standing in the pulpit
In this message we consider the minister under three topics: first as a burden bearer; second as a feeder of the flock; third as a plowboy, or plowman, of hope
10 While we're emphasizing this a little bit—no man break up new ground weed garden here—In the devil we call it death
You do all that work, prepare to do

all these things, listen to it, he does it in hope
He's got faith and hope that he's going to reap the benefits of it
Hmm?
The hardest thing ever I done one year— I didn't tell on one 'bout this in Mississippi; I was young and my bossman was young
15 Promised to give me a cow, and a calf to milk; I was sharecroppin' for him
I want to emphasize that—doesn't take me long to preach, cause I can talk
An' ahh this is the truth, I was through there a few years ago and laughin' about it
When time comes to give me the cow and the calf he give me the cow with no calf
I said you say you're gonna me a cow and a calf; he said, well she's milkin'
20 I said you said you'd give me a cow and a calf and this ain't gonna work
And we kept arguin', over that cow and the calf—the cow was milkin', but I wanted the cow and the calf

So that broke the treaty

Sharecroppin' for him; fact of it I
 didn't want to stay there

That would've been the hardest crop
 that ever I made in my life if
 I'd stayed there an' made it—
 but I didn't like it

25 Was sorry—if you don't like a thing
 —the thought of it—aaa, you
 shouldn't joined up

No man do these things—roll logs,
 join bricks, tow logs unless he
 does it in hope

It's the hope of reaping something
 more than he's putting out

Hmm?

The preacher bears the burden of
 the people and pulls the load
 of the church

30 I don't know whether you want to
 believe that or not, but it's true

Lot of times you don't want to do
 it, but you can't keep grumblin'
 about it—I'll get to that later—
 I say ya can't—I'm talkin' about
 preachin' today

He can't even grumble too much
 about what he does

He can't even have no fiftieth point
 set [?]

All right, let's see am I right about
 it

35 Paul is backin' me up as I travel
 through this desert land—

For it is written in the law of Moses
 Thou shalt not muzzle the
 mouth of the ox that treadeth
 out the corn. Do-eth God take
 of the ox?

I want you to answer me somethin'

Do-eth God take of an ox?

The minister here referred to as an
 ox

40 The ox is a very strong beast—
 stands a great deal of bruises
 and hard labor

He never complains in his suffering
 or hold any ill will against his
 punisher

Watch where you's goin'

The ox worked—not worked—at the
 will of others

The old ox was not free—not a
 freewill agent

45 He worked—ahh-at the will of his
 master

He never stopped in the shade when
 he was tired

He stopped when his master said
 stop

He did not eat when he was hungry,
 he ate when his master fed
 him

He did not eat what he wanted to
 eat, but what his master give
 him, to eat

50 The ox was a plowman, but at the
 reverse end of the plow stood
 a man

Ha ha, who do the hardest work?

I say at the reverse end of the plow
 stood a man

The minister usually gets the end
 where the hard work is to be
 done

The task of an ox was to plow half
 an acre in one day

55 The minister's job is to do an', to
   do—his job is to do and will
   require his best and full time
   —don't have no time for nothin'
   else
   Folks say why don't you go to the
   field an' chop cotton, why don't
   you pick cotton, why don't you
   cut some grape—he doesn't have
   time to do but one thing
   Umm? Jesus said to Peter, an' John,
   an' Andrew, and James on the
   lake—ahh drop your net and
   follow me
   You fishin' for yourself, I want you
   to fish for me
   C'mon an' follow me
60 Peter said to Him, I'm not educated, I'm just a—ahh—high
   school scholar—ahh—can only
   read and write my name
   I'm not able to follow you Jesus
   said, follow me
   Hear my cause, hear my cause
   [calls?]
   Hmm? Follow me
   The guys these days don't think
   they're a preacher unless they
   go into the seminary
65 Tryin' to put the seminary before
   they're being a fool
   The same 'postle Paul said the other
   day I count all my education
   nought
   I become a fool he said to gain
   Christ
   Didn't he say so?
   I had to become a fool to gain Christ

70 And to speak fourteen different
   languages
   Man—ahh—that was able to speak
   to anybody
   And we, ain't got that kind of
   learnin' these says, are we?
   No!
   A Mexican could come in here
   right now—and speak some
   about—wouldn't know what he
   was saying
75 Hmm?
   What I'm tryin' to tell you what
   Paul could do that
   Ahh, but he said I had to become
   a fool
   They're not lettin' you say it
   He said the letter will kill dead
80 Grace of God will make alive
   Didn't he say so?
   Ahh, he didn't eat when he wanted
   to eat
   But he ate when he—ahh—had the
   opportunity, by his master
   An then he—the minister usually
   gets the end where the work
   is the hardest
85 The task of the ox is half acre, the
   task of the minister is a con-
   tinuation
   Amen! everyday, even some nights
   on his bed
   Lyin' down at night, can't be at
   ease, there's somethin' wrong
   in the church
   That pastor's layin' there, all night
   long
   Thinkin', study what to do, prayin'

to God to give him wisdom an'
understandin'
⁹⁰ How to do these things, Amen
The ox has hitched to heavy loads
Uhh-huh, the ox was a very stout,
uhh, beast Amen and master
knew it
Therefore he got little sympathy, or
mercy
Umm-hmm
⁹⁵ By the church any man know that
the pastor—the preacher—is the
strongest man—should be the
strongest man in the church
They put all kinds of responsibilities upon the preacher
Amen an' he got to bear it
He don't have time, to have sympathy for hisself
He don't want nobody to have no
pity on him
¹⁰⁰ The minister should never get it in
his mind that he's being mis-
treated
Uhh-huh unnecessary loads are required of him
He must not have sympathy—umm-
hmm—with himself
Uhh-huh sympathize with others
The minister have no time to feel
sorry, for himself
¹⁰⁵ The ox—Amen—is used as a burden
bearer
Umm-hmm being strong, bearing,
a heavy burden, was often laid
upon, this old faithful ox
He grunt, sometime he groan
Amen sometimes falls to his knees

But he kept on pullin'
¹¹⁰ I wonder you know what I'm talkin'
about?
How the church lay a heavy burden, upon the pastor
Unnecessary burdens, such—umm-
hmm—as puts us in the home
Amen—disputes between husband
and wife
All these things—they laid it on the
pastor
¹¹⁵ God from Zion
Sometime, just [least?] a little for
nothin'
Look for the pastor, you think his
car burnin' gas?
Ride from house to house
See about these things—burden,
burden bearer
¹²⁰ What I'm tryin' to say is it's all
right, t'bear a burden
But Jesus said the other day
Bear ye, one another's burden
Didn't he say so?
Bear ye one another's burden
¹²⁵ That am, the motto of the church
Bear ye one another's burden
I think I'm right about it
And when the burden get too hard
Take 'em on the sheet
¹³⁰ Lay 'em down there to sleep
Tell Jesus about it
There He is, there He is
Tell Jesus about it
Oh bear my burdens
¹³⁵ Too hard for me to bear
Jesus'll take your burdens, all to
himself

I think I know what I'm talkin'
   about
But ya lay 'em on the preacher
An' look for the preacher
140 Amen!
Is the bearer of all your burdens
He just can't do it
I know I'm right about it
I say he just can't do it
145 Let's go on a little further
God from Zion
God's plowboy
Must feed
We're goin' on to the feedin'
150 I say God's plowboy
Must feed
His master's sheep
The Lord said to Peter
Feed, my lambs
155 And then he said unto him
Feed, my sheep
The Lord
Didn't have no flock
Didn't have no herd
160 He was talkin' about
God from Zion
He was talkin' about the lambs
Of new-born babes
In Christ Jesus
165 Such as had not yet, fully developed
He said to Peter twice feed my
   sheep
Said to him the last time
Feed my lamb
Ain't God all right?
170 Feed my lamb
Take heed
Therefore

Unto yourself
And to all the flock
175 Which the Holy Ghost have made
   thee
Overseer
To feed
The church of God
Huh let's think about it
180 God from Zion
God left the church
In the hands of the preacher
He feed
The church
185 Paul was speakin' here to the
   pastors
Who were
Feeders of the flock of God
Each 'n every pastor
Must not only feed
190 But properly feed
This what I'm tryin't to say to you
Some feed
The wrong kind of food
Some say
195 They don't have no sugar-tin
Some say
They don't have no sweet milk
I'm tryin' to say to you this evenin'
Every pastor
200 Must have a home
A sugar-tin
Along with him
Got Somebody in the church
Been there twenty years
205 And still needs a sugar-tin
God from Zion
Got Somebody here,
Umm-hmm

That need a sugar-tin
210 Every now and then
God from Zion
Let's see am I right about it
God
Went up on the mountain
215 The other day
To pray
And while He was up there prayin'
Some of the
Laborers
220 Said I'll be
I'll go out and get some stuff
And feed the people
Because they're hungry
Went out to pick vegetables
225 And got the wrong kind
Brought 'em on back
Put 'em in a pot
Begin to boil green
Had death in the pot
230 Ain't I right about it?
They tell me
That the pastor
Amen—must know
How to feed
235 And what thing to feed of
I'm going on to close now
God's
Plowboy
Has a right to plow
240 In hope
He that plows
Should plow in hope
It's only right
And fair
245 That the pastor should hope
To share in

The eternal
Things
Of all his members
250 God from Zion
Who
Ahh—goes
Warfare
Any time
255 Of his own
Charges
Who plants the vine-yards
And eateth not
Of the food thereof
260 Who feedeth
A flock
And don't drink the milk
Thereof
In this verse
265 We find Paul
Expressin'
To the Corinthian church
The diplomat forms
Of Righteousness
270 And able
Also
As he supported
As he
Of labor
275 Also
As he planted
He ate
Off his fruit Amen
As a shepherd
280 He drink
Of the milk
And let us consider
Separate
Each one of these things

285 No soldier
Go to the war
I don't care who he is
No soldier
Go over yonder
290 In that war
Unless his government/pay him so
    much a month
Give his family so much a month
No soldier
Volunteer
295 And went to war
Unless his government pays him
God from Zion
I'm tryin' to say here
That no soldier
300 Go here
In the army of God
Unless he looks for a reward
Ain't I right about it?
An' the reward
305 Shall be in the mornin'
In the mornin'
I said in the mornin'
When it's all over
Ohh, in the mornin'
    (long pause)
310 I read that—expect a man to prepare,
    the ground, get out there and
    cut down those trees
Break up the stumps, pull up the
    roots, and then hitch his tractor
    —pay a high price for his
    tractor
Go out there and tell 'em ain't got
    none
Get 'em ready to 'pare seed
An' then not do that any more

315 When he did it he believed it
In the fall there, he gonna reap—
    Amen—the work done
Jesus said you reap what you sow
When man does that he's gonna
    reap what he sows
God from Zion
320 He's gonna reap
A red horse
An' when a preacher preach the
    gospel
He's lookin' in the mornin'
For God to tell him
325 Well done
Ohh well done
Good and faithful servant
You been faithful
You preach some time in church
330 When there wasn't but a few there
Preach some time
When there wasn't but a half a
    dozen there
You preach some time
When there's nothin' but Sunday
    School students there
335 But you preach right on
Well done
Good and faithful servant
You been faithful over a few things
I'm gonna make you rule the whole
    day
340 C'mon, sit down, give ya the line of
    Jordan
I believe ya know what I'm talkin'
    about
After a while
It'll all be over
    (sings a few notes)

I said after a while
345 It'll all be over
We're goin' home
To get my crown
I love that song
I love to sing that song
350 When I've done, the best I can
I wear the crown
Pause to think about it

Missus Lacy used to sing the song
to me
When I'se in the pulpit preachin'
355 Sometimes she set me down
Singin' that song
When I've done
The best I can
Give me the crown
(sings)

GOD'S PLOWBOY

The Rev. Rubin Lacy delivered this sermon May 19, 1968, in Tulare, California. The importance of this sermon (when compared to its earlier version) to understanding structural changes in time has been discussed in Section VII. I recorded this purely by chance: Lacy had already delivered his sermon in the morning in his own church in Corcoran, and had no plans to do any further work for the day since his winter heart attacks were very much on his mind. However, when we arrived in Tulare (the New Mount Olive Baptist Church, the Rev. W. H. Henry, pastor) the guest preacher was not well and asked Lacy to fill in for him. With about fifteen minutes' notice Lacy preached the following sermon which was well received. The preacher established good rapport with the congregation early: he had been chatting amiably with them for several minutes before the sermon began so that once he started they responded readily. A faint chant begins around line 85 and is more metrical at line 120. Throughout Lacy held himself in check rather than risk taxing his heart. The performance turned out to be unique because he used materials from several sources, most of which I had been recording the year before; in this sermon he brings them together.

I better get it right
Me talkin' a little here about this
pastor
God almighty, umm
Obey them that have the rule over
you
5 And submit yourselves

For they watch for your souls
As they that must give an account
That they may do it with joy
And not with grief
10 For that is unprofitable
Not for me
But it's unprofitable for you

If I have to do it in grief
That's the text
15 You'll find it in Hebrew thirteen
     to seventeen
That's the text—the pastor of the
     church
Is more—have more responsibility
     than the King of England
Because the King of England
Has got to go to church
20 If he see God's face in peace
Hmm?
He got to shake the preacher's hand
And tell 'im I know God
An' I'm willin' to trust God
25 If he see God's face in peace
Yet he's a ruler
Over many people
But the preacher's over him
President Johnson
30 Can stay in the senate all week
With the senate and congress
And the House of Representatives
But on a Sunday mornin'
He gotta go to church
35 An' hear what the preacher says
Umm-hmm
Why?
Because Johnson
Can't watch his soul
40 But the preacher
Watches over your soul
Umm-hmm
When he's not there
He may be at home in the bed
45 An' you may be walkin' up an'
     down the streets
In your town

Sometime Mac is up yonder in
     Fresno
An' his people is havin' a big time
Mac is on bended knee
50 He may be in the bed
But he's on bended knee
Talkin' to God
About your soul
Umm-hmm
55 Sunday mornin'
When Mac comes down here
Down here to his church
First Baptist Church
He's ready to go
60 God has given 'im a message
An' I say he oughta use it
He oughtn'ta let a . . . preacher
He oughtn'to let nobody preach
If God gave it to you
65 You oughta deliver it to your folks
Umm-hmm
I know I'm right about it
You say you been here eighteen
     years
Umm-hmm
70 Good preachin' didn't keep ya here
Don't let nobody fool ya
Something else kept ya here
I know I'm right about it
God is on ya side
75 I know I'm right about it
God give ya a helpmate
That would stand by ya
Through dangerous seas
 . . . when you're hungry
80 She just be hungry with ya
When ya got a . . .
She's all right

I know I'm right about it
Umm-hmm
85 Talkin' about the man
That watches for your soul
The pastor
Is an overseer
Of souls
90 He watches, as one, that must give
    accounts
God, has entrusted souls, in his care
This tremendous responsibility
Of the pastor
Makes his work and duty
95 The most important
Man in the world
Yeah—we will consider the pastor
Under three headings
Let's see first
100 He as a watchman
Second as a preacher
Third as a pattern
Wanna say I may not go far on it
Wanna say this evenin' he's a
    watchman
105 One writer said he's a overseer
I know you know what it is
Some of you come off a plantation
Way down in Mississippi
In Arkansas
110 Out in Texas
They had overseers
What did the overseer do
The overseer
Told ya what to do
115 You didn't tell the overseer
But he told you
What to do
On the plantation

Ah—this writer said
120 Paul said
Pastors are overseers
God from Zion
Tell the church what to do
Tell the deacon what to do
125 And then everything's all right
Well it's changed around
They got to tell you
Jus' won't work
Not to save your life
130 Just won't work
The church is goin' backwards
Every day of his life
God from Zion
Yes he's a feeder
135 I said he's a feeder
Pastor must know how to feed
Just any old thing
Throw in the trough
Just won't do
140 Must know how to feed
Don't ya remember
When Moses went off that time
Up on the mountain
Left the boys down there
145 Somebody cried out I'm hungry
Went out there in the woods
Pulled up the wrong thing
Went on back there
Put it in the pot
150 Began to boil
Before Moses got back
Some of 'em was eatin' that stuff
Everybody begin to die
I want you to know Moses
155 Umm-hmm
Somebody said Death

Was in the pot
Pastor must know
What kind of food
160 Is to give his children
He got all kinds of children
Some of 'em's sickly
Some of 'em's healthy
And they all don't eat the same
thing
170 Some time
A healthy child
A good healthy member
Can die
On the wrong kind of food
175 Some time
A weak member
Can die
Tryin' to give him healthy food
Hark Halelujah
180 Pastor
Must be able
To feed his weak members
When they's gettin' weak
Some time
185 They got to lose time
Go around to his home
Pat him on the shoulder
Let somebody know
That you care about him
190 Ain't God all right
Some body
Every now and then
Some body
Want you to care
195 I wonder
Do ya know what I'm talkin' about
God from Zion
Yes he's a watchman

That stands
200 On the wall
Ezekiel said
Stand on the wall
Rap the gavel
Men don't believe you
205 Then their blood
Is not required at your hand
I'm wonderin' do ya hear me today
Somebody here
Soft-peddlin' the gospel
210 Tryin' to sooth somebody
Twistin' the Word of God
I'm here to tell ya today
Preach the Word
Preach the Word
215 Don't care who don't like it
I don't care who it hit
Ohh preach the Word
I don't care who don't like it
I don't care who get offended about
it
220 Preach the Word
Umm-hmm
That's another thing the pastor
must do
Oughta be glad to preach
Some of us say well
225 I know ya get tired sometime
But we oughta be glad to preach
Because God said preach
Umm-hmm
Preach
230 Umm-hmm
Because the gospel
Is the saving salt
That saves the soul
Umm-hmm

235 Preach
Because the gospel
Is the power of God
Unto those of salvation
To everyone that believe
240 Ohh preach the Word
Preach the Word
I said preach the Word
I'm glad God told me
A long time ago
245 To preach my Word
Ohh go eat
Therefore
In other words
Ohh men don't like you
250 I'm on ya side
Preach the Word
That's what He want you to do
Preach the Word
Yes He's a watchman
255 I'm closin' here
I say I'm closin'
Paul here says
I don't mean no harm but tell me
    what Paul says
Paul here says
260 The pastor must watch the enemy
Well—who is the enemy
For I know this Paul says
That after my departuring
Shall grievous wolves enter in
265 Among you
Not sparing the flock
Uhh-huh
These grievous wolves
I hate to say it
270 But sometimes
These grievous wolves

Sometimes is preachers
Umm-hmm
And they, will get good members
275 I don't mean bad members
Out of the church
An' go off an' organize another
    church
An' then take another one there
    with 'em
After they get off—I know what I'm
    talkin' about
280 I seen it done a few years ago
I know what I'm talkin' about
The preacher run off first
And then left the folks there
Without any preacher
285 After he's pulled out
And organized another church
Oh yes—said these grievous wolves
Do this to be bragged on
They want to be bragged on
290 Let me use the word pre-enium
It means to be bragged on
Lifted up high
When ya don't deserve it
But I say this
295 Jesus said
If any man exalts his self
He shall be . . .
God from Zion
If any man want to be exalted
300 Let him humble himself
Like Joseph did
When he was down in Egypt
Joseph
Stuck to God
305 He heard through God
Don't care what happen

When the woman caught Joseph
Pulled his coat off
Goin' 'round without his coat
310 Suffered to go to jail
Ain't I right about it
He suffered to go to jail
Wonder how many Josephs
Will we find now
315 Joseph suffered to go to jail
Stayed in jail
But listen friend
God was in jail too
Jailor
320 Was a mean man

But the jailer liked Joseph
Give him the key
Told him you take my place
Ain't I right about it
325 I want to say to you brothering—
     brother
Henry and Sister Henry
Stay on
You pray on
An' you preach on
330 Don't fool yourself good preachin'
     ain't keepin' ya here—they
     don't know what that is in
California

THE CHRIST OF THE BIBLE

Recited by the Rev. D. J. McDowell, July 30, 1967, in Delano, California, this sermon was received with great enthusiasm. The occasion was the anniversary service for the Rev. Mr. Moore (see lines 1 and 228) and was well attended by the local clergy. Mr. McDowell begins to chant sporadically at line 55, consistently at line 99. He is clearly singing the lines after 146, and this is sustained until line 306 when he very abruptly returns to conversational prose. The emotional build-up had been so great that the long denouement was needed. This sermon is noteworthy for its images (lines 24 and 34) and for its use of memorized themes. The major portion of the sermon was noted on a five-by-eight card which was kept on the pulpit and referred to from time to time. Memorized themes in this piece which have been used elsewhere are in lines 78-96; 235-245, 260-61; and 281-291.

Reverend Moore, Brown, Pastor
    Lacy, Sister Moore, Officers,
    our fellow citizens of the king-
    dom of God, and to our Center
    friends, if there be any with us
This is another opportunity for us
    to worship together

I would encourage each of you who
    are here today—let us take
    advantage of it
I'm honored to have this priviledge
    of closing out this appreciation
    service
5 Wanta invite your attention to the

sixteenth chapter of our
Lord's gospel by Matthew
And the sixteenth verse
And Simon Peter answered and
said, Thou art the Christ, the
son of the living God
Then John, chapter six verse sixty-
seven through sixty nine
10 Then said Jesus unto the twelve,
Will ye also go away?
Then Simon Peter answered him
Lord, to whom shall we go?
Thou hast the words of eternal
life and we believe, and are
sure that thou art the Christ,
the son of the living God, the
Holy One of God
Wanna talk to you this evening
from this thought, the Christ
of the Bible
The Christ of the Bible
I believe you will agree with me,
this evening, that if America
ever needed Christ in our life,
in our homes, on our jobs, in
our city government, state, and
internationally, we need Him
today
15 Turmoils, all around us
Frustration and confusion on every
side
Only the Christ of the Bible can
solve our problems
We want to talk about Him this
evening, if you please
Men everywhere seek for some form
of religion
20 Every man recognizes that there is

a God who made and controls
this wonderful world in which
we live
Even the atheist deep down within
knows there is a God somewhere
Ahh, and everyone in some way
wishes to have a connection
between himself and the Christ
of the Bible
The Bible is a book of revelations
based upon the Christ of the
Bible
He is a center-piece on every table
25 We may reach Him only by faith,
by faith
First—the first, foremost and final
task of the church is to teach
the word of God
And all other activities either con-
tribute to or grow out of an
understanding and an accept-
ance of the authority of the
word of God
When you see a man breaking the
law of the land, it only means
that he doesn't recognize the
law of God
When you see a man breaking the
law of God, it only means that
he's a lawbreaker in the land
30 We need God in our life—the
Christ of the Bible
Jesus—ahh—has come to the cross-
road in his earthly ministry
So He drew Himself away from the
scenes of His early labor
On the borderline of Palestine and

a Roman colony

At the foot of Mount Hermon, where the Jordan springs from the mountainside emptied themselves into the sea, as he would in a few short months empty himself in death for the sin of the world

35 C'mon, Holy Ghost

The Christ of the Bible

It was here in this—ahh—secluded place where Jesus called upon His

Disciples to give a definite statement of their faith in Him

Whom say ye that I am?

40 Simon Peter answered and said, Thou are the Christ, the son of the living God

Talkin' about the Christ of the Bible

Ahh, my friends, we must be able to answer this question today

Right now in our hearts, for the whole weight and worth of our salvation hinges upon the answer to this question

To know the Christ of the Bible is to know the gospel

45 Whom say ye that I am?

What do you say about him this evenin'?

We have found Him Whom Moses in the Law and the prophets did write

Jesus of Nazareth, the son of Joseph; the Christ of the Bible cannot be described in words

Language loses its signifisence [sic], tryin' to pay proper homage to the Christ of the Bible

50 Nathaniel ask him 's there any good thing come out of Nazareth

Phillip said unto him, come and see.—John one forty-five and forty-six

Talkin' about the Christ of the Bible

You see words, are only symbols of an artist, that are used in creating images in the human mind

But mere words fall short—Amen— and become insufficient and images dissolve and vanish because the Christ of the Bible is not an aggregation of words but the perfect embodment of the living God Himself—Isaiah chapter six verse three, Colossians, chapter two and verse nine

55 Isaiah, Isaiah declared the other day that he saw Him, high and lifted up

Sitting on the throne

He said His strain filled the temple

Amen! and he asked me a question

And I had the knowledge that I'm unworthy

60 I am not fit to serve on your program

I—I dwell among men of unclean lips

Even my lips, myself they are unclean

For that reason I can't go
He said—he said, I kept on
    watching
65 And in a moment and twinkling of
    an eye
He ordered one of His seraphim
    angels
And he took a pair 'o tongs
And took a live coal
For the (order) of God
70 And Isaiah said He came even to me
Touched my lips
Purged my sins
Amen! And dissipated my
    iniquities
He asked me again who will go for
    us
75 I said here I am Lord, send me
Talkin' about the Christ of the
    Bible
The only description that be given
    to Him that describes Him as
    the Christ of the Bible comes
    from the names and titles given
    in the Holy Word of God
All the world cannot contain Him
All oceans cannot bear Him
80 All questions cannot confound Him
All judges cannot condemn Him
An' all courts cannot try Him
And all rules cannot discipline Him
All orders cannot compel Him
85 And all graves cannot hold Him
    down
I'm glad about it this evening
There was no grave that could hold
    Him down
Help me Lord Jesus, tell your story

In education, He is the period at the
    end of every sentence
90 The logic, in every phrase and the
    glowing beauty and meaning
    in every syllable
Nominations would not elevate
    Him
Nations could not entangle Him
Campaigns did not elect Him
Parties could not influence Him
95 Epidemics did not surprise Him
Death had no power on Him
This is the Christ of the Bible
Help me Lord Jesus, I feel some-
    thing coming now
There is no secret, which He does
    not know the smallest detail
100 There is no problem, that He does
    not have the solution for
You have a problem in your life,
    you oughta tell Jesus about it
The Christ of the Bible
Ahh, no poet can describe His
    character, nor the meaning of
    His being
No—no, no one could describe Him,
    no one could pin the character
    of my Lord and Savior Jesus
    Christ
105 In Genesis, He is the seed of the
    woman
Oh yes He is
In exodus He is the burning bush,
    that stopped old man Moses
Am I right about it?
In Leviticus He is the image of
    holiness, standing in the center
    of the sanctuary

110 Help me Jesus
    In Numbers He is the star, that
        came out of Jacob
    The brazen serpent
    The smitten rock
    And the city of refuge
115 I'm talkin' about the Christ of the
        Bible
    In Deuteronomy He is the interpre-
        tation of the Law
    I'm talkin' about the Christ of the
        Bible
    Ahh, in Joshua, he is my battleaxe,
        in time of war
    Not only that but in Judges, He is,
        the separator
120 In Ruth, He is the true-bred, in
        Bethlehem
    In First Samuel, He is the true
        potentate, for all mankind
    In Second Samuel, He is anointed
        Shepherd
    And knows each of his sheep by
        name
    I wonder are you prayin' with me?
125 Goin' on now, in First Kings, He is
        Solomon's counsellor
    In Second Kings, He is the troubler
        of all men He have
    And the destruction of Sister
        Jezebel
    In First Chronicle He gives Israel,
        an everlastin' name
    In Second Chronicle, He is, the
        complete structure, of
130 Solomon's temple, and a buildin'
        made, without hands
    In, in in Ezra, He is Zerubbabel's
        leadership

In Nehemiah, He—He is Israel's,
    pure religion
I'm wondering, is He your pure
    religion this evening?
In Esther, He is the consolation,
    of the Jews
135 And in Job, He is my heart's
    pouring in yonder valley
In Psalms, of David, He's the
    mighty shepherd
Am I right about it?
In Proverbs, He is the wisdom,
    that passes all understanding
In Ecclesiastes, He is the gaining,
    of more wisdom
140 Songs of Solomon, He is the bride-
    groom, looking forward to a
    bright morning
I feel something coming now
In Isaiah He is the warrior, wrapped
    in a dyed garment
Walkin' in the strength of his own
    power
In Jeremiah, He is, the message, to
    the weeping prophet
145 In Ezekiel, He is the wheel, in the
    middle of the wheel
Help me Lord Jesus tell your story
Not only that but in Daniel, He's
    the stone
Cut out of the mountain, moving
    down through the world
Tearin' down the kingdoms of the
    world
150 Am I right about it?
In Hosea, He is, a mighty search-
    light
Am I right about it?

In Joel, He's a plague of locusts
I'm talkin' about the Christ, in my
    Bible
155 Not only that but in Amos, He's the
    plowman, overtakin' His
    reaper
I know that's right
Will you pray with me?
In Obadiah, He is Israel's, mighty
    deliverer
I don't know about you but he
    delivered me one day
160 Ever since that day, I been risin' an'
    fallin' in His name
C'mon church, and help me tell
    God's story
In Jonah, He is the speed-cop,
    overtakin' the mighty violator
Have you violated? if you've vio-
    lated he'll overtake you bye an'
    bye after a while
In Micah, He's the hope of the
    church
165 In Nahum, He's a whirlwind, in a
    cloud of dust
In Habbakkuk, He is the triumph
    of all missions
I know that's right
In Zephaniah, He is the foundation
In old man David's house
170 Not only that in Malachi
He is the refiner's fire
He'll purify you whole
He'll purify your soul
If you want purifyin'
175 I know that's right
In Matthew, he is the lion, and the
    tribe of Judah

Pray with me church
In Mark, He is, the high-cost
    servant
I know that right
180 In Luke, He's the great Physician
In John, He transcends time both
    ways
He's grace and truth
Help me Lord Jesus, tell your story
In Acts, He's the spirit and scope
185 Of all Evangelism
Help me Lord Jesus, tell your story
In Romans, He is the one, Who
    ascended way up to heaven
I know that's right
In Ephesians, He is, my spiritual
    weapon
190 Am I right about it?
In Philippians, He is my abdicator
In Colossians, He's my all and all
What about yours?
In First Thessalonians, He's the
    head of the church
195 I know that's right
In Second Thessalonians, He is the
    returning Lord
Are you lookin's for him? Are you
    lookin' for Him Saint Paul?
He's in His dressing room right
    now, coming back out to His
    church
In First Timothy, He is, the finish
    of all my pain
200 He's my courage, He's my hope,
    He's my all and all
Are you prayin' with me now?
In Second Timothy, He's the joy of
    my salvation

Am I right about it?
I feel all right right now
205 Something moving in my heart
In Titus, He is my sound doctrine
My signpost, my guideline
Am I right about it?
In—in Jude, yes He is
210 He's my doxology, and my
    benediction
In Revelation, I'm alpha and omega
I know that's right
I started this business, I'm goin' to
    see it to the end
Am I right about it?
215 I don't worry, about man destroyin'
    God's world
God started this world
And God will end this world
Man might destroy himself
But he cannot destroy God's
    creation
220 Am I right about it?
If you don't hear me no more
    Saint Paul
Keep your hand in God's hand
Keep your eyes, on the starpost in
    glory
Step by step
225 You'll have to make this journey
I know that's right
But step by step
I'm gonna make an end, some day
Am I right about it?
230 Brother Moore if I don't speak, in
    your church no more
Keep your hand in God's hand
And your eyes, on the starposts in
    glory

Lord said He would fight your
    battles
If you'd only be still
235 You may not be a florist
Am I right about it?
But you must tell them, that He's
    the Rose of Sharon
I know that's right
You may not be a geologist
240 But you must tell them, that He's
    the Rock of Ages
I know that's right
You may not be a physician
But you must tell them, that He's
    the great physician
You may not be a baker,
245 But you must tell them, that He's
    the bread of life
Am I right about it?
You must tell them
That He's a friend
That stick close t'his brother
250 He said I'll not cast ya out
In the sixth hour, and in the
    seventh hour
I didn't know I was turnin' you out
If y'keep your hand in God's hand
Let me stay in you
255 And high in you
I'll lead ya t' high heights
And deeper depths in my fire
Am I right about it?
And not only that
260 You may not be a builder
But you must tell them, that He's
    the chief cornerstone
Am I right about it?
I believe

Right now Saint Paul
265 He's in His dressing room right now
Putting on His Judgment garments
Gettin' ready to come back t' this
    church
We will be waiting
Are you waiting?
270 Are you waiting?
Are you waiting Saint Paul?
Keep your hands in the Lord's
    hands
Keep your eyes, on the starpost in
    glory
Walk, and never get tired
275 Run, and think 'bout the saints
Cause He's the strength
Of my salvation
Promise, said the Lord
In my life
280 And my salvation
Whom do I have to fear?
He's the strength of my life
Whom do I have to be afraid of?
He's my all
285 He's my all
He's my bread
When I'm hungry
He's my water
When I get thirsty
290 He's my shelter
When they throw me outdoors
I know that's right
When I don't have a leaning post
I can lean on Him
295 Am I right about it?
He won't turn me out
For the Psalmist said forty-six
God is our refuge

And strength
300 A well-proved helpmate in trouble
I'm in trouble this evenin'
Yes I am
I said I'm in trouble this evenin'
I need someone to go all night long
305 If you never hear me no more
Keep your hand, in God's hand
He'll make a way for you
The Christ of the Bible
No grave, could hold him down
310 This is the Christ of the Bible
Overtaking the reaper, overtaking
    the violator
Amen!
Don't worry Saint Paul about folk
    misusing you
No no don't worry about folk
    misusing you
315 The Christ of the Bible sooner or
    later, is gonna overtake them
He's my speed-cop
See he's my speed-cop
Amen!
He's the chief speed-cop
320 He may misuse me and think he's
    getting away with it
But at the moment—at the moment
    —when he least expect—you
    know this is true—
Amen those of us who have gotten
    citations
You're in a hurry, left late
Amen and you're overspeedin'
325 Oh yes I've gotten them
Amen
And the moment that you least
    expect, the Highway Patrol

You look up in your rearview
    mirror and you see a red light
Blinkin' in your face
330 He's overtakin' you.
So it is with the Christ of the Bible
You may mistreat me
You may talk about me
But just keep on livin'
335 The speed-cop gonna take care of it
When you don't know anything but
    red lights, gonna be blinkin' in
    your face
And it's no use to say you didn't do
    it
Amen
Because he was your record
340 He have our everything
Amen you can't deny it
And it signed in your name

And you can't deny it
I like that
345 Amen everybody's gonna have to
    read their own title prayer
And you can't deny your own
    signature
Oh yes I've wanted to deny mine
I've signed mine, Amen and found
    out that it was very difficult for
    me to pay that bill
And Amen, I wondered, well now
    wait a minute here did I sign
    that—yes I signed—there's the
    signature right here
350 Yes that's my signature I won't
    deny it
So, if we violate he's gonna catch up
    with us after a while
The Christ of the Bible

PREACH THE WORD

This sermon was recited by the Rev. Elihue H. Brown, July 16, 1967, in Bakersfield, California. It was delivered in honor of a Rev. Mr. Thompson of Bakersfield's St. Immanuel Church; the occasion was his twentieth ministerial anniversary, which must have made him one of the first Negro ministers who had settled in Bakersfield and was still alive in the community. The many references to the preacher in the desert are a tribute to Thompson's early years. As with all of Brown's sermons, the chanting begins early, here on line 30. Brown stays fairly close to his basic comparison throughout, that of Thompson to Ezekiel, though he makes a number of digressions which are triggered by thoughts in the "main stream." Thompson is a prophet; Brown is reminded of the prophet Daniel (line 54) and then of Ezekiel (line 89). Then he thinks of the Word of God and this reminds him of John (line 124) and then of his own life (line 142), back to the Word and then to Jesus (line 172). The remainder of the sermon employs all the themes and associations that Brown has used earlier. For example, the lines, "Tell them/I know my redeemer live/Because he lives in me" (172-74) is repeated in lines 209-11. Although the Rev. Rubin Lacy has preached (ostensibly) on the same subject there is little overlapping.

Son of man I have made thee a
    watchman in the house of
    Israel
Therefore hear the words at my
    mouth and give them warnings
    from me
You'll find these words and noted
    expressions comin' out of the
    Book of Ezekiel chapter three
    verse seventeen
Son of man I have made thee a
    watchman
5 Unto the house of Israel
Therefore hear the word of my
    mouth
And give them warning from me
Thank you
To Pastor Thompson, and all of my
    brother ministers, visitors, and
    members of the Saint
    Immanuel Baptist church
10 All our other visiters, we are very
    gratified that God has made it
    possible for us to be present
    here this evenin'
That we can say we thank God for
    He has brought us another
    milestone in life
There have been many voices
    hushed up since one year ago
But I can remember when we were
    here
On this same occasion

15 I can remember some of the words
    came from some of the mem-
    bers that they had been along
    with pastor Thompson a long
    time
But one and all we want to thank
    God for a man who was able to
    stand on the wall twenty years
And bring men warnings from God
You know no man could do what
    pastor Thompson done out in
    the midst of a desert
Unless that God would direct him
20 Just can't do things of yourself
It takes the Lord to help you
So as God warned and give these
    ever-kind words to the listenin'
    ear of one of the major
    prophets
So as He warned Brother Thompson
    as he traveled twenty years
    journey
I want you to know God is still
    asking Thompson to bring
    them warnings from me
25 There is no way that a man could
    walk out in the midst of a
    desert and call enough men and
    Christians together
And say let's build God a house
Unless'n God is with him
In warnin' men every now and
    then, you can't warn 'em off

your opinion, but you have to
warn them what God relate to
you
Then you confer to them what God
has told you to say
30 I believe this evenin' that we stay
with God's word, everything
will be all right
He said son of man I have made
thee
A watchman over the house of Israel
I want you to listen to my voice
And I want you to warn Israel and
at my commandment
35 So it was with Brother Thompson
and still is
I want you to warn Saint Immanuel
With my voice
What I'm talkin' about Brother
Thompson preached soul
That men can hear God in your
voice
40 Want to walk soul
That men can see God in your walk
Then you can climb to the bars of
Jesus
While the celestial light shines
And men may see your good works
45 I want you to know that God this
evenin'
He was warnin' Ezekiel
One of the major prophets
Who had been through the sun
Who had been through the rain
50 Men who had gone down in
captivity
And stayed down there under old
Nebuchadnezzar's rule

Stayed down there in Babylonia
They were able to stand up and
speak up for God
I tell you Ezekiel and Daniel
55 Or some of the major prophets can
tell you that God will carry
you through your troubles
If you wanted to talk about prayer
this evenin'
You'd talk to Daniel and Daniel
would tell you
Just stand in the window
And face Jerusalem
60 And prayer will be all right
I know as for myself
In nineteen years
Thompson had to face Jerusalem
Started out here brotherens
65 In the desert
Didn't have no place to worship
Started out in old tent
But he kept on preachin'
Until the Lord build a house
70 Now now now
Devil done told somebody
Thompson is gettin' old
He's worryin' all the people
Need a younger man
75 Man that walked along here
With this responsibility
On his shoulders
Sometime he cry all night long
Tell the Lord
80 Take care of Saint Immanuel
Have a little difficulty at Saint
Immanuel
I know you can take care Lord
I'm not able to Lord

To take care o' little difficulty
85 Ohh I know if you hold my hand
He'll make every thing all right
I want Brother Thompson
To be obedient
Like Ezekiel
90 Ezekiel said
The Lord carried me out one day
Carried me out in the valley
Set me down in the midst of dry
    bones
Set right there brotheren
95 Ohh after a while
The Lord said to Ezekiel
Son of man
Can these bones live
Ezekiel said in these words
100 Oh Lord thou knowest
One thing about it Brother Thomp-
    son
If we wait on the Lord
Let the Lord know what we want
    Him to do
Everything will turn out all right
105 Ezekiel sittin' out there
In a valley of many dry bones
Voice of the Lord said
Can these dry bones live
He said Lord God thou knowest
110 Say I want you to prophesy to them
    now
What you want me to say to them
    Lord
Tell them Ohh ye dry bones
Hear ye the word of the Lord
One thing I want you to know this
    evening
115 If you preach the Word Brother

Thompson
Everything will be all right
Somebody may go home
Just keep on preachin'
I know he will this evenin'
120 These words, in solid rock
These words will stand the terrible
    fire
These words will be here when
    everything is gone
Because God, is aware
I believe you'll read in the Book of
    John
125 That in the beginnin'
Was the Word
And the Word was with God
Ond the Word sure was God
Don't ya know God is all right this
    evenin'
130 Ohh Lord
To God some change in him
Stay with His Word
If His Word was able enough to
    come to this world and develop
    itself in Him
And dwell among us thirty-three
    long years
135 Don't you know the Word is all
    right to trust y'in
I know the Word this evenin'
It'll lift you up
When it seems like all your friends
    are gone
It'll give you strength
140 When you get weak
I know the Word this evenin'
Will bring you a long ways
The Word churnin' me up

It started my heart to fear
145 The hour I first believe
Long time ago
In the state of old Arkansas
Thompson I know it saw it then
Every now and then
150 I stay by the Word
Ohh the Word
Ohh the old preacher's sermon
    begin
Come on to me all you who are
    able
And heavy laden
155 And I will give you rest
Take my yoke upon you
And learn of me
My yoke is easy
And burden light
160 Kept on settin' there
One evenin'
Somethin' got all in my head
Started my mouth to talkin'
Started my feet to walkin'
165 I don't mind runnin' for Him this
    mornin'
Because the Word is in my heart
Don't mind cryin' for the name
Because every tear I shed/ is shed
    for a good cause brotheren
I'm gonna read the . . . some day
170 Stay with the Word
What I'm sayin' Immanuel every
    time Brother Thompson
Tell them
I know my redeemer live
Because He lives in me
175 Tell 'em that Job said
Ohh the appointed time

I'll wait on the change comin'
So many time men try to move
    before the change comin'
But stay right here
180 Stay here
And bring them warnings from me
Warn them out of God's word
Tell men when they're right
Doesn't matter how much money
    he pay in church
185 But tell him when he's wrong
Am I right
So right
To stand on His word
It's all right
190 To cry upon the man
I know it's all right
Carry your trouble to the Lord
Ohh have you ever carried your
    burden to the Lord
And leave 'em right there
195 I declare you're about to this
    evenin'
Never lost a patient
And friend this evenin'
He's a friend
Above all others
200 Don't you know His word this
    evenin'
To go on out with Ezekiel with
    the dry bones
And start a-rattlin' and shakin'
Don't you know He's gonna let this
    old body . . .
If they're started them old bones
    a-shakin' out there in that
    valley
205 Well, I know it will make me move

It getting my feet
I don't mind walkin'
Ohh, get on in the voice
Tell men
210 I know my redeemer lives
Because he lives in me
In the later years
In my flesh
I shall see God
215 Somebody
Somebody this evenin'
May be sayin' in your heart
There is no God
Search the Scripture over
220 I heard the Book of Psalms say
That fool
Said in thy heart
There is no God
I know this evenin' there is a God
225 God's somewhere
Every now and then brotherens
He's been close to me
Tell me
When I get weak
230 Hold on a little while longer
Some time
Some times
I hold against His courage
But there's a little old fistful
235 To keep on moving
Ohh after a while
He's sure to be all right
I gotta keep on
Carryin' my heavy load
240 Cause some of these days
I'm gonna lay down my heavy load
But I got somewhere, Funches
I made a long time ready to go

Ohh the Word this evenin'
245 Warn 'em brother Thompson
If they don't hear you
You gonna lose your reward
But if you fail to tell Saint
    Immanuel
And they die in the change
250 God will require of your hand
Ohh tell men
I know, for myself
That I been changed
You know what we don't have now
255 We don't have enough changed
    men in the world
We have men too scared
To let the world know they been
    changed
Oh I don't mind tellin' the world
I know I been changed
260 I know for myself
Ever since that Monday evenin'
I'm goin' home
To live with God
When I lay my burden down
265 I'm going to get my calendar
I'm not sufferin' here in this old
    world brotherens
For some body to say I'm a sufferer
But I'm sufferin' because of the
    grace of God
In my heart
270 Warn them on Brother Thompson
Twenty years of service
Bringin' warnin's to one hard-head
    group of folks
God will give you a reward
Who had his wife to stand by him
275 Until sickness came along and say

you take a rest for a while
The same is goin' to happen to all
    of us some of these days
I want to say to the members of the
    Saint Immanuel Church
Let us stay by our pastor
He is my pastor like he is yours
280 We want to stay here by him and
    throw around him—our arms
    of protection
Give him his flowers while he live
That he can enjoy the heat of the
    sun
Give me my flowers while I live
Doesn't matter how many we would
    bring down through the hour
285 After God has called him home
But bring—give him the flowers
    now while he can enjoy them
We pray His blessing that he will
    serve many many more years
I want you to know Brother
    Thompson it's just hot in here
God will give you victory
290 If you'll just hold to His hand
Stood on the wall and watch
It doesn't mean watchin' what folks
    do

But watching Thompson
And you can see what others do
295 Am I right brother preachers
If you stand on a corner tryin' to
    watch all of these folks they'll
    cut a corner around that-a-way
But if you just watch yourself
Tell the Lord every every now and
    then give me strength
I am weak but thou art strong
300 God bless you
I wants to see Jesus
Do you
I have a father gone
I have a brother gone and sister
305 But out of all of that I want to see
    Jesus
Do you want to see Jesus
Do you know you're on the right
    road only way that you can
    see Jesus
You must be on the right road
By and by
310 I will see Jesus
By and by
I will see Jesus
    (singing)

DRY BONES IN THE VALLEY

Recited by the Rev. Rubin Lacy, July 16, 1967, in Bakersfield, California, this sermon was, despite its poor beginning, moderately successful. Lacy was slow in getting started because he spent a lot of his time on politics, local and international. In all of the sermons recorded little time was spent on such matters. Lines 42-46 refer to the Arab-Israeli "Six-Day War," then just a month old; lines 87 ff. have to do with a telecast Lacy had just seen, though he would not identify the speaker.

From this "false prophet" Lacy turns to the duty of the true preacher and finally gets around to the main point of the sermon. Most of the opening remarks (the first 120 lines) appear to have been lost on the congregation as well; most of them had not seen the TV program Lacy was criticizing. The chanting begins at line 157, with a set piece about John's life as a preacher. Although off the subject (Dry Bones), Lacy undoubtedly used it for two reasons: he was talking about preachers already and this theme was psychologically related; and since it was a memorized (or nearly memorized) theme he could use it to his best advantage to establish a rhythmical pattern in his audience. A consistent chant begins at line 203; he had been chanting sporadically since line 162. From John's life as a preacher Lacy moves to Moses in the desert and then to the wilderness experience of Ezekiel. Momentum had begun to build up (by line 268) when he decided to use material from the gospel song, "Dem Bones." Near the end he comes to the main story (lines 287 ff.), occasionally breaking into song (lines 337 ff. and 363-78).

We're gonna talk today from Ezek-
    iel thirty-seven, and fourth
    chap—verse
Ezekiel thirty-seven and fourth
    verse
Son of man, can these dry bones
    live?
Son of man, can these dry bones
    live?
5 Ezekiel said to God, Oh Lord, thou
    knowest
Ezekiel way back there reminded
    me of Peter
God asked Peter feed my sheep
Asked him again to feed my sheep
He said Peter do you love me?
10 He said Lord thou knowest
You know you know I love you—
    gotta feed my lambs
So Ezekiel here tells God Lord thou
    knowest

And the Lord said in the fourth
    verse then you prophesy
Go out there and prophesy
15 Prophesy to the dry bones
That they might—tell 'em to get up
    and walk, to live again
We find here that old—that Ezekiel
    was obedient
Obedience is better than sacrifice
It wasn't Ezekiel's business to see
    how God would make those
    bones live
20 Wasn't his business
You know, we as a whole, if we are
    told to do something, that we
    don't see any sense in doing
    that we don't think it oughta
    be did
We talk back
But this prophet didn't argue with
    God, neither did

Abraham—Abram argue with God
25 God said to Abram take that boy
    and take him on out yonder
Just go on goin' 'til ya get to Mount
    Moriah
And when ya get there I'll show
    ya which one of the peaks to
    get up on
There's a heap a peaks out there
When ye get there I'll show ya the
    one to go up on
30 Take him on out there and kill 'em
Offer 'em up as a sacrifice
You know Abraham thought about
    that God had said that outta
    that boy would come the seed
    of all nations
Of the tribes to be brr-blest
You know that he thought of that
35 But he didn't argue with God
He did not argue with God
Ahh, he just don't be
So, we know Ishmael was here
Son that's begotten by the concu-
    bine we know he was here
40 And he's here today
Amen I say he's here today
Ishmael is troubling Jerusalem
    today
Ishmaelites—they're called Arabs
But they're troublin' Jerusalem
    today
45 Israel, is God's chosen people
They're here there standing up for
    their rights
They've fallen many times, every
    time they fall, God reaches
His outstretched hand and picks
    them up

You know, if God is for ya He's
    more than the world against ya
50 Yes, we, love to argue too much,
    with leadership
Because we can't see it, hmm?
But I think if we do more obeying
    than we do arguing we'd get
    along better
God has chosen people, to tell you
    what to do
Hmm?
55 Paul said, Timothy, to be mindful
    over the flock which the Holy
    Ghost have made thee overseer
Word overseer here doesn't mean
    a slave
Hmm?
But the overseer is to tell you what
    to do, not to tell him
Amen
60 Speakin' of the boss of the church—
    if the church have any boss on
    earth it's the preacher
I know some folks don't like to hear
    it but it's true
Because the church is left in the
    hands of the preacher whether
    he like it or not
Hmm?
Said the hands of the preacher
65 Jesus said to Peter the other day I
    give unto thee the keys of the
    kingdom of heaven
All that walks around here loose,
    will loose in heaven
All that you bind here on earth,
    I'll bind in heaven
Hmm?

The keys not the key, but the key
    that means the skeleton keys or
    the pass keys or whatever ya
    wanta call it—not like the
    other keys
70 Thought he'd ask Ezekiel here a
    question, can these dry bones
    live?
It spell-bound Ezekiel cause he
    didn't know
But I love him because he sub-
    mitted himself to God: you
    know, you know, tell me what
    to do
God said go out there and speak,
    God wants men today that'll
    speak for Him
Hmm?
75 We got people here now—ahh—
    speakin' for the folk, not God
I want this on the record—I want
    this on the record
I say we got men, here, that
    speakin' for men and not God
    and sayin' they're preachers—
    ministers of the gospel
Hmm?
No ministers, of God, is gonna let
    no dollar buy him
80 Hmm?
Simon Peter and John hail a man,
    here come a rich man, and
    offered to pay 'em
If you just gimme a token so I can
    do that—Amen!—I do—I'd
    make you rich
Peter turned around and told him
    this don't come from money

I know it's all right, this don't come
    from money
85 Tryin' to say to you this evenin',
    we have here in Bakersfield
We have preachers in Bakersfield
    that's preachin' for the folk
    and not for God
Ahh, I know what I'm talkin' about
    because God is not a segregated
    God
I say God is not a segregated God
Hmm?
90 I know a man here in this town
    Pastor seventeen or eighteen
    hundred people
Hmm?
Got on the public TV the other day
And publicly announced that was
    canvassin' for white supremacy
Amen—Wallace, George Wallace
    of Alabama
95 That man—if he's pastorin' two
    thousand people every one of
    those people is with him
'Cause if they wasn't they'd leave
    the church
I know I'm right about it
God is displeased at that
That isn't doin' anything—that's
    not doing the town any good
100 That's stirrin' up more trouble
More confusion, more hate into our
    town
And it's comin' from the church
The Missionary Baptist church of
    Bakersfield
Seventeen or eighteen hundred
    members

105 If he didn't hide it I didn't have no
          right to hide it
    I wouldn't speak about it if he
          hadn't got on TV with it
    But I have to answer—some way or
          another to answer him
    I want to tell you he's not the
          preacher of God
    But he's a preacher for the white
          supremacy folk, not God he's
          not a preacher but a business
          of the people in Bakersfield
110 I know that
    God is no respecter of persons—you
          had that in your lessons this
          mornin'
    They was tryin' to segregate way
          back then Peter was the hard-
          est-hearted one there was in
          the bunch, but God had con-
          vinced him on the housetops
          that He wasn't no respecter of
          persons
    Hmm?
    Ahh—but I want you—to remember
          that if God's for you, He's
          more than the world against
          you
115 Ezekiel here—ahh—believed in God
    When he was a young man he
          didn't do like some of us now
    All stiff-necked
    Hmm?
    And didn't wanna deal, with
          nothin' but the big members of
          the church
120 But he went out and sat down in
          sackcloth and ashes with the
          people
    Yes he did, I say he sit down there
          with the people
    God wants the shepherd to be with
          the sheep
    How can you feed—Amen—your
          sheep when you're in New
          Orleans and your sheep's in
          Bakersfield
    You can't do it to save your life
125 A shepherd is a feeder
    And to feed you gotta be there
    I know what I'm talkin' about/'an
          you gotta know how to feed
    Everybody that said they can feed
          can't feed
    I can't come here and feed this
          man's sheep like he did
130 Why? because these are his sheep
    Amen, I can come along here and
          boost him
    Maybe give them a boost
    But the regular feeder—haveta be
          the shepherd
    He never said shepherds—no he
          didn't—over no flock
135 But he said the shepherd of the
          flock
    Not shepherds over the flock
    Therefore one shepherd at a time
    If one—one—shepherd is removed,
          God always have been able to
          place another one there
    Ahh, so Ezekiel I said, was a
          shepherd
140 He's almost a gospel preacher
    One that God told him to stand on
          the wall

And rap the gavel
And if men don't believe him, then
    —ahh—their souls is required
    at their own hands
But if you stand to rap the gavel,
    then if they die in sin
145 You are responsible for it
Ahh—so many of us—ahh—ministers
    of the gospel
Is responsible today because we're
    scared to tell the truth
Afraid we'll lose a dollar
Afraid we'll lose a church
150 I say unto you this evenin', if God
    calls me to preach, and not
    able to give me no preachin'
    to do, it's all right with me
If He wanted me to sit down, He
    say Lacy you've done enough
That's all right
I can sit down, but I'm not dis-
    chargin' myself
Because I think God oughta do the
    dischargin'
155 Ahh—I'm not like some people,
    sayin' that a preacher oughta
    retire
There's no retirement to no
    preacher
Amen—he keeps on—keepin' on—
    let's see about—am I right
    about it
John was young man
When he started out
160 About twenty some-odd years old
Like him now, make a conclusion
    to the book of Revelation
Way up yonder, in his nineties

I said in his nineties
Fixin' to go home
165 But yet he never had sat down
And—uhh—discharge his debt
He might have got to the place,
    brother pastors
Where he didn't shout as much as
    he used t'
And do much evangelistic work as
    he used t'
170 But at this particular time
He was sitting down in the city of
    Ephesia
Pastoring a church
That Timothy—Bishop Timothy—
Ahh—had founded a long time ago
175 Tryin' to say to you we can't give
    up, as ministers of the gospel
Yes sir!
Take this young prophet, out
    yonder in the valley, where
    many of 'em had disobeyed
    God
Y'know, t' hear the light, stay in the
    wilderness, forty long years,
    all of that was because of
    disobedience
They could have been to the land
    of Canaan in two or three days
180 Ahh—but they stay there on account
    of they was disobedient t'God
Uhh-huhh, and, God, set there an'
    wandered right there in the
    wilderness
But he was good to them
He didn't let them starve to death
For food and neither water
185 He smote a rock out yonder

Water come up out of the foot of
   the mountain
They drink—Amen—the good cool
   pure water
An' then it rained down bread
I'm told it was angel's food
190 Food that the angels ate
And they were disobedient about
   that
He told them to gather just what
   you could eat on one day
Don't put up nothin' for tomorrow
Ahh—God has always been particular about men stackin' up a
   whole lot
195 Because you're here today, and
   tomorrow you may be gone
I see then they disobeyed God
And began to stack back-stuffs
They just wasn't obeyin', not to
   save their lives
And God said the other day, I'm
   gonna kill all of ya
200 Every one, that help out the land
   of Egypt
With Moses fulfilled with Joshua
Ahh—I'm gonna say if you do that,
   the people'll go out with the
   news
That you wasn't able to get 'em
To the land of Canaan
205 God said I don't care what the folks
   say
They've been so disobedient
God from Zion
They've hurt me time and again
That He ain't gonna put up with
   them no longer

210 God began to kill 'em
Out there in the wilderness
Died out there
Old Moses
Go get your serpent
215 Is rarin' up out there
Go tryin' an' get 'em
See what it all been
Go and got a golden serpent
Rarin' up there out in the
   wilderness
220 All of you
Wanna stop dyin'
And wanna get well
Just look up and live
Went out there
225 Stood under the serpent
So me-an
So contribuous [sic]
Stood there with the head down
Just wouldn't look up
230 Stood there rather die
That don't be the word of God
Ain't God all right?
See here
Some years after
235 Ezekiel come on the scene
That great prophet of God
Told him Ezekiel
Go out yonder
Go an' pastor that land
240 Save everybody
Way they die out there
By the millions
Out yonder in the valley
Prophesy
245 To the Dry Bones
The Word

The valley is white
Bleached with dry bones
Go out yon
250 And phophesy to 'em
Tell 'em
To wake up
And hear the word of God
Ain't God all right
255 God from Zion
Ezekiel went out there
Begin to prophesy
Dry Bones
Ezekiel said
260 I heard
A mighty rattlin'
The rattlin' of bones
Shakin' through the valley
Hark halelujah
265 Rattlin' of a livin' God
Set the bones
Began to get together
Toe bone
Connected to the foot bone
270 Foot bone
Connected to the ankle bone
Ankle bone
Connected to the leg bone
Leg bone
275 Connected to the knee bone
Knee bone
Connected to the hip—thigh bone
Thigh bone
Connected to the hip bone
280 Hip bone
Connected to the back bone
Back bone
Connected to the head bone
—To the neck bone

285 The neck bone
Connected to the back bone
And I heard
Him prophesy again
The Word of God
290 Come to the dry bones
Rise and live
God from Zion
Said to Ezekiel
Prophesy again
295 Prophesy
Said again
Came over the bone
Layin' there
With skin on the bones
300 Said prophesy
Some manage t' get up
Prophesied again
Wind was still
No wind blowin'
305 Said to Prophesy
Four winds to blowin'
God blowed His hardest
On the winds
Winds blow
310 Breath came into the bones
These bones
Got up shouting
Praisin' God
Ain't God all right?
315 Ohh He'll give you another chance
I love the Lord
Cause He'll give you
Another chance
Ain't God all right?
320 Heard Jesus
Say the other day
To those Pharisees

God from Zion
It'll be more trouble
³²⁵ For you
In the resurrection mornin'
Than it was
With those people
In Sodom and Gomorrah
³³⁰ Ain't God all right?
Ohh He's a warrior
Fightin' your battles
Ohhh, take my hand
Take my hand
³³⁵ If you'll hold my hand
I'm going on anyhow
Lord, hold my hand
Ohh, hold my hand
I don't want to hold His hand
³⁴⁰ Cause I might turn it loose
There's old folks used to sing
You better mind how you walk on
     across
Your foot might slip, and your soul
     be lost
I don't want, to hold His hand
³⁴⁵ I might be weak and turn it loose
But I want Jesus, to hold my hand
When ya leave here brother McRoy
We hit the daily highway
Ya tell God to hold me
³⁵⁰ Guide me

Ohh, lead me
Lead me
I know him-what you're doin'
I'm on the highway
³⁵⁵ I may get a guide to show me
Don't let the race-rod [sic] come
     loose
Umm-hmm
Ohh all alone
Sleep with Him
³⁶⁰ I say, to tell Him to sleep with ya
And wake ya in the mornin'
And everything will be all right
Give me wings
Just give me wings
³⁶⁵ Oh wings of faith
To fly away
To be at—my soul is . . .
Give me wings
Give servant wings
³⁷⁰ And I'll fly
To be . . .
Just give me wings
Servant wings
Ohh wings of faith
³⁷⁵ To fly away to be . . .
My soul is where I'm at . . .
Ohh give me wings
     (dissolves in humming)

I CAN DO ALL THINGS

This sermon was recited by Assistant Pastor William Robinson, August 13, 1967, in Santa Barbara, California. The failure of this sermon (as an oral performance) can be attributed to Mr. Robinson's lack of experience. At the time of recording he had not mastered the technique of organizing his words into metrical units. As a result he had to think about each line: he was not able to achieve any metrical consistency until near the end (line 181); pauses between lines were excessive, and he was unable to give any sense of metrical continuity. Between lines the regular pastor, C. Earl Williamson, shouted encouragement: "pray with him church," "yes, yes," and "you tell it, preacher." At first the congregation was sympathetic but after several minutes they became restless so that by the time Robinson was able to begin a chant he had lost them completely. The length of the lines and the flexibility of the syntax mark them as more akin to written prose than to oral delivery, especially oral presentation in this tradition. There is little of the parallelism characteristic of oral delivery; in lines 26 and 27 the repetition of "through Christ" came about because Robinson couldn't think of what to say next. It was, in other words, an unintentional stall formula. The first traces of oral style—and the first sign of metrical consistency—come at line 93 but could not be sustained. Robinson begins to sing at line 174; the lines remain just as irregular, but at that point we begin to have much more repetition and parallel syntax and resistance against introducing new ideas. Lines 186-88 nearly repeat phrases which have been used earlier; to the end of the performance the language is noticeably repetitive: the last lines at least Robinson has mastered.

Pastor Williamson, Officers, first
    lady, members and visitin'
    friends
Truly I am grateful to the Lord
For blessing me and keeping me
And I am grateful to you for this
    opportunity
5 It is always good to be able to say
    something for the Lord
I want to call your attention at this
    time to the Epistle of Paul to
    the Phillippians
That is the Epistle of Paul or the
    letter of Paul to the 'lippians
In chapter four of that letter and
    the thirteenth verse you will
    find these words

I can do all things through Christ
    that strengthens me
10 I can do all things through Christ
    that strengthens me
To put our hearts in one tune will
    you repeat after me these
    words
I can do all things
    (response)
Through Christ
    (response)
That strengthens me
    (response)
15 So said Paul, apostle Paul
I would like to use, these words, for
    my main thought
For the main thought of my mes-

sage, this morning
Could say for the theme, but I say
    main thought of my message
Reason I say this is because, if you
    don't get anything else, from
    the message this morning you
    can carry these words away
    from the sanctuary with you
20 You can carry this thought with
    you
These are the words of Apostle Paul
And I am moved or I am touched
    with this saying
Now the main—the key word in our
    thought this morning
I think—I think would be that I
    can do
25 I can do—I think this would be the
    key word
But I would like for you to think—
    think mainly on these words
    through Christ, through Christ
Through Christ
This is the lesson that Paul had to
    learn
It's the lesson
30 I will go as far to say that this is the
    lesson that some of us will have
    to learn
That it is through Christ
Not through President Johnson
Not through Rap Brown, Stokely
    Carmichael
Not even through Pastor
    Williamson
35 Oh no
But through Christ
I can do through Christ

But without Christ then I don't
    think that we can do anything
We can't do anything, anything
    without Christ
40 I said Paul had to learn this lesson
Now I think first of all we should,
    take a look at the life of Paul
The man that spoke these words
See, in the epistle and at this pres-
    ent time we think of him as
    apostle Paul
But it wasn't so from the beginning
45 No
There was some time before he was
    known as Paul
Umm-hmm
Well first of all he was born—born
    in Tarsus, Tarsus
A few years after the resurrection
    of Christ
50 And was named Saul
Lord help us today
Was named Saul
He was born of Jewish parent
Who held the rights and privileges
    of Roman—Roman citizenship
55 He was instructed in the Jewish law
    to the extent that at the age of
    thirteen he would call—he was
    called a son of the law
A son of the law, meanin' that he
    knew the law so well
That he was honored to be a son of
    the law
But I would like for you to think
    that—think on the idea of Paul
    bein' a Jew
And his parent bein' also Hebrews

that held the rights and privileges of Roman citizenship
60 Because it is—it means something
It means something, it means something
You see that first of all there were
many Jews that did not believe
in Christ
Did not believe in Christ
Now they believed in God
65 But there were many that never—
and some even today—that
don't believe in Christ
Some of them are still lookin'—
lookin' for the risen Christ
And do you know that there are
many of us today that don't
believe in Christ
And some of us don't even believe
in God
After we are able to look on the
altar of nature and see the sun
and all of His handiworks
70 Read His divine word but some of
us still don't believe in God
We say we believe in God
But Pastor William has said that
he's gonna talk about it and I
want to hear it—All Shook
Up
And you know when you fail to believe in God—when you be fail
—when you fail to believe in
Christ then you are goin' to be
shook up
Oh yes goin' to be shook up
75 I said that Paul was a Jew
And it seemed as though that he

was destined
To be a great man to be a great man
—it was discovered in the early
stages of his life
Because we find that he was
brilliant
There was a time when our poor
parents thought of their children to the extent that they
could look at them and predict
what they would be when they
grew up
80 They would say if you had—if you
had—a large head he's going to
be a preacher
I know when I was a child—very
small—my mother used to say
one day you are going to be a
preacher
I had no thoughts but today here
I am
I am—and I am what I am but I
want you to know I am a servant of the living God
That is—I feel that is what's important
85 Not to the point of being a preacher
but being a servant of the true
and living God
Paul said I can do all things,
through Christ
But we also find here that maybe
someone we should talk about
this to our [?] that you may
have a better understandin'
All things, not all things you know,
there must be some limitation
to this
Anything

90   Through Christ—no no not any-
        thing—not all things
     Now reverend what do you mean—
        you just made this statement
        all things
     But Paul goes to say here in this
        eighth verse
     Finally brotheren, whatsoever thing
        is true
     Whatsoever thing are honest
95   Whatsoever things are just
     Whatsoever things are pure
     Whatsoever things are lovely
     Whatsoever things are good
     Report
100 You know he named those things
     Whatsoever things are right
     Things that are good
     Things that are pure
     Those things we can do through
        Christ
105 No He can't—I don't think—don't
        get the idea that you can jump
        the jack through Christ—it's
        through the devil
     But through Christ
     What did Paul start out to do
     And I think we should call him
        Saul at this time
     That we may better identify him
110 What did Saul start out to do
     Right off hand we could say that he
        started out to destroy the
        Church
     He started out to get rid of the man
        —the idea of this Christ
     But do you know one thing
     God stopped him

115 This Christ stopped him
     He could have stopped altogether
        but He just delayed him
     Gave him to know that I am the
        Christ
     Jesus after His baptism you know
        became the Christ
     At Nazareth—Jesus—but don't get
        confused about Jesus Christ
        'cause the Father an' Son an'
        Holy Ghost they're all in One
120 Jesus hears—I'm talkin' about Christ
     We find that Paul, as I said, went
        to the synagogue school
     And he achieved so much in the
        synagogue school
     The teachin' of the rabbis
     That he was honored as the son of
        the law
125 And up on his graduation from
        synagogue school
     We find that he went to Jerusalem
        to further his schooling
     And there he was taught under
        Gamaliel
     People like to say that he was
        taught at the feet of Gamaliel
     Gamaliel was a great teacher of the
        law
130 And he—he was the leadin' figure
        in the Sanhedrin council—
        whenever they needed council
        they would turn to him
     He was one that knew the law
     So Paul received further learning
        in the council
     He was taught more about the law
     This is the Sanhedrin council

135 The same council that passed the
    judgment upon this Christ
They knew about it
Paul received training there—
    learned more about the law
Increased knowledge and wisdom
But it is said that while he there
    attendin' law school in Jeru-
    salem he came in contact with
    the new Christian movement
140 And it is said that it aroused his
    hostility
And after the death of Stephen
    which he had a share
He was around some place
It is said that he was employed by
    the Sanhedrin council
To further destroy—to further
    destroy this Christian move-
    ment—Lord help me a little
    while
145 And to make the arrest of all of
    Stephen's followers
And it was while he was exercising
    this commission it happened
Because if you recall on the road
    to Damascus
As he drew near to the city
And it was along about noon day
150 Paul said that somethin' happened
    —this same Christ appeared
    unto him—came before him
    this same Christ—and He ap-
    peared, and He appeared in the
    form of a light, a light that was
    so bright
Until it was even brighter than the
    sun

Was so bright until it blinded—and
    Lord help when I say it—Paul
    because it was Saul
Blinded Saul—the light was so
    bright—Lord help us—until it
    blinded Saul's eyes and he fell
    on the ground
While he's on the ground Paul said
    he saw someone in that light
155 Someone that he had never seen
    before
Not only did he see someone but
    Paul said he heard a voice
A voice said Saul—Lord help us
    this morning—
Saul—Saul—Saul why persecute
    thou me
Saul why—why—why are you tryin'
    to fight against me
160 Tell me that Saul said who was
    Thou Lord
Who are Thou Lord
He said that I am Jesus
Meanin' the Christ
The One that you are tryin' to
    destroy
165 An' my mind go back to God's word
    —to Jesus' word when He said
    upon this rock I build my
    church
And the gates of hell shall not pre-
    vail against it
Upon this rock I build my church
You see Paul didn't know that
    which he was tryin' to destroy
Founded by that same Christ
170 Paul—Paul didn't know that he was
    playin' with Someone that was
    much bigger

But you know today—today we have
those that are still tryin' to destroy that which is right that
which is holy and that which
is just
You still have those who are tryin'
to destroy the church of a true
and a living God
Last Sunday I had the privilege of
hearing a young man stand behind the rostrum—the pulpit
here and say that who would
believe in this Christ idea
He said that I don't think there
anything to this idea of Christ
175 And he tried to make a joke about
it 'cause he said if you had a
wife an' you would come home
and she told you she was with
child
She told you that she received it by
the Holy Spirit what would
you think of it
I'm tryin'—what I'm tryin' to say to
you today that there are those
that not only are so far out that
they no longer believe in the
Christ idea
That they are tryin' to teach others
Umm they're tryin' to teach others
that there is no such thing as
Christ
180 They are—they are proclaiming and
saying that God is dead
Trying—and you know what they
are trying to do—they are
trying to destroy the church
But my Bible tell me

Umm-hmm my Bible tell me
That the gates of hell shall not
prevail
185 And I want to say—say—to you that
is a mighty dangerous thing
Umm to go around tryin' to destroy
that which is right
Tryin' to destroy that which is holy
Tryin' to destroy that which is just
Umm and as I close this mornin'
190 Paul had to learn this lesson—had
to learn his lesson
And we find him saying here—saying here today
That I can do all things through
Christ
Umm at one time in my life
I thought that I could do all things
through the law
195 At one time in my life I thought
that I could do all things
through—under my own power
I thought I could do all things
under my own strength
Oh Lord but ah—but ah today—
today I'm sayin' that I can do
all things through Christ
Umm because I realize today that
my strength lies in Christ Jesus
My strength lies in Christ Jesus
200 Everything that I attempt to do I
shall put Christ before me
And everything that I do I should
want to know is this the will
of Christ
If it isn't the will of Christ—umm—
I should feel like that I'm
going to fail

The same Christ—the same Christ
The same Christ Pastor William
205 The same Christ He is available
    today
The same Christ the same Christ
    lives today
He is here today in the form of the
    Holy Spirit
You may not be able to see the same
    Christ
Umm but if you will just open up
    the door of your heart
210 Behold I said at the door and knock
    He said

And if you'll open up I'll come in
    and sup with ya
The same Christ is available today
Have you met Him
Do you know Him
215 Open up your heart today
And receive Him
Because if we are to succeed it must
    be through Christ
And if we fail it is because we fail
    to recognize that Christ
He lives today—open up your heart
    and receive Him

PERILOUS TIMES

Recited by the Rev. T. J. Hurley, May 12, 1968, in Oklahoma City, the two versions of this sermon were performed before Hurley's church, the Oneness Pentacostal, but the second version was also broadcast live on Radio Station WBYE. These are the only sermons that I have ever recorded by the same man on the same day on the same subject, and for that reason are valuable in what they may show about near-term retention. The atmosphere in white Pentacostal churches differs from that in Negro Baptist. The members of the congregation are not inclined to express themselves rhythmically, although they are far more demonstrative of their emotions than the members of any other church I have visited. Since they are so well prepared beforehand, the preacher can begin his chant early, in Hurley's case around line 15 in both sermons. Hurley is not musical as are his Negro counterparts: however his rapid delivery becomes metrical, anaphoric passages develop, and then he abruptly breaks off and reverts to normal speech for several lines. These sermons, typical of his style, contain several such ups and downs. Only those lines which are repeated within these two sermons are underlined: their placement within the sermon as well as their number is important in studying the preacher's technique.

Version I

The Bible say, if you want to read
    with us today, in the second
    Epistle of Paul the Apostle to
    Timothy
Second Timothy the third chapter
    and the first verse
This is very familiar and no doubt
    you have read it—you've heard
    it many times
And some times the Word of God
    is just like pouring water off a
    duck's back—it just goes in one
    ear
    and out the other
5 Or some folks it goes in both ears
    and out the mouth but
The Word of God is something we
    need to pay attention to
Praise the Lord
The Bible said this know also
It didn't say you think on it but it
    said know
10 Amen somethin' you know you're
    not in doubt about
You come up and say well what's
    your name—oh I don't know
    the last time I heard it was
    T. J. or
Where do you live—well I don't—I
    think it's 2934 Southwest Fifty-
    seventh or I really don't know
    —you're in doubt but the Bible
    said to know this
And rest assured that it is so—that
    it is true
That in the last days perilous times

    shall come
15 For men shall be lovers of their own
    selves, covetous boasters, proud
    blasphemers disobedient to
    parents
Unthankful and unholy and it goes
    on and names everything from
    here to yon that men are doing
    today
It said this know that in the last
    days
Perilous times shall come
An' I'm not going to tell you that
    perilous times are coming
20 I'm not going to tell you that
    they're on the way because I
    personally do not believe that
I don't believe that the perilous
    times that the Word of God is
    talkin' about are on their way
I don't believe that they're comin'—
    I believe that they're already
    here
Amen—we are livin' in the last days
And perilous times are surely here
    today
25 Amen—what is it that makes a man
    go into a student nurses' dormi-
    tory and take the lives of eight
    student nurses
An' what is it that makes a man
    climb to the top of a tower and
    kill thirty-two people in one
    day
An' what is it that causes an eight-
    een-year-old boy to walk into

a beauty shop
An' cause 'em to lay down and blow
   their brains out on the floor
What is it that causes people not to
   want to live for God
30 That when ya' preach the truth
   they get mad and storm out the
   door and slam the door and say
   I'll never come back again
What is it that causes people to quit
   payin' their tithes
And to start lyin' and cheatin' and
   killin' and murderin'
What is it that causes people to quit
   livin' right
And to go out and start doin' every
   wicked and imaginable thing
   in the world
35 It's the thing my friend
It boils down to one thing
That we are living in perilous times
Not the perilous times
Not the world we're talkin' about
40 They're in the land today
Men are lovers of their own selves
They're fightin' they're killin' and
   they're cheatin'
For their own profit
Brother Williams you leave me
   alone
45 Don't you do anything to bother me
I don't care if you starve to death
Just let me eat good
I don't care if you walk just let me
   ride in a Cadillac
I don't care if you don't live in a
   nice home
50 Just let me live in a brick mansion

Those perilous times
That the Bible is talkin' about
Are here today
Amen we're covetous
55 People in the land today are
   covetous
Amen they don't want you to have
   anything if they can't have one
   just like it
Amen—you know I'm telling ya the
   truth an' you might as well
   say amen
Amen
Lovers of our own selves—covetous
60 Boasters—my God if I ever heard of
   anything
That makes me wanna vomit out
   my toes it's people that get up
   —all the time braggin' about
   themselves
And folks that say look at the good
   works that I did
Look at everything that I'm a-doing
   —look at all my great works
Friend the Bible says that when a
   man thinks in his heart
65 That he's somethin' he winds up to
   find out that he's really nothin'
Amen—but those days are here
People say oh look at me
There's nobody like me
I want you to know my friend
70 That the reason you are what you
   are today
Is because of the love
And the grace and the goodness of
   almighty God
And when you get t' thinkin' that

you're somethin'
An' that you know it all
75 An' that you're somethin' great
My God that made you what you
    are
Can cut you down
And make you to be nothin'
Amen
80 I realize that I'm nothin' today
What I am I know where I got it
Amen it was almighty God that
    brought me this far
If I make it through another day
If I ever make it up in the mornin'
85 It'll be again because of the Lord
And the grace of almighty God
It's not any good thing in me
Because the Bible said that my
    righteousness
And your righteousness
90 Is as filthy rags
Amen we ought to be like Jesus
When he prayed in the garden of
    Gethsemane
He said Oh Lord
It's not my will
95 It's not my way
It's not my thoughts
It's not my ideas
It's not my opinions
It's not my theories
100 It's not what I think
It's not what I do
It's not what I say
No God it's your will be done
What you think
105 How you think it oughta be done
What you want me to say

What you want me to do
Oh God not my will but thine be
    done
Perilous times have come to the
    world
110 The thing that shocks me beyond
    measure
Is that perilous times are also
    creepin' into our united
    Pentacostal Churches
In our free Jesus' name churches
Amen
It's comin' in brotheren
115 You just might as well get ready for
    it
What is it that causes people
Want to come and sit on the pew
What is it that makes a man come
And think that he can smoke
    cigarettes
120 And lay 'em down and come to th'
    house of God
What is that makes a woman think
    that she can go home
And watch television all day
And sneak out to a movie once in
    a while
And then come and sit on the pew
125 And claim the air of Christianity
What is it that's gotten in our
    preachers
That they get up
And they got fear
And they got fame among the
    people
130 And they won't preach the Word
    of God
Like it's written in the book

They compromise
And they belly-wash around
What is it that's causin' all this
    trouble in our churches
135 If we recall that perilous times are
    comin'
And men are lovers of their own
    selves
They're lookin' out for their own
    good
And nobody else
An' I want you to know my friend
140 I'm workin' for you
I'm workin' for myself
I want to go to heaven
That's all I want in this world
Amen
145 Praise God
Heard a song the other day
Somebody drew my attention to it
Certain part of this song said some
    preachers preach
What others want to preach
150 Amen
Some preachers preach what others
    want to preach
Praise God I preach what God
    wants me to preach
Amen
I preach what God wants me to
    preach
155 Amen—if people don't like it I can't
    help 'em
Amen—if you don't want to live
    right
There's nothin' that anybody can
    do
If you want to live like the devil

my friend
There's nobody that can help you
    but the devil
160 If you want to live like the world
There's nobody that can help you
    but the world
I want you to know
That if you want to live a holy
And a Godly an' a sober and a
    righteous life
165 That my God will stand beside ya
My God'll fight ya battles for ya
He'll never forsake ya
He'll never leave ya
He'll never let ya down
170 He's always there to lead ya—
    guide ya
And He'll take care of ya
If you'll only put your trust in Him
The Bible said finally my bretheren
Lookin' around you and seein' all
    these things
175 That are happenin' in the world
    today
Lookin' around you
An' seein' all the people
That don't want to live for God
Lookin' around you
180 An' seein' all the people
That want to get mad if one time
    things don't go their way
Lookin' around you
An' seein' all the people
That'll take one story and make a
    mountain out of it
185 Lookin' around you
And seein' all these things
The Bible said finally my bretheren

Be strong in the Lord
190 I want you to know my friend
What we need today
Is we need people that'll be strong
    in the Lord
Amen
We need some hard heads
195 I said we need some hard heads
Praise the Lord
'Cause I want you to know my
    friend somebody's gonna be
    throwin' stones until we all die
Amen
Somebody make a statement while
    I know that the devil hasn't
    got me 'cause he's still after me
200 Amen—well I want you to know
    friend that when people quit
    throwin' stones at ya there's
    somethin' wrong with ya
Amen—these people that are sittin'
    around always rubbin' their
    head—oh somebody hit me
Oh I got hit and I'm hurt
Oh somebody said somethin' I
    didn't like
Oh they hit me Oh somebody said
    somethin' I didn't like
205 Friend we need some hard heads
Amen
Amen
Brother we need some people that
    can stand up
And brace against the storm
210 And say regardless of what comes or
    goes
Let the winds blow and rains fall
    and the storms come

I'm gonna stand up and fight the
    devil on his own ground
I'm gonna make my stand
I'm gonna stand on the Word of
    God
215 Regardless of what anybody says or
    does
Regardless of who turns against me
Regardless of who's for me
Let 'em mock let 'em scoff
Let 'em make fun and make shame
    of me
220 I'm gonna live for God
We need people
That'll be strong in the Lord
Amen
We don't need compromisers
225 We don't need belly-washers
We don't need people with a back-
    bone like a jelly-fish
What we need is somebody
That'll stand up
And say live—die—sink or swim
230 My God I'm gonna stand on your
    Word
I'm gonna live for ya
I'm gonna do what's right
Regardless of what comes
Amen
235 Said put on the whole armor of God
That you may be able to withstand
The wiles of the devil
Amen
Bless God—you people that are
    goin' around here
240 I'm not makin' any accusation
If you're here today I want to
    preach at you for a while

Amen—people that are always goin'
    around, and comin' to church
    and sittin' there and their teeth
    are draggin' the floor and they
    just can't hardly do anything
An' they just can't get up
Every time somebody says some-
    thing I want to get offended
245 Every time somebody does some-
    thing I don't like
I'm just gonna bow down
And go out the door
And jus' never come back again
I didn't like the way Brother Wade
    looked at me
250 I didn't like Sister Marie's hand-
    shake
Friend ya might as well get used to
    those kind of things
'Cause I'll be shakin' her hand all
    my life
And she never does put any fire
    into it
I been gettin' those looks from
    Brother Wade ever since I
    been in Pentacost
255 An' we just might as well get ready
    for those things
People that are always goin' around
Oh I didn't like what's goin' on
I don't like the way he beats those
    drums
Those people just make too much
    noise in my ears
260 I don't like the way Sister Hale
    plays that organ
And I don't like anything that's
    going on

My friend the only thing that's
    wrong with you
Is you haven't put on the whole
    armor of God
If you had on the whole armor of
    God
265 You'd be able to withstand
All the wiles of the devil
You'd be able to come to church
With some victory down inside
You'd be able to come to church
270 And raise your hands
And worship almighty God
Open your mouth
And sing the praise of God
Clap your hands
275 And stomp your feet
If ya had on the whole armor of
    God
Oh, the devil just been after me
    all day
I'm tellin' you
Been runnin' in and out of the—
    kids 've been runnin' in and
    out an' slammin' doors an'
280 And everybody forgets me an'
The devil's been fightin' so hard
One poor old sister sit down and
    . . . Pentacostal Church
Everything's just been goin' so
    badly
I just feel like going right to the
    doctor
285 That's what'll happen to ya when
    ya get your mind on that kind
    of thing
That's what she said in her testi-
    mony—she meant to say suicide

but she let the devil work for
her and she let the wrong word
come out
Amen—that's the reason the Bible
said set your affections on
things above
Amen—set your affection on things
above
I want you to know friend
290 That if you go around with your
eyes on God
If you go around with your eyes
above
Up in heaven
An' worshippin' almighty God
You wouldn't see the things that
the world's doin'
295 You wouldn't know what's goin' on
here around you
If you had your affections set
To things above
You couldn't see all the things
That the devil's got layin' for you
300 You couldn't be offended
Every time somebody spoke up
against you
No my friend
What we need in Pentacost
Is people that'll put on
305 The whole armor of God
So that when the devil comes up
against them
They'll be able to stay on the
ground
And say devil
You get away from me
310 You folks that are comin' to church
Oh—oh—its a hard life

. . . God
It's just worse then I can hardly
take
It's just almost more than I can bear
315 But you know what the Bible said
friend
The Bible said the way of the
transgressor
Is hard
Amen
Said the way of the transgressor
320 Is hard
Amen I want you to know friend
When you're livin' for God
My God'll take care of ya
He said I won't put more on ya
325 Than that what you're able to bear
Amen when the load gets to gettin'
too heavy
I'll lift it up on ya
My friend when you come draggin'
your face sayin' everything' too
hard
Everything too bad
330 You're just plainly gettin' up an'
sayin' I'm a transgressor
I haven't done what God want me
to do
I haven't obeyed His Word
I left off
No my friend
335 If ya put on the armor of God
The devil and the forces of hell
Cannot come up against you
They can't drag you down
They can't get ya down
340 If ya put on the whole armor of
God

Amen
For we wrestle not
Against flesh and blood
Amen
345 Brother Wade you and Brother
    Williams—you're not fightin'
    me
I haven't lost any teeth yet—have
    no black eye either and I
    haven't bloodied your nose
We're not fightin' against flesh and
    blood
Amen
That's not what's the matter with
    us
350 Do you know what we're fighting
We're fighting powers
Principalities
Against the rulers of darkness of
    this world
And against what—spiritual—oh a
    lot of people don't like this one
355 We're fighting people's spiritual
    weakness in our places
Amen—that not the president of
    the United States
No sir that's not Senator Harris
No that's not Governor Rockefeller
No sir that's not Governor . . .
    that we're fighting
360 What we're fighting my friend
Is people that claim to be Christians
And claim to be deacons
And board members
And pastors
365 And saints
And Sunday school teachers
And people that claim to be high

In organizations
And think—somebody
370 We're fightin' those kind of people
That'll stand up
And say you can do anything
And live for God
You can do this
375 You can do that
You don't have to live right
This church is too hard
The Pentacostal Church is too strict
If ya can't live it come over here
380 What we're fightin'
Is the devil
In sheep's clothing
We're fighting the devil my friend
And we might as well
385 Put on the whole armor of God
So that we can stand
Amen
Amen
I read a story when I was in high
    school
390 We were studying Greek mythology
I read a story of one of the greatest
    men at that time
He was a mighty warrior
He had never—he had never been
    injured, and he had slain
    thousands of the enemy
He was a mighty warrior
395 As the story went on that this man
    was never caught
Without his armor on
He was never caught
Without his armor on
You know the reason people are
    backslidin' today

400 You know periods of people were
    gettin' to thinkin'
You know the reason that people
    are goin' around
With their sticks stickin' out of
    their shoulder
It's because they put off the whole
    armor of God
Amen
405 You know what that Bible said
    within our hearin' the other
    night
The Bible says the devil never sleeps
He goes about his . . . day and
    night
Seekin' whom he may devour
I want you to know
410 That if the devil catches you
At home or on the job
He will
He'll pull off your armor
And you don't have your armor on
415 He's lookin' for that
He can't wait for you to put it off
And when you do
My God
The devil's gonna move
420 And get a-hold of you
One man got smart
An he found out the man that made
    this man's armor
He said is there any part of this
    body that is not covered up
Is there any way I could get an
    arrow into some part of this
    body
425 My friend, Sampson said if we
    . . . .

Amen
How many of ya ever saw a baby
    that didn't have a soft spot
They've all got 'em don't they
430 I never saw a Christian that didn't
    have a weak spot
Some where
Amen
Amen
I'm not sayin' we all got weaknesses
435 Brother if we let the devil know
    that
We better beware
I said you better beware
Amen
C'mon folks can't ya say amen
440 If it was double-A Allen up here
    everybody'd be shoutin'
Praise the Lord
I guess I'm not puttin' on a big
    enough show for everybody
Praise God
And this man told him—he said that
    there's one part in the calf of
    his leg
445 In the bend of his knee where his
    armor—where he spreads out
    his leg he's got a spot where
    it's open
That's the only place
And this soldier he waited and lay
    for him
I want you to know that the devil
    lay for you
Amen I said the devil will lay for ya
    friend
450 He finds out where your weak spot
    is—he finds out where your

weakness is

He's gonna be hidin'—he's gonna be
    waitin' for ya

Amen

This man he got him a poisonous
    arrow

He caught this soldier's leg
    straightening out one time an'

455 He sent his poisonous arrow into
    his leg and he killed him

Amen

This is a myth

It's a story

But I found it to be so true

460 In our ancient myths

The devil finds out our weak spot

He finds out where its kept

He finds out when we pull off our
    armor

He finds out when we're really
    relaxed and we pull off our
    armor

465 An' brother he's got a poisonous
    he's just waitin' to inject into
    our body

He's just waiting for that right
    moment

He's waiting for the right day and
    the right hour and the right
    time

When he can inject that poisonous
    arrow

Into your body

470 And drain the very spiritual life
    out of you

My friend

If ya wanna live right

If ya wanna go to heaven

You must put on the whole armor
    of God

475 And keep it on

And don't let down

'Cause . . .

The devil will get us

Therefore

480 Stand therefore having his loins
    gird about with truth

With truth

An' I want you to know

That the reason America

Is what it is today

485 'Cause America is tryin' to do what's
    true

They stood up for truth

Amen

And I want you to know friend that
    the truth is always gonna win

An' lies never wins

490 Amen

You talk to a man for thirty or
    forty minutes an' you'll catch
    him in three or four of them

He'll tell a lie an' then he'll tell
    another to get out of that one

Amen

Truth is always gonna win

495 Truth is always gonna win

Heavenly love is gotta abound with
    truth

Having on the breast plate of
    righteousness

Righteousness

Righteousness

500 Righteousness

I'm not talkin' about our righteous-
    ness

'Cause that's nothin' but filthy rags
I'm talkin' about that righteousness
    that ya get from God
I'm talkin' about that righteousness
    that ya get from on high
505 I'm talkin' about that kind of right-
    eousness brother that keeps ya
    from sin
I'm talking' about that kind of
    righteousness
That's keeps people livin' for God
    day after day
Month after month
Year after year
510 Year after year
And I'm talkin' about that kind of
    righteousness
That God gives
And we must be righteous
If we ever make heaven our home
515 Brother you just put on your whole
    armor
You put it on
You let your hair grow long
You let your skirts get long
You let your sleeves get long and
    your necks high
520 You don't wear any jewelry no
    make-up and you let your hair
    grow
My friend you put on all the rest
    of your armor
But you leave off the breast-plate
    of righteousness
And the devil will still get you
Amen brother
525 When you clean up the outside
And you dress holy

You must be righteous on the inside
I'll let ya know just exactly how
    I feel about it
I don't believe that everybody that
    talks in tongues is gonna go to
    heaven
530 I believe that everybody that goes to
    heaven is gonna talk in tongues
I don't believe that everybody that
    claims a hollow victory is
    gonna go to heaven
But I want you to know that every-
    body that goes to heaven is
    gonna have victory
I want you to know
That it's not everybody that dresses
    holy
535 That's goin' to heaven
But everybody that goes to heaven
    Is most definitely gonna dress holy
Holiness is more than skin-deep
Amen
540 Lot of folks say the first thing they
    gotta do when they get into
    church is start dressing right
First thing you do when you get
    to church is ya gotta get your
    heart right
Amen
You can be holy on the outside
But that's not gonna take care
    of your heart
545 You can be holy on the outside
Without being holy inside
But there's no possible conceivable
    way
It's absolutely impossible
To be holy on the inside

550 Without bein' holy on the outside
If ya clean your heart up
It'll automatically clean you up on
    the outside
You're wastin' your time tryin' to
    clean up the outside
An' look holy
555 An' dress holy
Without first
You clean up your heart
An' ya get right inside
Praise God
560 And your feet shod with the prepa-
    ration of the gospel of peace
Gospel of peace
A lot of folks are—their feet are shod
    with the preparation of the
    gospel all right but it's the
    gospel of gossip
The gospel of turmoil
Amen
565 The gospel of stirrin' up trouble
The gossip of causin' trouble
Great God some people Brother
        Williams—one time Brother
        Cavage preached—Duke Cav-
        age preached—he could explain
        it so well
A lot of people in our Pentacostal
    Churches
Can't see a man or woman walkin'
    down the road
570 And just casually look at a beer
    joint
And before it gets all the way
    around back to the church
    and back to the poor old boy
They got him goin' in there and

staggerin' back out fallin'
    drunk
Amen a lot of people have got their
    feet shod
With the preparation
575 Of the gospel of gossip
The Bible said the gospel of peace
Amen
Praise the Lord
I want you to know friend
580 That if me and Brother Williams
        have a fight today
It's not all my fault
An' it's not all his fault
I don't want ya takin' sides with him
And I don't want ya takin' sides
    with me
585 Let's start standin' up like a man
Stand up like a woman
And shoot it right down the middle
And say right's right
Wrong's wrong
590 And I'm gonna stand up for what
        the Word of God says
Praise God
Don't believe in bein' lopsided about
    anything
An' I want you to know I don't want
    no favors from this church
I love Brother Hale just as much as
    I love brother Wade
595 I love brother brother . . . just as
        much as I love Brother
        Williams
He don't mean a bit more to me
    than anybody else does
An' friends when you get to pickin'
    sides an' to sayin' I'm not goin'

to sit beside anybody but Sister
Hale
I'm not gonna sit by anybody but
Brother Wade
I'm not gonna invite anybody over
my house but Brother so and so
600 I'm not gonna have anything to do
with this man because he made
a mistake
I'm not gonna have anything to do
with this woman because she
made a mistake
I'm just gonna pick my own little
group
We're gonna go away and have our
own precious time
You're just as wrong as . . .
605 Bible didn't say blessed are the
troublemakers
Blessed are the gossipers
But the Bible said blessed are the
peacemakers
Praise God—I don't know why I'm
sayin' all this but I don't guess
it hurts
I won't charge anything for that—
I just thought I'd throw it in
for nothing
610 . . . more than anything take the
shield of faith
Of faith
Friend you can lose your pride
You can lose your home
You can lose your automobile
615 You can lose your friendship
You can lose everything you got
But don't lose your faith
Don't lose your faith in God—Amen

When you've lost faith in God
you've lost your real and your
purpose for living
620 Takin' the helmet of salvation
And the Word of God
And the Word of God
Let me tell ya somethin' friend
You office-holders in this church—
an' teachers
625 I believe that it is most definitely
wrong
For a woman to cut her hair
Trim her bangs burn 'em or do
anything I believe it's wrong
And I believe that a man must be
born again just like Jesus told
it would be
That you must repent be baptised
and receive the Holy Ghost
630 I believe it with all my heart
But I also know friend that if ya
take the Word of God people'll
accept it
Amen
Brother Williams you can't pick a
man up off the street and say
listen here you're going to hell
because you're in the wrong
church
If we don't watch it that's where
we'll go
635 Amen
Amen
You know the only way to do that
is to say listen friend the Bible
says that if you want to go to
heaven you must be born again
Take the Word of God

You can't go out on the street and
    say woman you're goin' to hell
    for cuttin' her hair
640 Who are you
She may be older than you
She may be a Christian all her life
And you go up to a stranger and
    say you're goin' to hell for
    cuttin' her hair
Don't say nothin' friends you can't
    back up with the Word of God
645 When you take it to her take it with
    the Word of God
Say listen friend I'll show ya
It's not what I'm sayin'—I'm not

sayin' this—it's what the Bible
    says
It's what the Bible says
Praise the Lord
650 All of ya now
If you can live for God
Ya don't have to fall
Ya don't have to fail
If you'll just put on the whole armor
    of God
655 God'll take care of ya
I said God'll take care of ya
Let us stand and worship God this
    morning

PERILOUS TIMES

Here in 1968 Bible prophecy is
    being fulfilled
The Bible said in the Book of Sec-
    ond Timothy the first chapter
    and the first verse
This know also that in the last days
    perilous times shall come
Now I want you to know my
    friends that these perilous times
    are not coming
5 They are not on their way
They will not be here soon but they
    are here today
They are already in the land today
Perilous times have come when men
    are lovers of their own selves
They are killing they are lying they
    are cheating for their own
    profit

10 They don't care about anyone else
    —it's just them and them only
As the old saying goes, me myself
    and no more
We are living in perilous times
And the Bible also says but as the
    days of Noah were so shall also
    the days of the coming of the
    Son of Man be
For as in the days before the flood
    they were eating and drinking,
    marrying and giving in mar-
    riage until the days that Noah
    entered into the ark
15 As it was in the days of Noah so
    shall it also be in the days of
    the coming of the Lord
My friends we are living in the last
    days

And the perilous times are here
The Bible tells us that in the days
    of the flood the Bible said that
    the earth was corrupt before
    God
And the earth was filled with vio-
    lence and God looked upon the
    earth and behold it was corrupt
20 For all flesh had corrupted His way
    upon the earth
And God said unto Noah the end
    of all flesh is come before me,
    for the earth is filled with vio-
    lence through them, and be-
    hold, I will destroy them with
    the earth
And as it was in those days today
    people are preaching and being
    married
They are giving in marriage the
    man and having a grand time
The way of sin they don't know
    they think that everything is
    all right
25 They think that there is no sin—
    oh I realize that they'll say well
    you can sin and you can be
    lawless but they think they'll
    go along with everybody
They'll say you don't have to do this
    and you don't have to do that
It's all right to smoke it's all right to
    drink it's all right to curse
It's all right to commit adultery it's
    all right to commit fornication
It's all right to lie it's all right to
    cheat
30 It's all right to steal

It's all right to murder
It's all right to do these different
    things
And the ark today
Is like it was
35 In the days of Noah
This earth has corrupted itself
The imagination of man is on evil
    continually
They cannot think decent thoughts
They can't talk right
40 They can't even say a half a dozen
    words without cursing vilely
They can't talk right
Their mind is on evil continually
All they think about is getting re-
    venge on somebody
All they think about
45 Is fulfillin' the lust of their eyes
Or the pride of life
Or the lusts of the flesh
Now I want you to know my friend
That as it was
50 In the days of Noah
So shall it also be
In these last days
That we are now livin' in
God would not tolerate sin
55 God would not tolerate preachers
That would not preach the Word of
    God
God would not tolerate
Men and women goin' against the
    law of God
And transgressing
60 And sinning against the law of God
I want you to know surely
That in these last days

In the latter part of this nineteenth
  century
That my God still will not tolerate
  sin
65 My God will not tolerate preachers
That will not preach the Word of
  God
My God will not tolerate people
That transgress
And sin against the law of almighty
  God
70 My God said the Word of God
He said behold
All souls are mine
All souls are mine
My friend you people that are out
  there
75 An' you believe in evolution
You need to read your Bible a little
  more carefully
You're here today
The only reason that you're a comin'
  on the face of God's green earth
Was because that one day
80 My God reached down
And picked up a ball of dust
And He called it man
And He created a man
And He breathed into him
85 The breath of life
And man became a living soul
And you're here tonight
Or today
Because God has given you
90 He said all souls are mine
I give
And I take
He said I give

And I make alive
95 And the soul that sinneth
It shall die
My friend God looked on the earth
And He said behold
It is corrupt
100 Men down there commit adultery
  and doin' everything
They're doin' everything that come
  into their mind
And the heart can imagine
That they can possibly think of
They're goin' around and doin' it
105 They won't listen to my prophesy
They won't listen to Brother Noah
As he preaches unto them
The Word of God
And He said I will destroy man
110 Who I have created
He repented
And God said I'm sorry
That I ever even made a man
And my friends tonight
115 I want you to know
That my god made you
And he placed you in the world
And he gives you a job to do
And that job was to be holy
120 And to live right
Live holy
And righteous in the sight of God
And if you will not do it
My God will repent
125 That He ever made you
And He's gonna destroy you
From off the face of the earth
Amen
God never has tolerated sin

130 And God never will tolerate sin
Amen
You friends that are out there in
    radioland
Our goal and our ambition and our
    desire is—is to fulfill what we
    say
We claim to bring the whole gospel
    to the whole world
135 An' our goal and our desire is to
    bring you the whole gospel
Not just a part of it
Not just the part that you like
Not just the part that somebody else
    likes
Not just the part that I like
140 Not just the part that you write in
And tell us that you like
But the whole gospel
We're gonna—we're gonna preach it
    just as far
As these radio waves will let us go
145 Amen—and I mean we're gonna
    tell ya
We're not gonna compromise
My God never could stand anybody
That would compromise
My God wanted somebody
150 That would put their feet on the
    floor
And say live die sink or swim
Let the rains come and the winds
    blow and the storms rage
I'm gonna serve my God
I'm gonna stand up for what's right
155 I'm gonna preach the Word of God
I'm gonna obey the Word of
    God . . .

I'm gonna do what my preacher tell
    me to do
I'm gonna obey the Word of God
My friend, if you're in a compro-
    misin' belly-washin' church
160 That won't preach you the truth
I want you to know
That if you want to go to heaven
You're gonna have to obey truth
You may have to get down on your
    knees
165 You may not like it
You may have to sacrifice
A little bit of the flesh
And go against your kind of way
But if you go to heaven
170 You're gonna obey truth
And the only way that you can obey
    truth
Is a preacher that'll preach you the
    truth
And if your preacher's not doin' this
I want you to know
175 That our doors swing wide open
And we believe
And we teach and we practice the
    whole Word of God
Amen we believe
. . . that a man must live right in
    the sight of God
180 But the Bible says
As it was
In the days of Noah
So shall it also be
In the days of the comin' of the Son
    of Man
185 They were drinking
They were makin' merry

They were doin' what they thought
    was right
God was their enemy
That's not the way I intended things
    to go
190 That's not the way I intended things
    to be
He repented that He made man
He said behold I will destroy them
    with the earth
I will destroy them with the earth
There's one verse of Scripture that
    I like in this chapter
195 Bible said but Noah, found grace,
    in the eyes of the Lord
I want you to know friend that my
    God is a-lookin' down on this
    old world today
He sees all the wickedness
He sees all the evil
He sees that the imagination of
    men's hearts is on evil con-
    tinually
200 That they can't think right they
    can't act right
They can't walk right
They can't talk right
They can't do anything right
And my God is grievin' today be-
    cause men have come to this
    way up upon the earth
205 And God said I will destroy you
I'm gonna destroy ya
He said I'm gonna rain down fire
    and brimstone
I'm comin' back in a flamin' fire
Seekin' vengeance upon them
210 That don't know God

And those that will not obey the
    Word of God
My friend if you want to escape
    that great
And judgment day of almighty God
You want to escape the wrath of
    God
215 What you need to do
Is to obey the Word of God
Amen and know God
And get on down and show your
    heart
You say how can I do that
220 By the . . .
If you wanna be saved
If you want to go to heaven
Jesus told me to . . .
You must be born again
225 And Nicodemus said how can I
    when I'm old
Can I enter a second time in my
    mother's womb and be born
And Jesus said no
That's not what I'm talkin' about
He said you must be born again
230 Of the water
And of the Spirit
And ladies and gentlemen I want
    you to know
You that are listenin' to this broad-
    cast today
That if you want to go to heaven
235 I don't care what you think about it
I don't care what I think about it
But it's the spirit of the Word of
    God
My ideas
And my feelings

240 And my opinions will get me
       nowhere
   And neither will yours
   What we must do
   Is sit down
   And open the Word of God
245 And the Bible said
   That you must be born again
   Of the water of faith
   I want you to know my friend, that
       every time, God got ready to
       pour His wrath, He had a way
       for people to escape
   He saw and loathed the world
250 I'm gonna destroy these people that
       I made
   I'm gonna cause a flood to come and
       I'm gonna wash them all away
   But you know what He did
   He went to Noah—He said listen
       Brother Noah I'm gonna cause
       a flood to come upon the earth
   I want you to build an ark
255 And I want you to preach my Word
   Everybody that'll get inside of that
       ark can be saved
   God was makin' a way
   God was makin' a way
   I want you to know friend that my
       God will make a way for you
       too
260 I said my God will make a way for
       you too
   When He said that He would rain
       down fire and brimstone
   Upon Sodom and Gomorrah
   He sent an angel to warn the people
   You got to leave here because God

   is going to send down fire and
       brimstone
265 He was makin' a way for 'em
   He was sayin' if you wanna live
       right
   If you wanna do right
   I'm gonna stand by ya
   I'm gonna make a way
270 I want you to know my friend
   That my God will never
   Let His children
   He will never let His saints
   That want to live right
275 Who try to do right
   He will not let them down
   He said I'll never leave
   Ya I'll never forsake ya
   I'll never turn away from ya
280 Then, my God will make a way for
       you
   You know the trouble with people
       today
   The very same thing that was wrong
       with them in Noah's day
   Noah preached
   If I read my Bible right it took him
       one hundred years to build the
       ark
285 For one hundred years every day
       Noah preached
   Noah preached
   He said listen people
   It's gonna rain
   It's gonna rain
290 God's gonna send a flood down
   God's gonna destroy ya
   If ya don't come in this boat that
       I'm makin'

But the same thing's wrong with
   those people—they laughed and
   said oh no Noah
   It can't be
295 We never had a rain around here
We never had a flood around here
It's just not logical
It's just not right
I want you to know
300 That the ways of God
Sometimes may not be logical
According to your ideas
And according to your theories
But old brother Noah
305 He'd had a clear revelation from
   almighty God
And he tried to preach to them
   people
And say ya better come on
For one hundred years
He begged and he preached and he
   pleaded and he cried come on
310 God will destroy ya
But they sit on the . . .
And they hung their hearts
And they would not hear him
Let me ask you a question now
315 How long have you heard that the
   Lord's coming back
How many times has a preacher told
   you that He's soon to come
Noah told them for one hundred
   years every day
How long have you been told that
   Jesus is gonna come again
That Jesus is gonna rain down His
   wrath
320 That He's gonna come back in a

   smoke of fire
. . . .
And that won't obey Him
How many times
Have you been told
325 That He's soon to come again
And you shrugged it off
And you brushed it aside
And you wouldn't pay any attention
   to it
You say I'm gonna call the Lord—
   He's never come to me in a
   revelation
330 He's never told me
That He's gonna do this
I never saw anything like that
Those children had never saw rain
They never saw a flood either
335 And my friend it was just as true
   whether they saw or not
And whether you believe it or not
   today
My God is gonna come back
And if you're not ready to go
He's gonna leave you behind
340 Amen
Amen
But God made a way for these
   people to get out of there
Took care of His people
If ya want God to take care of you
   friend ya better get to be His
   people
345 This world that we live in
You say we're not livin' in perilous
   times
Lot of folks sit at home and they
   never get out much and they

don't really know, exactly
everything that is going on in
the world today
I want you to know that perilous
times are comin'
Amen
350 I want you to know that this world
cannot last very much longer
One of our professors on the West
Coast—this is a statement that
he made—and he made it pub-
licly and it was printed in the
newspapers, so I guess I have
a right to quote him on it
He said these sexual aberrations on
the West Coast will destroy us
by the year 2000 even if the
Russians don't
I want you to know my friend
That the way that this world
355 Is a-shapin' up
We got a rebellion goin' on
They say we got a new morality
We've got hippies and things a-livin'
We've got civil rights marchers
360 Marchin' up and down the streets
Causin' all the trouble that they can
We're livin' in perilous times
It's like it was
In the days of Noah
365 My friend, we . . .
In the gutter dark drunk
We've got people
That are spit upon
Because of alcohol
370 We've got children
In the orphanage homes today
Because of divorces

We got people there
Today because
375 Of cigarettes, LSD, and all sorts
of dope
I want you to know
That it's just as it was
In the days of Noah
And my God
380 Looks down upon this earth tonight
It's more than He can take
And He swears
That I'm gonna destroy man
God is makin' a way
385 He's makin' a way
He's makin' a way
That way
Peter preached on the day of
Pentacost
He said you have taken this man
called Jesus
390 And you've crucified Him
You've taken Him and you've done
away with Him—you've
destroyed Him
You've murdered Him
And he said now this man that you
have killed
He said God has made Him . . .
395 And he said someday He's gonna
come back and He's gonna
judge you for your worth and
for your deeds
These people began to get troubled
Conviction began to grip their
hearts
And they were grippin' their hearts
And they said well listen brotheren
400 You've told me what I've done

You've told me I've sinned
You've told me I've done wrong
You've told me that I'm wrong
And that I'm done for
405 And that some day
He's gonna come back
And judge me
What can I do
What can I do to rid myself of this
410 What can I do
And Peter told him
He said all you must do
Is repent of your sins
And be baptised in water
415 In the name of Jesus Christ
For the remission of your sins
And you shall receive
The gift of the Holy Ghost
And
420 . . . .
And . . .
And . . .
God is makin' a way
God is makin' a way
425 My friend I wish that you could
    realize, exactly what this world
    is headed for today
I wish you could only know, what
    this world is a-comin' to
There's something wrong with the
    nation
When people are takin' the lives of
    other people
There's somethin' wrong
430 When an eighteen-year-old boy
Walks into a beauty parlor
And causes five women to lay down
And blows their brains out on the
    floor

There's somethin' wrong
435 When a man goes to the top of a
    tower
In Austin Texas
And murders thirty-two people in a
    matter of hours
There's somethin' wrong
With the world my friend
440 When people go into a dormitory
And slaughter eight student nurses
In one night
There's somethin' wrong with our
    country
When our morals are breakin' down
445 When nudity is fast bein' accepted
And a fashion
There's somethin' wrong my friend
When we're selling liquor by the
    drink
And we're doing every thing
450 That can possibly be done
Every moral
Every law's bein' broken down
There's somethin' wrong
When our policemen
455 And our officers
Cannot arrest a man
And convict of bein' . . .
There's somethin' wrong
With our country
460 And it's all over the world
And the only thing is
Is that the Bible prophesied
That these times would come
And they're here
465 They're here
If you want to get out of it
If you want to escape

The wrath and the judgment of
    almighty God
All you must do is repent
470 Repent
Repent
Sad to say but that's the hardest
    thing for a lot of people to do
To realize they're wrong and say
    God forgive me
An' if you ever get to heaven you're
    gonna have to repent
475 To repent they'll have to baptise
    you in water in the name of
    Jesus

And receive the baptism of the Holy
    Ghost with . . . speaking in
    other tongues
You say will God have me
Yes God'll have ya friend
God'll have ya
480 You say where can I find this
    experience
Where can I come in contact with
    God
At the Oneness Pentacostal Church
At 3400 Southwest Twenty-fifth
    Street, in Oklahoma City

THAT WHICH IS RIGHT

Brother Dorance Manning recited this sermon May 5, 1968, in Norman, Oklahoma. Manning deserves a place in this book because his sermon is characteristic of the non-metrical oral style. He handles a guitar well and strums it softly while his congregation testifies before the sermon; after, he leads them in devotional music with his singing and playing. Yet he never chants or sings his sermons. The similarity of this style to printed rather than to the metrical sermons in this book has been discussed. As with all Pentacostal churches the congregation was receptive and participated actively in the service, exclaiming as the Spirit moved them. Later, several were moved to speak in tongues.

All right if you have your Bible and
    would like to turn, let us turn
    to the Book of Ruth
We want to read a few verses found
    in the Book of Ruth
In the first chapter and then the
    first two verses in the Book of
    Ruth
Now it came to pass in the days
    when the judges ruled that

there was a famine in the land
and a certain man of Bethlehem—Judah went to sojourn in
the country of Moab, he and
his wife and his two sons and
the name of the man was Elimelech, and the name of his
wife Naomi and the name of
his two sons Mahlon and Chilion, Ephrathites of Bethlehem

—Judah, and they came into the country of Moab, and continued there

5 Lord Jesus we come to you tonight thankful for this opportunity of preaching the Word of God to this people and as we come to Thee we realize that in ourselves we are not a preacher but if we have the help of God through the power of the Holy Ghost, Lord we pray that Thou canst anoinst us and help us to preach, and give forth these things that the people should have

Help us now to pray and anoint as we ask and bless this people keep Your hand upon each one we pray and move by Thy Spirit is our prayer, in Jesus' precious name, praise God

I suppose that you noticed in the first sentence I read that this portion of Scripture that I read to you about Ruth happened during the time of the judges

Some of you can possibly recall who some of those judges were

There was Deborah there was Barak there was Samuel there was Jephtha and Elam—several of those judges that ruled over those children of Israel during the time of the judges

10 There was Gideon there was Sampson and many others

And this story about Ruth

happened during this period of time

Now this period of time was characterized by something that is characterized in our age today

In the last verse of the Book of Judges we have these words written

In those days there was no king in Israel every man did that which is right in his own eyes

15 That's what's happening around us today throughout our nation every man is doing that which is right in his own eyes

As we look at this first portion here of Scripture, we see man and a woman living in Bethlehem

They have two boys approximately from eighteen perhaps even twenty—twenty-five years of age

And they realize that there's a famine in the land

This famine has been quite severe for some time

20 Bethlehem—the very meaning of the word means that there is food there—there is a place for them to have food and to worship

And there's a famine in the land

And as Elimelech watches his family

As he sees the flowers of health fade from their cheeks

He decides he must do something about it

25 And so they talk about it sometimes
 at night after the boys have
 gone on to bed perhaps around
 the—what little there is to eat
 in the evening or the morning
They talk about what are we going
 to do
And finally they make their decision
 that they shall go to the land
 of Moab
Now leaving the story for a few moments, in the twenty-sixth
 chapter of Leviticus God speaks
 to the children of Israel and He
 says to them to do at least four
 things
He says I want you to refrain from
 all types of idolatry
30 I want you to keep my sabbaths
I want you to reverence my
 sanctuary
And I want you to respect my law
Now these are the four things I
 want you to do Israel
And if you will do these things He
 told them I will in turn do
 something for you
35 I will give you rain so that your
 crops will grow
I will not only give you rain but I
 will give you rest from your
 enemies and your enemies shall
 not bother you
You can lie down at ease and at
 peace and know that no harm
 shall befall you
I'll not only give you rest but I'll
 give you victory over your en-

emies when they do come I'll
 give you the victory and you
 can overcome them
I will give you plenty—there will be
 plenty to eat
40 The vineyards will give forth of
 their fruit and the fields will
 give forth of their ears of corn
 and you'll have plenty to eat
And then I'll give you a place of
 worship—my sanctuary shall
 dwell among you
And He said not only that but I will
 come down and dwell with you
Now these are the things that God
 had promised the children of
 Israel
And as we come to this place in the
 life of Ruth—ah Naomi rather
 and the time of Elimelech we
 find a famine in the land
45 And we find them doing something
 typical that most of us do in a
 like situation
Instead of them examining the situation and then saying now
 what is the problem here
Why do we not have rain
Why do we not have a place of
 worship
Why has our crops failed and why
 has this come upon us
50 And searching the answer out in
 God
They decide that they will run
They decide they will evade the
 issue of facing up to God
And so they decide they'll just leave

the country

Now that's not of course the first
time that that's has happened

⁵⁵ And God really gives—and He gave
these children of Israel two
choices

He said you can take the way of
obedience and happiness or you
can take the way of disobedi-
ence and unhappiness

And if you obey me I will keep the
famine and the drought and
the war and all of these things
from coming your way but if
you disobey me in these areas
of which I mention then I'm
going to send these things upon
you

Isn't that the way we are a lot of
times

When we cease to pray

⁶⁰ When we cease to read God's Word

When we cease to have the spiritual
victory that God intends for us
to have

There's coming a time in our lives—
now mark it down because it's
true

There's coming a time in our lives
when something is going to
happen to us down the way

You might say now will God actually send something along our
way—yes He will because He
wants to wake us up from the
place that we're in

⁶⁵ He doesn't want us to reach the
place to where that we'll go

finally the way of the world
and so He'll send something if
nothing else He'll send judgment upon us

And the New Testament backs this
out as well

So this man and this woman decided
they would move

Now we find in the Bible that
there's three places that the
children of Israel moved to

Whenever they were afflicted whenever the drought came whenever bare circumstances arose
there were three main portions
of country that the children of
Israel moved to

⁷⁰ They either moved to Egypt—that's
the first country that was
mentioned

Or they moved to Babylon or were
carried there in captivity

Or they went to Moab

Now throughout the Scripture we
find that various places in the
Bible have tremendous import

They are types of various things

⁷⁵ We find as the preacher preached
this morning that Egypt was a
type of sin

It's a type of the sinner down in the
world and he cannot get loose

And for a moment if you'll pardon
me for taking this amount of
time

Here was the children of Israel in
the land of Egypt—they were
slaves there

Pharaoh had gotten complete
control over them
80 He had completely dominated their
national life
Now they were slaves working out
—making bricks
Building pyramids building cities
for Pharaoh
Tilling the fields and so on and so
forth while the Egyptians lolled
in comfort and in ease and were
the taskmasters and did no
work while these slaves done
their work
You might say well why didn't the
children of Israel just get up
and leave
85 Because they weren't able to leave—
they were not organized for
one thing—they were slaves and
had no will of their own
They had no where to go and so
they were helpless in the grip
of Pharaoh and his armies
And brother and sister that's the way
the sinner is in the grip of
Satan
And those hosts that this brother
talked about a while ago—Satan
knows how to keep people in
his grasp and they can't get out
by themselves they must have
the help of the Lord
And so oftentimes in fact all
through the Old Testament
Egypt is mentioned as a type of
sin and the sinner
90 And Pharaoh as a type of Satan and

their inability to get away
Then we have Babylon—Babylon is
a type of the backslider—the
apostate
The children of Israel you remember had had a national life for
hundreds of years
And for hundreds of years God had
warned them, now you obey
my laws you obey my statutes
and I will bless you
And on and on this had gone but
as time elapsed the children of
Israel's repenting and getting to
the Lord were fewer and
farther between
95 And God sent prophet after prophet
to warn the children of Israel
that unless you repent I'm
going to send into captivity and
finally Nebuchanezar came
with his forces and carried the
children of Israel into Babylon
And you remember those children
of Israel as they sat on the
banks of the Euphrates
And those people come around to
them they said sing unto us
some songs of the Lord
And these children of Israel said
we cannot sing—they'd weep
and they'd cry
And they hung their hearts on the
willow and they said we cannot
sing the songs of the Lord
100 Why? they were apostates they had
backslid they had gone away
from the Lord and they refused

to repent until the Lord had carried them captive

And you'll notice the unhappiness that characterized them

You'll notice they were unhappy down there—there were tears of sorrow, and tears because they were not right with their God, and they couldn't sing these songs of the Lord down in that captive land

Brothers and sisters there's a lot of people that way in this day and time

There's people that have backslid and there's people that has gone out from us as John said if they had been of us it is evident if they had been of us they wouldn't have left us but they've gone out from us and it's evident that they were not of us

105 And so—and I don't mean that individually as a church I'm talking about people that have gone away from God

And they're unhappy—they're not happy in their hearts they're not happy in their souls

But they're sad there's a sadness that grips them

You might say well how do you know this well I've been down that road myself

I was a backslider I was away from God

110 And when I'd get in the service and when I would hear the preaching on the Word

And when I was around the people who knew God there was a sadness

And even though it seemed sometime I was having fun in the world as soon as the fun was over I was still searching and hunting for something and it was that lost—that satisfaction that I'd had as a Christian serving the Lord

Yes they went to Babylon

And then there was some that went to Moab

115 And Naomi and Elimelech they looked at their two boys and they looked around them and it seemed there was no hope

It seemed like the rains would never come

It seemed like that the famine would never be over

They done everything that they could to stay as long as they could but instead of facing up to the situation—actually that's what the children of Israel usually done

But it took them longer and longer to do it—usually they'd say God what's this all about

120 How come and the prophet would come along and preach to them repentance—repent of your ways repent of your sins and get right with God

Then they'd fall on their faces before God and they'd repent and
God would send the rain
And God would send—would loosen
the famine and God would
bless them and God would
help them get rid of their enemies and the blessings of God
would flow upon them
But Naomi and Elimelech didn't do
this
They decided that they would leave
125 And so they moved their family and
sold their land and headed for
the land of Moab
Now let's turn over to Jeremiah the
forty-eighth chapter for just a
moment
And let's find out what the land of
Moab is talking about
What is the land of Moab
In chapter forty-eight, if you have
your Bible and would like to
turn
130 In the eleventh verse we read these
words
Moab hath been at ease from his
youth, and he hath settled on
his lees, and hath not been
emptied from vessel to vessel,
neither hath he gone to captivity, therefore his taste remained
in him, and his scent is not
changed
Now here we have described to us
the land of Moab
And this is a place that a lot of
Christian people are living

today in the land of Moab
Then my face struck to the fact that
they need to repent
135 And my face struck to the fact that
they need to get a new experience in the Lord
And they're living in the land of
Moab
Let's look at it for just a moment
Moab had been at ease from his
youth
In other words the people who live
at Moab are unconcerned and
don't we find a large amount of
the church world today
unconcerned
140 One of the writers of the Old Testament said words of this effect
that all—every passes by and
laith it not to heart
In other words he's unconcerned
about people that are on their
way to Hell
Unconcerned about people that
need an experience with God
to make them happy and to get
them ready for heaven and to
live on this world—you know I
was noticing in our songs and
so forth that we was talking
about heaven about heaven
about heaven it's great to talk
about heaven and it's great to
have a religion that'll take you
to heaven but it's better to have
a religion that'll help you to
live on this earth and be happy
and to enjoy this life

And so if you have a religion like
    that you'll have a good religion
    to die by to take you to heaven
But there's a lot of people that are—
    that are like these that have
    lived in Moab, they are
    unconcerned
145 And I think sometimes that we're
    like this
We're unconcerned about people
    because we don't love them as
    we ought
If we really believe what God says
    —that they're going to Hell
That they're going to be lost—then
    we'd care more about whether
    they're saved or not
Amen
150 And yet so many church people
    today are living in the land of
    Moab they're completely
    unconcerned
And that's what he said of this
    people
Moab had been at ease from his
    youth
From early in his Christian experi-
    ence he's not concerned about
    the lost, he's not concerned
    about doing anything for God
Brother and sister if we're ever to do
    anything for God we'd better
    get started in our own genera-
    tion because the time is fast
    passing by when we'll be able
    to do anything
155 And then he says that he had
    settled on his lees

Now you say well what does that
    mean
Well someone has described it
    thusly that the longer that the
    wine sat in the bottles and the
    dregs drifted down to the bot-
    tom it's sorta like a medicine
    bottle that sets for a while
You read about some medicines and
    it says on there on the bottle to
    shake well before using—you've
    probably read that on various
    bottles—shake well before
    using
Now why do you suppose that the
    pharmacist or the doctor puts
    that on that bottle
160 Because some of the medicinal
    properties that are in that
    medicine goes down to the
    bottom
The dregs of it or the properties they
    go to the bottom
And if you take that medicine
    without shaking that bottle
    those medicinal properties in
    the bottle go down to the bot-
    tom and they won't do you any
    good
And so that's what he's saying down
    here
He says he had settled on his lees
165 And so he's unfaithful
He's content to set at home when
    other people are going to
    church
He's content to miss the regular
    services

He's content to be unfaithful in
every avenue of his life
concerning Christ
And because he's this way he has
gone to the land of Moab
170 And brother and sister aren't we
finding more and more people
like this
And I'm not talking about what we
call the nominal churches I'm
talking about Pentacostal
people
I'm talking about people that once
had the fire of God in their
souls
The joys of the Lord in their heart
and a faithfulness down in
heart planted there that made
them want to come to the house
of God and be there without
fail at every service but now
they've settled on their lees
They've settled on their seats of
unfaithfulness and you can't
get 'em out to the various
services
175 Now he goes ahead and says, and he
hath not been emptied from
vessel to vessel
In other words he is unengaged in
the business of the Lord's
activity
And there's so many Christian people today that are unengaged in
the activity of the Lord
You know when I contemplate our
twentieth-century church
I'm made to want to compare it with

the early church
180 That early church the Lord had
planted that church through
the power of the Holy Ghost
on the day of Pentecost
And you know it wasn't the preachers that done all the work
But every member every person that
an acquaintance with the Lord
Jesus went everywhere talking
about Jesus
They talked it over the back fence
They talked it to everywhere they
went
185 And as a result down at Antioch
sprang up a church
They didn't even have a pastor they
didn't even have a preacher
And finally the apostles up at Jerusalem said we'd better send
somebody down there to see
how that thing's going and
they sent Barnabas down there
And when he got down there the
church was already called
Christians
The first place in history of people
being called Christians
190 Why because they were demonstrat-
ing and I used to think it was
this
I thought well now they were first
called Christians because they
showed forth Christ in their
lives
But those people didn't know Christ
they'd never heard of Christ
They didn't know who Christ was

or what He stood for

But they were first called Christians because those members of that church were everywhere talking about what Christ had done

195 And so these said they're Christians they're Christians

And so brothers and sisters when we compare the twentieth-century church with the church of yesteryear we find that we are unengaged about the things of the Lord, aren't we

We find that we've gone to Moab and we're sitting there unengaged

And that's what happened to Naomi and to Elimelech

Then we find that he's yet unpunished

200 He says that neither hath he gone into captivity

Now you might say well now preacher this all relates to the Old Testament but you know the Old Testament church was our example today

And it points back to that Old Testament church as our example

And it says he's unpunished and as yet there's many people today that are going the way I've been talking about here that are completely unpunished

But did you know the Bible says they are going to be punished

205 The Word of God says in the Book of Revelation that there is a church that is going right in to the tribulation period

He says of one church—the Thyatira church—he said I will cast you into the bed of great tribulations unless you repent

And he says to that last church—the Laodicean Church—he said I will spew you out of my mouth

And so that church—while those that have been faithful while those that have been concerned while those that have been engaged in the work of the Lord are around the marriage supper of the lamb enjoying the good things of the Lord there are some that have yet been unpunished that are going to be punished in the tribulation period

And then he says that he's unchanged he says therefore his taste remained in him

210 Naomi and Elimelech went down to Moab

And they got down there and a year or so went by

And that boy—those two boys married girls

They done the very thing that God had told them not to do—to marry into another lineage—He said to keep 'em all Israelites but they married Moabitish girls

Diametrically opposed to what God
    had said
215 More than likely they had some
    idolatrous type of ceremony
    that was performed as they got
    married
Why? do you say—do you really
    think that—they were in the
    land of Moab
They had gone there of their own
    free will
And brother when you get away
    from God and go down to the
    land of Moab you'll do things
    that are not right according to
    what God has to say about the
    thing
And so brother they had slipped a
    long ways
220 He say they were unpunished and
    he said that they were un-
    changed there he said therefore
    his taste remained in him
Brother there's a lot of people that
    has lived in Moab—you know
    we talk about a religion that'll
    change ya—isn't that the kind
    of religion we really want
Isn't that the kind of thing we
    really want—and someone said
    that Sister Wilson said salva-
    tion—yes there's a difference
    between religion and salvation
Salvation is that which cleans ya up
    and makes ya a different person
Makes ya walk and talk with the
    Lord—everybody has religion
    of some kind but not every-

body has salvation
225 And brother and sister there's a
    salvation for ya, and when that
    salvation comes along it
    changes you
Praise God forever—it changed
    Zachias—Zachias said Lord if
    I've wronged anybody I'll give
    'em back fourfold
And brothers he went back—payin'
    back the money he had cheated
    people out of
There wasn't a person in that you
    could have proved or you could
    have got to say anything against
    that man
You hada' said he's got something
    he's something's happened to
    that man because he's never
    been like that before
230 Brother he straightened his life up
    and finally when it's all over he
    said Lord the rest of my goods
    I'll bestow on the poor
Praise God forever
Brother listen good old time salva-
    tion will change a person and
    make him a different person
But he said his taste has remained
    in him, he still has the same old
    appetites for this world
He still wants to do the same old
    things that he done before he
    ever got saved
235 Brother when that happens he just
    didn't get the experience that
    he ought to have, did he
Praise God forever

And then he says his scent is not changed—in other words his ability to smell his ability to discern right from wrong is unchanged

He can't discern the right from the wrong and isn't that what is one of the main things that is afflicting our world today

We have so many people that can't discern right from wrong

240 As that Scripture in Judges—that last verse said

He said that every man done that which was right in his own eyes

And brother you take someone that's convinced they're doin' right in their own eyes it takes the Holy Ghost to get 'holt of them and convince them that they're doin' the wrong thing

Amen?

No preacher can do it, no individual can do it, you look 'em in the two eyes and tell 'em what they're doin' wrong but unless the Holy Ghost gets 'holt of them there's nothing in this to convince them of wrong-doing, why?

245 Because we're doing right in our own eyes

His scent was unchanged

He couldn't tell right from wrong

Brother that's exactly what's happening in our day and time, Amen?

And so judgment came upon them

250 One day Naomi went in to get Elimelech up for breakfast and as she shook him she found that he was very sick

She waited on him and she done everything she could but he went from bad to worse

And in a few days he passed on

She was heart-broken wondering how now can I live without my husband

But he was gone

255 A year went by and Mahlon got sick—his name means sickly

He got sicker and soon he too died

A few weeks passed by and Chilion got worse

His name means consumptive

And the first thing you know Naomi had buried her husband, had buried her oldest son and had buried her youngest son

260 Naomi means happy

Means happy

She had been out of Bethlehem—Judah the place of worship the place of bread—she had gone out happy

But now she had lost everything she'd lost it all

Finally she decided I'm goin' back—I'm goin' back to the place of worship

265 I'm goin' back to the place where there's plenty to eat

She'd heard that God had visited Bethlehem

Notes

CHAPTER I

1. Albert B. Lord, *The Singer of Tales* (New York, 1965), p. 137.
2. Over one hundred articles and books have appeared as a result of the stimulus provided by Francis P. Magoun, Jr., "Oral Formulaic Character of Anglo-Saxon Narrative Poetry," *Speculum,* XXVIII (July 1953).
3. For a summary of this criticism and a sound analysis of the situation, see Larry D. Benson, "The Literary Character of Anglo-Saxon Formulaic Poetry," *PMLA,* LXXXI (1966), 334-41.
4. Milman Parry, "Studies in the Epic Technique of Oral Verse-Making. I: Homer and Homeric Style," *Harvard Studies in Classical Philosophy,* XLI (1930), 80.
5. See Newman I. White, *American Negro Folk-Songs* (Hatboro, Pa., 1965), pp. 126-28: the artistic and sometimes elaborate "stage directions" suggest an editor's hand; Edward C. L. Adams, *Congaree Sketches* (Chapel Hill, 1927), pp. 41-47; Edward C. L. Adams, *Nigger to Nigger* (New York, 1928), pp. 211-13: suspiciously fluent; Orlando Kay Armstrong, *Old Massa's People* (Indianapolis, 1931), pp. 226-27: short fragment and patronizing tone; Alan Lomax, *The Rainbow Sign* (New York, 1959), pp. 185-209: the sermon is given completely, but the editor's comments are overly dramatic; Marcellus S. Whalley, *The Old Types Pass Away* (Boston, 1925), pp. 84-97: the sermon is fragmentary and the editor's tone condescending; and J. Mason Brewer, *American Negro Folklore* (Chicago, 1968), pp. 119-38: the most authentic collection of sermons so far.
6. James Weldon Johnson, *God's Trombones* (New York, 1948), p. 1.
7. Harry Caplan, "Classical Rhetoric and the Medieval Theory of Preaching," *Classical Philology,* XXVIII (1933), 96.
8. Johnson, *God's Trombones,* p. 1.
9. Throughout, an Uher 4000-L with twenty-foot extension cable was used. This made it possible to record the preacher clearly so long as he stayed

behind the pulpit; I stayed with the congregation so as to observe their reactions better. A multidirectional microphone is necessary with this kind of preacher because there is a lot of movement behind the pulpit and a lavaliere microphone would have been too restrictive.

10. More than two hundred sermons of about fifty preachers from about a dozen states were examined for this study. Some men, such as the ones cited most frequently in this paper, were studied intensively, while others were sampled. Field work was conducted in the four geographical areas mentioned in the text; radio sermons from relatively inaccessible areas were also monitored.

CHAPTER II

1. Joseph R. Washington, Jr., *Black Religion* (Boston, 1966), p. 173.
2. E. Franklin Frazier, *The Negro Church in America* (New York, 1964), p. 7.
3. Frazier, *The Negro Church in America*, p. 28.
4. John Hope Franklin, *From Slavery to Freedom* (New York, 1967), pp. 162-63.
5. Marcia M. Mathews, *Richard Allen* (Baltimore, 1963), p. 18.
6. Perry Miller, *The New England Mind: The Seventeenth Century* (Cambridge, Mass., 1963), p. 352; see also Robert Henson, "Form and Content of the Puritan Funeral Elegy," *American Literature*, XXXII (March 1960), 12.
7. William Warren Sweet, *Revivalism in America* (New York, 1944), p. 108.
8. Alan Heimert, *Religion and the American Mind* (Cambridge, Mass., 1966), pp. 228-31 and *passim*.
9. Washington, *Black Religion*, p. 190.
10. Heimert, *Religion and the American Mind*, p. 230.
11. George Pullen Jackson, *White and Negro Spirituals* (New York, 1943), pp. 80-83. Mrs. Francis Trollope describes a camp meeting she attended in 1829 in which Negroes were numbered among the 2,000 or so faithful. Her account is contemptuous of the sobbing, shrieking, groaning, and screaming all around her, so that her picture of American life must be accepted with reservations: *Domestic Manners of the Americans* (New York, 1901), pp. 237-41.
12. Frazier, *The Negro Church in America*, p. 8.
13. Washington, *Black Religion*, pp. 194-95.
14. *Ibid.*, pp. 196 ff.
15. Frazier, *The Negro Church in America*, p. 3.
16. Don Yoder, *Pennsylvania Spirituals* (Lancaster, Pa., 1961), pp. 1-32.
17. The history of this phenomenon has been efficiently summarized by Bruce Jackson, "The Glory Songs of the Lord," pp. 108-19, in Tristram P. Coffin, ed., *Our Living Traditions* (New York, 1968). For an early description of an antiphonal service of lining out and response, see Bruce Jackson, *The Negro and His Folklore in Nineteenth-Century Periodicals* (Austin, Texas, 1967), pp. 122-23.

18. See Jackson, "Glory Songs," pp. 115 ff.

19. Lacy's etymology is not particularly creative in this instance; on another occasion he told his congregation that "Sunday" was named for the "Son" of God, which was why we all went to church on that day.

20. The tradition of which I speak in this book is that of oral preaching in which the sermons are metrical and are spontaneously composed. Almost all such preachers either come from the South or learned this style from a southerner. Often the preacher is Negro, although some whites, in Kentucky, Ohio, and Pennsylvania, also preach this way.

21. Albert B. Lord, *The Singer of Tales* (New York, 1965), pp. 21-26.

22. After several weeks of attending services I was myself able to make a rather specious leap into the second stage by reciting a formulaic "testimony" I had devised. In most Baptist churches guests are asked to "say a few words" before the congregation is dismissed: I found that the testimonies were heavily fomulaic, and after listening to several such performances I was able to give my own. What I lacked in years of experience in making such statements I overcame because I knew the linguistic principles on which such short speeches were made. Professor Donald R. Howard thinks that Chaucer would have had a place for people like me among the Canterbury pilgrims, but I hope that my "testimony" will be understood as a verbal exercise rather than as religious hypocrisy:
    Thanking the Lord above all things
    It's good to be in His house this mornin'
    And it's good to hear the words of the preacher
    We thank him for his message
    I thank the Lord for giving me another night's rest
    I thank Him for letting me rise this morning
    And I thank Him for letting me have another day
    God bless this congregation
    God bless the pastor
    God bless the deacons
    And bless this house

23. Lacy once insisted that his favorite preacher was John Allen Chalk, whose Sunday morning sermons originate in Abilene, Texas, and who is heard in Bakersfield over KUZZ. It is obvious, however, that Chalk is a manuscript preacher and not the kind Lacy usually admired. Curiously, on the several mornings when I asked Lacy questions about Chalk's sermon, that day he said that he had not listened. Certainly Lacy did not admire Chalk's style of delivery; one can only speculate about the "real" reason.

24. Charles Keil, *Urban Blues* (Chicago, 1966), pp. 7-8, notes that speaking in tongues, healing, "possession," frenzied dancing, hand-clapping, tambourine playing, singing and screaming, and constant participation by the audience are alien to the "prevailing conception of Protestantism." The ineffectiveness of a white minister in a black church was noticed over a century ago: see Bruce Jackson, *The Negro and His Folklore*, p. 66.

CHAPTER III

1. This literature is surprisingly widespread. The Gospel Book House of Atlanta publishes several by John C. Jernigan: *My Text Books, Semons in Nutshells, The Preacher's Gold Mine, Homiletic Treasure, Advice to Ministers,* and several more. Other volumes are available by other men. For a different appeal a minister may refer to the sermons of Paul Tillich, *The Eternal Man* (New York, 1963), Harry Emerson Fosdick's *Riverside Sermons* (New York, 1958), Elton Trueblood's *The Yoke of Christ* (New York, 1958), and countless others.
2. Harold Courlander, *Negro Folk Music, U.S.A.* (New York, 1963), p. 42: songs about Moses, Joshua, and the visions of St. John were most appealing to slaves.
3. A-T Type 1613 has been traced to the eighteenth century, and very close analogues of Tyler's version have been found in England, for instance the Frank Kidson Collection, Mitchell Library, Glasgow (folio collection of Broadsides, vol. 1, p. 125). Ed Cray found an identical version in the United States around 1915: "The Soldier's Deck of Cards Again," *Midwest Folklore,* XI (1961), 225-34. Nevertheless most recordings give Tyler credit for authorship. A year after Lacy first credited the "Deck of Cards" to Tyler, he recalled that it was popular in Mississippi years before Tyler recorded it, having been preached by C. H. Jackson, Chris Gallion and "Rapfoot" Gayden.
4. Matthew 25. As with all sermons (and all preachers), Freeman claimed that his was original.
5. Fred N. Robinson (ed.), *The Works of Geoffrey Chaucer* (Boston, 1957). All citations of Chaucer's work in this book are from this edition.

CHAPTER IV

1. James Weldon Johnson, *God's Trombones* (New York, 1948), p. 5.
2. Mainly, I think that the art of the oral preacher who chants his sermon is not as precise as that of other allegedly oral poets, Homer and the author of *Beowulf.* When a poem such as the Anglo-Saxon epic gets written down, whether by a scribe or by the poet himself, care can be taken to regularize the lines. This asumes that the performance is less regular than the text that has survived (in the case of *Beowulf,* Cotton Vitellius A XV). Lord found that the *guslars* were fairly regular metrically even during performance, but in such poetry there is (apparently) a tradition to be so. And, the *guslar* maintains pretty much the same meter from the beginning. However that may be true of Lord's experience, when I visited Yugoslavia during the summer of 1969 I found the performances of the *guslars* even less songlike than those of most of the preachers I had recorded; also more hypometric and hypermetric lines than in the chanted portions of many sermons.
3. Gordon Hall Gerould, *The Ballad of Tradition* (New York, 1957), p. 269:

"Better than any other singers, who have been carefully observed, they [Negroes] show the power of instantaneous response to a stimulus of any kind and a very general habit of composition under stress of excitement."

4. The matter needs closer study. Harold Courlander mentions some spirituals that may have originally been sermons: *Negro Folk Music, U.S.A.* (New York, 1963), pp. 52-56; he also describes some songs as having a "preaching style of delivery, with sermonizing and singing interspersed" (p. 64).

5. Johnson, *God's Trombones*, p. 6, mentions the similar histrionics of other preachers; Alan Lomax, *The Rainbow Sign* (New York, 1959), p. 190, calls the preacher "a trained actor."

6. W. B. Yeats, *Ideas of Good and Evil* (London, 1903), pp. 247-48.

7. A former colleague at the Santa Barbara campus of the University of California spent a good part of his youth in Texas at Baptist revivals and Sunday services; he recently admitted to me that the selection of hymns was crucial to the amount of the offering on any given day. His father was—still is—a Baptist minister. My friend would begin certain services with a slow song, follow it with a fast-paced number, slow down again during the third, and then in subsequent songs rapidly escalate in tempo (and consequently in emotion) which was designed to hit its peak just before the offering. This informant, who has asked that he not be named, claims that stimulating a congregation is a commonly practiced art, though not usually for personal profit.

8. The scriptural authority for glossolalia is in Acts, 2:2-4: "And suddenly there came a sound from heaven as of a rushing mighty wind, and it filled all the house where they were sitting. And there appeared unto them cloven tongues like as of fire, and it sat upon each of them. And they were all filled with the Holy Ghost, and began to speak with other tongues, as the Spirit gave them utterance." (King James version).

9. *Miracle Magazine*, XII (July 1967), 3 and 22.

10. Johan Huizinga, *The Waning of the Middle Ages*, trans. by F. Hopman (New York, 1956), pp. 12, 13.

CHAPTER V

1. As defined by Albert B. Lord, *The Singer of Tales* (New York, 1965), p. 30: "A group of words regularly employed under the same metrical conditions to express a given essential idea."

2. Lord, *Singer of Tales*, p. 68: "Groups of ideas regularly used in telling a tale in the formulaic style of traditional song . . ."

3. This is now a matter of some controversy, but the original conception of "formula" depended upon repetition; in the matter of verbatim repetition of phrases the sermons are even more formulaic than any epic Parry or Lord recorded.

4. James Weldon Johnson, *God's Trombones* (New York, 1948), p. 5.

5. Also observed by Johnson, *God's Trombones*, p. 11.

6. Lacy, like most preachers, builds towards an emotional climax which is timed to arrive near the end, and a denouement closes it out. However, J. Charles Jessup's climax is usually near the middle of the sermon—a structure popular in ancient Greece—and he descends gradually from that peak.

7. This compares favorably with the ratio of formulas found in *Beowulf* by Magoun: 74 per cent of the first fifty lines occur elsewhere in the corpus of Old English verse and "at least fifteen per cent of the verses of the poem are to all intents and purposes repeated within the poem": see Francis P. Magoun, Jr., "Oral Formulaic Character of Anglo-Saxon Narrative Poetry," *Speculum*, XXVIII (July 1953), 449-50, 454.

8. Donald K. Fry, "Old English Formulas and Systems," *English Studies*, XLVIII (June 1967), 193-204.

9. Milman Parry, "Studies in the Epic Technique of Oral Verse-Making I: Homer and Homeric Style," *Harvard Studies in Classical Philology*, XLI (1930).

10. H. L. Rogers, "The Crypto-Psychological Character of the Oral Formula," *English Studies*, XLVII (1966), 89-102.

11. Lord, *Singer of Tales*, p. 37.

12. Donald K. Fry, "Old English Formulas," 203.

13. Old English heroic poetry also uses this technique.

14. Milman Parry, "The Distinctive Character of Enjambement in Homeric Verse," *Transactions of the American Philosophical Association*, LX (1929), 200-220.

CHAPTER VI

1. This theme is by no means unique to Brown. In a sermon recited in Charlottesville, Virginia, on March 17, 1968, Elder Jerry H. Lockett recited the following three passages during a sermon entitled "That Same Man":
This same Jesus
No other Jesus but this same Jesus
Back—gave sight to the blind
Cause the dumb to talk
Cause the lame to walk
Cause the deaf to hear
This same Jesus

. . .

I'm talkin' about Jesus
I'm talkin' about Jesus
Talkin' about the One
Who brought us up a mighty long ways
We seen a child way up in Jerusalem
Seen Him up there sittin' with the doctors
Seen him up there with the lawyers
Settin' up there with those highly educated people

. . .

This same Jesus
Told the woman one day
Same Jesus
That gave sight to the blind one day
This same Jesus
Spoke to the dumb one day
Caused them to speak
The deaf to hear one day
That same Jesus

Elder Lockett was adamant in his insistence that "the Lord" gave him the words, and would not acknowledge any other source. Polygenesis seems unlikely, given the amount of details in this theme cluster; Lockett has never been to Arkansas or Bakersfield, nor has Brown ever been to Virginia. "This same Jesus" occurs only once in the Bible (Acts 1:11) but the miracles are not enumerated in this passage. The possible source is a spiritual which Hays only vaguely remembers whose first lines are:

This same Jesus
Walked at Galilee
This same Jesus
Made the blind to see . . .

I have not been able to find this song in any of the spiritual collections available to me.

2. The reader may wish to compare the findings in this section with those in Lord's *Singer of Tales*, pp. 68-98. The major difference appears to be the use to which the Yugoslav and American themes are put, and the ramifications of that difference.

3. The metaphor comes from—but is also an elaboration of—Revelations 1:14-16:
His head and hairs were white like wool, as white as snow; and his eyes were as a flame of fire;
And his feet like unto fine brass, as if they burned in a furnace; and his voice as the sound of many waters.
And he had in his right hand seven stars: and out of his mouth went a sharp two-edged sword.

4. Frieda Goldman-Eisler, "Speech Production and the Predictability of Words in Context," *Quarterly Journal of Educational Psychology*, X (May 1958), 96-106; "Hesitation and Information in Speech," in *Information Theory: Fourth London Symposium* (London, 1961), pp. 162-74; "Continuity of Speech Utterance, Its Determinants and Its Significance," *Language and Speech*, IV (1961), 220-31; and "The Distribution of Pause Durations in Speech," *Language and Speech*, IV (1961), 232-37. Professor Richard Bauman of the University of Texas was kind enough to bring these articles to my attention.

5. The tendency of subjects to recall aspects of narrative by word association rather than idea or story element was first noted by F. C. Bartlett, "Some Experiments on the Reproduction of Folk Stories," reprinted in Alan Dundes, *The Study of Folklore* (New Jersey, 1965), p. 249.

CHAPTER VII

1. Several experiments have been performed with repeated reproduction: F. C. Bartlett's is perhaps the best known (especially pp. 63-94 of *Remembering* [Cambridge, 1932]). But Bartlett did not use stories that were native to his subjects, who were in any event university students and not members of a homogeneous folk group. Most important, Bartlett's subjects read their material and then wrote them out so that their transmission was likely to be quite different from oral transmission. Albert Wesselski (*Versuch einer Theorie des Märchens*, Prager Deutsche Studien [Reichenberg, 1931]) used young girls rather than adult storytellers. And the informal experiments of Walter Anderson were also conducted in writing. The comparisons of the sermons in this study were of the adult bearers of their own tradition orally transmitted. Bartlett allowed about thirty minutes between reception and transmission; the comparisons here were made, for the most part, eleven months apart. For a discussion of the achievement of fluency and the relationship of it to content and initial performance, see Frieda Goldman-Eisler, "Continuity of Speech Utterance, Its Determinants and its Significance," *Language and Speech*, IV (1961), 220-31.
2. William Faulkner's description in *The Sound and the Fury* is quite accurate (New York, 1946), pp. 310-13.
3. A type of self-correction similar to Anderson's "Law." See also Goldman-Eisler, "Continuity of Speech," 229-31.
4. F. C. Bartlett, "Some Experiments on the Reproduction of Folk Stories," reprinted in Alan Dundes, *The Study of Folklore* (New Jersey, 1965), p. 249, remarks that "relations of opposition, similarity, subjection, and the like, occurring in the original, are very commonly intensified. This forms one illustration of a deep-rooted and widespread tendency to dramatization . . ." One might supplement Bartlett's observation by citing Axel Olrick's "Epic Law" of the tendency to polarize characters and their qualities in oral transmission—also reprinted in Dundes, pp. 135-37.
5. Bartlett, "Some Experiments . . ." p. 249 found visual imagery readily retained and often intensified.
6. Cf. *Ibid.* pp. 249-50: in repeated reproduction elements that are forgotten are called "under potent"; the "normally potent" are reproduced; and the "over potent" will gain in importance. This is tautological and merely supplies scientifistic terms for what is observed, as though naming the phenomenon somehow explains it.

CHAPTER VIII

1. Especially the recordings of such chants made for the Library of Congress by Charley Berry, Thomas J. Marshall, and Iron Head: LC Albums L8 and L59.
2. Melville Jacobs, *The People Are Coming Soon* (Seattle, 1960), pp. x-xi; and *The Content and Style of an Oral Literature* (Chicago, 1959), pp. 268-69.

3. Albert B. Lord, *The Singer of Tales* (New York, 1965), p. 54.

4. A word needs to be said about the effect of anaphoric passages on the congregation and the preacher's attempt to exploit these effects. Parallelism of this type can have a profound cumulative dramatic impact. Perhaps the reader will have heard sermons by the late Rev. Martin Luther King, Jr., or the Rev. Ralph Abernathy, and will have felt this impact personally. The Rev. Mr. King's "I Have a Dream" speech, though written, is rich in anaphoric development. Yet nearly all of the preachers interviewed for this study were unaware of creating such parallel passages, and claimed to have been concentrating exclusively on the problems of composition. However, in the case of Dr. King and other preachers of comparable learning who preach spontaneously, it is hard to believe that they were not aware of the effect on the audience.

5. Actually Lord makes this point, though it is often overlooked: "I believe that we are. justified in considering that the creating of phrases is the true art of the singer on the level of line formation, and it is this facility rather than his memory of relatively fixed formulas that marks him as a skillful singer in performance": *Singer of Tales*, p. 43.

6. Frieda Goldman-Eisler, "Speech Production and the Predictability of Words in Context," *Quarterly Journal of Educational Psychology*, X (May 1958), 96-106.

7. Lord, *Singer of Tales*, p. 20.

8. See Larry D. Benson, "The Literary Character of Anglo-Saxon Formulaic Poetry," *PMLA*, LXXXI (1966), 334-41.

9. Milman Parry, *Serbocroatian Heroic Songs*, I (Cambridge, Mass., 1954), 116.

10. Nora K. Chadwick and Victor Zhirmunsky, *Oral Epics of Central Asia* (Cambridge, England, 1969), p. 31.

11. Lord, *Singer of Tales*, p. 127; but Lord does not mention what happens to stall formulas when a song is dictated at leisure.

12. It is the thesis of Professor Alan Jabbour of The Library of Congress that *Beowulf* is neither formulaic (in Lord's sense) nor improvised, but entirely memorial. Chadwick speaks of a strong tradition of epic memorization in central Asia (pp. 17-18), and analysis of the sermons suggests that Jabbour's thesis is possible. His theory thus accounts for the absence of all stall formulas as well as the presence of certain repetitions (þæt wæs god cyning). The contemporary parallel might be the actor who remembered, by heart, all of Shakespeare's tragedies, or the symphonic conductor (such as Sir Thomas Beecham) who has memorized the entire score of an opera: see "Memorial Transmission in Old English Poetry," *Chaucer Review*, III (Fall 1969), 174-90.

13. Chadwick and Zhirmunsky, *Oral Epics*, p. 326.

Index

Henry, Rev. W. H., 181
Henson, Robert, 252
Hesitation pauses, 67-68
Holiness Pentacostal Church, 77
Holy Ghost, as sermon source, 23-24, 27-30, 38, 53, 75-76, 111
Homer, 3, 6, 102, 116
"The Horse Paweth in the Valley" (sermon), 28
Howard, Donald R., 253
Howland, Rev. Robert, 32, 45
Huizinga, Johan, 255
Hurley, Rev. T. J., 89-91, 93-94

"I Can Do All Things" (sermon); transcription, 208-15
Interviews with preachers, 6-8, 20-28, 46, 53, 64-67, 72, 102, 112-13

Jabbour, Alan, 11-12, 14, 259
Jackson, Bruce, 252, 253
Jackson, George Pullen, 252
Jacobs, Melville, 104-105, 258
Jernigan, John C., 254
Jessup, J. Charles, 6, 22-23, 33, 42, 54, 106-7, 121, 256
"Jesus Will Lead You" (sermon), 29
"Jesus Will Make It All Right" (sermon), 29
Johnson, James Weldon, 5-6, 47, 251, 254
Johnson, President Lyndon, reference to in sermon, 210

KBYE, 89
Keil, Charles, 253
Kennings, 102, 113
Kentucky, 4, 8, 10, 14, 16, 17
King, Rev. Martin Luther, 259
Kirghiz, 4, 115
Kuhlman, Sister Katherine, 22
KUZZ, 253

Lacy, Rev. Rubin, 6, 7, 8, 20-25, 27-44, 47, 50-51, 53-55, 57-58, 60, 62-72, 74-76, 79-88, 91-95, 100-101, 103, 113, 253, 256

Liberty Baptist Church, 74
Literacy, as criterion of oral composition, 4, 97-100, 113-14
Lockett, Elder, Jerry H., 256-57
Lomax, Alan, 5, 251, 255
Lord, Albert B., 3-4, 10, 24-25 34, 46-47, 49, 51, 62, 74, 77, 96, 100, 110-11, 113-14, 116, 251, 253, 255, 257, 259

McAllister, Rev. Otis, 88, 96
McCoy, Joe ("Hallelujah Joe"), 28
McDowell, Rev. D. J., 16-17, 20, 22, 31, 40, 41-42, 48-55, 59, 72, 78-79, 96-97, 101-3
McElroy, Brother Bob, 22
McRoy, Rev. W. G., 74

Magoun, Francis P. Jr., 3-4, 256
Manning, Brother Dorance, 77
"Manuscript Preachers," 9, 30
Master Sermons Outlines, 29-30, 31, 75, 82
Mathews, Marcia M., 252
Memory: in oral composition, 4, 19, 30, 42, 55, 64, 67-69, 73, 78-79, 102, 103, 111, 115-16, 259; "creative memory," 116; in catalogue retention, 116
Meter, 5, 38, 39-40, 48, 53, 57, 72, 83, 99, 101-3. See also Rhythm.
Middle Ages, clergy of, 22; sermons of, 32, 45; literary style of, 94; rhetorical exercises of, 116
Middle-class churches: interests of ministers, 32; taste of congregation, 45
Miller, Perry, 14, 252
"Ministerial Promotion" (sermon), 87-88
Miracle Magazine, 22, 254
Missionary Baptist Church, 22, 45
Moore, Rev., 186
Moses, 34, 108
"Moses at the Red Sea" (sermon), 28, 33, 107-9
"Mujo and the Shepherd" (Parry Song #8), 114-15.
Mukes, Mrs. Lucille, 43